T0358682

ASIAN FREE TRADE
AGREEMENTS AND
WTO COMPATIBILITY
Goods, Services, Trade Facilitation
and Economic Cooperation

World Scientific Studies in International Economics
(ISSN: 1793-3641)

The complete list of the published volumes in the series can be found at
http://www.worldscientific.com/series/wssie

32 World Scientific
Studies in
International
Economics

ASIAN FREE TRADE AGREEMENTS AND WTO COMPATIBILITY

Goods, Services, Trade Facilitation and Economic Cooperation

Shintaro Hamanaka

Asian Development Bank

World Scientific

NEW JERSEY • LONDON • SINGAPORE • BEIJING • SHANGHAI • HONG KONG • TAIPEI • CHENNAI

Published by

World Scientific Publishing Co. Pte. Ltd.

5 Toh Tuck Link, Singapore 596224

USA office: 27 Warren Street, Suite 401-402, Hackensack, NJ 07601

UK office: 57 Shelton Street, Covent Garden, London WC2H 9HE

Library of Congress Cataloging-in-Publication Data
Hamanaka, Shintaro.
    Asian free trade agreements and WTO compatibility : goods, services, trade facilitation and
economic cooperation / by Shintaro Hamanaka (Asian Development Bank, Philippines).
        pages cm. -- (World scientific studies in international economics, ISSN 1793-3641 ; volume 32)
    Includes bibliographical references and index.
    ISBN 978-9814460408
    1. Free trade--Asia. 2. Asia--Foreign economic relations. 3. Asia--Commercial policy.
4. Asia--Commercial treaties. 5. World Trade Organization--Asia. I. Title.
    HF2294.H36 2014
    382'.71095--dc23
                                                            2013038714

British Library Cataloguing-in-Publication Data
A catalogue record for this book is available from the British Library.

In-house Editor: Alisha Nguyen

Typeset by Stallion Press
Email: enquiries@stallionpress.com

Printed in Singapore

To my parents

Preface

The trend toward regionalism has continued to grow in the recent decade and a half, while the concept of regions continually evolves across time, too. In Europe, the "domino effect" took the form of outsiders' participation in the existing regional framework, although in Asia, it leads to the proliferation of new bilateral free trade agreements (FTAs). Meanwhile, at the multilateral level, trade negotiations have been facing serious challenges and difficulties without any concrete prospect of conclusion.

Given the changing dynamics of regionalism and multilateralism, it is timely to re-consider the relationship between the two, especially from an Asian perspective. In the past, before the proliferation of FTAs, there had been serious efforts to theorize "open" regionalism by Asia-Pacific scholars, but the discussion then mainly focused on preferential tariff treatment. However, the FTAs proliferating in Asia actually cover not only tariffs but also other issues such as trade facilitation and services.

In my previous book, *Asian Regionalism and Japan: Politics of Membership in Regional Diplomatic, Financial and Trade Groups* (Routledge, 2009), I emphasized the "exclusive" aspect of regionalism mainly from international relations standpoint. Regionalism can be best understood as a political project pursued by an unconfident "leader" to assume exclusive influence within the limited geographical area. In contrast, in this research, I analyzed regionalism, especially trade regionalism, from the opposite angle. I considered how to make regionalism covering various issue areas as open as possible from economic standpoint.

There is a genuine concern that the proliferation of FTAs ruins the function of the multilateral trading system. This is because recent policy-makers and scholars, faced with the overwhelming status of FTAs in Asia, tend to focus on issues that may be too unrealistic or technical. However, neither dreams nor tricks can solve the problem. Rather, conscious policy efforts are necessary to make regionalism open in order to reduce their negative external effects on outsiders, just like what was practiced in the past. It is important to re-emphasize the significance of open regionalism in the context of the 2010s as it is simply natural to expect reform-oriented regional cooperation to be very open.

Finally, I would like to emphasize the importance of having an *academic* critical mind in conducting research, especially *policy-oriented* research. Karl Popper's *critical rationalism* is highly important in tackling contested topics both in theory and practice such as the relationship between regionalism and multilateralism. The confusion on the relationship between the two "-isms" can be partly attributed to lack of serious studies conducted by scholars with *academic* critical minds who are not overwhelmed by the current situation. I believe that this study has made a good attempt in this regard.

Summary of Contents

Table of Contents

List of Illustrations

List of Abbreviations

ACP	African, Caribbean and Pacific Group of States
ADB	Asian Development Bank
AEM	ASEAN Economic Ministers (Meeting)
AFAS	ASEAN Framework Agreement on Trade in Services
AFTA	ASEAN Free Trade Area
APEC	Asia-Pacific Economic Cooperation
APTA	Asia-Pacific Trade Agreement
ASEAN	Association of Southeast Asian Nations
ASFTA	Australia–Singapore FTA
ATIGA	ASEAN Trade in Goods Agreement
BTA	Bilateral Trade Agreement
CACM	Central America Common Market
CAN	Andean Community
CARICOM	Caribbean Community and Common Market
CBTA	Cross-border Transport Agreement
CECA	Comprehensive Economic Cooperation Agreement
CEMAC	Economic and Monetary Community of Central Africa
CEPA	Comprehensive Economic Partnership Agreement
CEPT	Common Effective Preferential Tariff
CIS	Commonwealth of Independent States
COMESA	Common Market for Eastern and Southern Africa
CRTA	Committee on Regional Trade Agreements
CTD	Committee on Trade and Development
CU	Customs Union
CVA	Customs Valuation Agreement
DSU	Understanding on Rules and Procedures Governing the Settlement of Disputes
EAC	East African Community
EC	European Community
ECO	Economic Cooperation Organization
ECOTA	Economic Cooperation Organization Trade Agreement

ECOWAS	Economic Community of West African States
EEE	Electrical and Electronic Equipment
EFTA	European Free Trade Association
EIA	Economic Integration Agreement
EPA	Economic Partnership Agreement
ESCAP	United Nations Economic and Social Commission for Asia and the Pacific
EU	European Union
FOB	Free on Board
FTA	Free Trade Agreement
GATT	General Agreement on Tariffs and Trade
GATS	General Agreement on Trade in Services
GCC	Gulf Cooperation Council
GPA	Agreement on Government Procurement
GSP	Generalized System of Preferences
GSTP	Global System of Trade Preferences among Developing Countries
IPR	Intellectual Property Rights
ITO	International Trade Organization
JETRO	Japan External Trade Organization
JIEPA	Japan–Indonesia Economic Partnership Agreement
JMEPA	Japan–Malaysia Economic Partnership Agreement
JPEPA	Japan–Philippines Economic Partnership Agreement
JSEPA	Japan–Singapore Economic Partnership Agreement
JTEPA	Japan–Thailand Economic Partnership Agreement
JVEPA	Japan–Viet Nam Economic Partnership Agreement
LAIA	Latin American Integration Association
LDCs	Least Developed Countries
MERCOSUR	Southern Common Market
MFN	Most Favored Nation
MRA	Mutual Recognition Agreement/Arrangement
MSGTA	Melanesian Spearhead Group Trade Agreement
NAFTA	North American Free Trade Agreement
NIEO	New International Economic Order
OECD	Organisation for Economic Cooperation and Development
ORRCs	Other Restrictive Regulations of Commerce

OTA	Open Trading Agreement
PACER	Pacific Agreement on Closer Economic Relations
PICTA	Pacific Island Countries Trade Agreement
PSA	Partial Scope Agreement
PSI	Agreement on Preshipment Inspection
PTA	Plurilateral Trade Agreement
PTN	Protocol on Trade Negotiations
ROOs	Rules of Origin
SAARC	South Asian Association for Regional Cooperation
SAFTA	South Asian Free Trade Agreement
SAPTA	South Asian Preferential Trade Arrangement
SMEs	Small- and Medium-sized Enterprises
SPARTECA	South Pacific Regional Trade and Economic Cooperation Agreement
SPF	South Pacific Forum
SPS	Sanitary and Phytosanitary (Agreement)
TA	Technical Assistance
TBT	Technical Barriers to Trade (Agreement)
TPR	Trade Policy Review (Mechanism)
TRIPS	Agreement on Trade-related Aspects of Intellectual Property Rights
UNCTAD	United Nations Conference on Trade and Development
US	United States of America
WAEMU	West African Economic and Monetary Union
WCO	World Customs Organization
WTO	World Trade Organization

CHAPTER 1

Introduction

Conceptualizing the WTO Compatibility of FTAs

1.1 WTO Compatibility, WTO Consistency and WTO Friendliness

In considering the pros and cons of regionalism,[1] the central question is always whether or not it is compatible with multilateralism.[2] In the case of trade,[3] where regionalism mainly takes the form of a free trade agreement (FTA), which is the object of analysis in this study,[4] an FTA's compatibility with trade multilateralism becomes the question. While the term "multilateralism" or "multilateral" has various meanings, in this study, the multilateral trading system[5] refers to the system at the global level, not

---

[1]In general, regionalism is defined as a state(s)-led project designed to reorganize a particular regional space along defined economic and political lines (Gamble and Payne, 1996). But others simply define regionalism as intergovernmental collaboration on a geographically restricted basis (Ravenhill, 2001). The difference between the two definitions is important. The former only includes collaboration among regional governments that intends to reorganize the region, while the latter includes any collaboration among regional governments.

[2]The nominal definition of multilateralism is "the practice of coordinating national policies in groups of three or more states" (Keohane, 1990, p. 731). Ruggie (1992) argues that multilateralism refers to coordinating relations among three or more states in accordance with certain principles. Three critical principles of multilateralism are (i) generalized principles of conduct, (ii) indivisibility, and (iii) diffuse reciprocity. See also Caporaso (1992) on the concept of multilateralism.

[3]The compatibility of regionalism with multilateralism is not an issue limited to trade-related matters. In the case of finance, the compatibility of regional financial agreements with the International Monetary Fund (IMF) becomes the problem. For more on this topic, see Henning (2002) and Hill and Menon (2013).

[4]FTAs are usually regarded as examples of regionalism. However, there are many FTAs that are not based on geography in terms of membership.

[5]Despite the wide usage, there is little literature that defines the term multilateral trading system. Irwin and O'Rourke (2011) define a multilateral trading system as "cooperative

a trade agreement among multiple parties. More specifically, the (global) multilateral trading system is used to mainly refer to the World Trade Organization (WTO) system.[6] Because both multilateralism and regionalism (and other preferential arrangements) play an important role in liberalizing and facilitating international trade transactions, we should always have dual perspectives in analyzing the contemporary trade governance structure (Goldstein, Rivers, and Tomz, 2007, p. 39).

When we discuss the appropriate relationship between FTAs and the WTO, it is important to avoid endless debates based on tautological arguments, which are common but not fruitful, especially from the policy perspective. Some may argue that regionalism is only the "second" best option, suggesting that FTAs are unlikely to be perfectly WTO-compatible. Others may argue that FTAs are the second "best" option, implying that the proliferation of FTAs is the reality with which multilateralism should live. However, we should bear in mind that the issue of WTO compatibility of regionalism is not about which one, regionalism or multilateralism, is a more ideal or realistic option. We should think about the appropriate relationship between FTAs and the WTO, especially the former's compatibility with the latter, avoiding dichotomy of debates. We tend to have this type of tautological argument partly because we do not have a good framework to analyze the WTO compatibility of FTAs.

However, conceptualizing the WTO compatibility of FTAs is not a straightforward task. WTO compatibility is a complex concept that includes several different types of ideas about the relationship between FTAs and the WTO.[7] A clear distinction of related concepts to WTO compatibility, such as WTO consistency, makes our lives as researchers much easier. It is always

---

efforts of various countries in the realm of trade policy." However, in this study, the multilateral trading system means the trading system at the global level.

[6]To be precise, the multilateral trading system and the WTO system are not synonymous; the latter is the central component of the former. In fact, not only the WTO, but also other global multilateral institutions, such as the World Customs Organization (WCO), play an important role in forming the multilateral trading system. However, in this study, the multilateral trading system and the WTO system will be used interchangeably.

[7]Many studies tend to use the terms compatibility and consistency interchangeably to refer to regionalism that satisfies the rules of the WTO. However, in this study, the term "WTO compatibility" is used to refer to an overarching concept to describe the relationship between an FTA and the WTO, which includes WTO consistency.

Figure 1.1   Concept of WTO compatibility of FTAs

Source: Author's illustration

very important for us to have a clear understanding about which type of WTO compatibility we are talking about, so that we are conscious of the angle from which the relationship between the two is analyzed. Several key terms are used by different authors in a different way, while different terms are sometimes used to refer to the same concept by different authors. Such a situation causes unnecessary confusion.

There are two interrelated concepts that constitute the WTO compatibility of FTAs: (i) consistency with the WTO, and (ii) friendliness with the WTO (Figure 1.1). WTO consistency refers to whether FTAs are consistent with the rules on the formation of regional agreements as stipulated in WTO Agreements.[8] As we will see in detail later, the various WTO Agreements set many conditions that should be satisfied by regional agreements in trade-related fields. Only when these conditions are met can we regard an FTA as being WTO-consistent. Thus, WTO-consistency is mainly a legal matter.

WTO friendliness is a different concept from WTO consistency, though the two are related. The WTO friendliness of an FTA is a more pragmatic, rather than legal, issue. The non-violation of rules does not mean that there is harmony. In other words, just because an FTA satisfies the conditions set by WTO Agreements does not mean that it is a friend of WTO. A harmonious relationship between the WTO and an FTA can be achieved only when the latter is WTO-friendly, if we take the current form of the multilateral

---

[8]Some literature uses the term WTO compliant to refer to the legal consistency between an FTA and the WTO (Schaefer, 2007). Other scholars use the term WTO compatibility to refer to such legal consistency.

trading system as a given. Thus, WTO friendliness is an issue regarding how open or exclusive an FTA is, though assessing the openness or exclusiveness of FTAs is not an easy task. In this study, two terms, the WTO friendliness of an FTA and the openness of an FTA are used interchangeably.

The WTO friendliness of FTAs has two subcategories: (i) friendliness (openness) to other WTO Members that are non-members of the FTA (hereafter, non-member friendliness) and (ii) friendliness (openness) to the entire multilateral trading system. First, a non-member-friendly FTA (an FTA that is friendly to non-members as well) means that the FTA does not have serious adverse effects on non-members, especially on other WTO Members that are not members of the FTA. This is the problem associated with the insider–outsider dynamic; theoretically, the insiders can be better-off at the expense of the outsiders (Keohane, 1984, p. 79). Thus, the central focus is the economic aspect of FTAs. In particular, the impact on outsiders' trade flows and economic welfare is the question.[9] When the benefit of FTAs is exclusive, such FTAs should be regarded as non-friendly FTAs to non-members.

Second, a system-friendly FTA means that an FTA is friendly to the multilateral trading system, namely the WTO system. As suggested by the WTO, the critical question at the system level is "whether [F]TAs favored or contradicted mutual development of the multilateral trading system; that is, whether [F]TAs have functioned as "building blocks" or "stumbling blocks" *vis-à-vis* the multilateral process" (WTO, 2000, p. 4). The issue is the impact of regionalism on the development of multilateral trading systems and/or the credibility and usefulness of multilateral trade negotiation processes. Thus, this is the problem that is emphasized by political scientists, especially some international political economy specialists as well as trade economists. Bhagwati (1991), who was the first to use the term "building blocks or stumbling blocks" in discussing the role of FTAs in the multilateral system, argues that FTAs that contribute to the multilateral freeing of trade in a dynamic time-path sense can be called building blocks.

Naturally, the friendliness to outsiders and friendliness to the system are closely related. Thus, the overlap between the two types of WTO

---

[9]From the trade perspective, the size of the trade diversion effect is critical in assessing the negative impact on outsiders (Viner, 1950). In terms of welfare, Kemp and Wan (1976) demonstrated that FTAs can be formed without deterioration in the welfare of third parties.

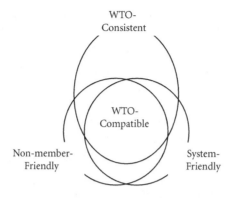

Figure 1.2   WTO consistency and WTO friendliness
WTO = World Trade Organization
Source: Author's illustration

friendliness is large (Figure 1.2). When the benefits of an FTA are exclusive, it has harmful effects on others and does not seem to contribute to the sound development of the multilateral trading system, because it may lead to the formation of another exclusive FTA based on defensive interests. Likewise, an exclusive FTA seems to have large negative impacts on the system, because such an FTA seems to create little incentive for its members to multilateralize the preferential treatment. However, it is also not true that the two types of WTO friendliness always co-exist. This is because a certain aspect of openness of FTAs may have a larger impact on one type of friendliness, but not on the other. An FTA that brings benefits to both members and some non-members, especially in the short-run (a non-member-friendly FTA), may have some negative impacts on the multilateral process in the long run. There is a risk of declined interests in multilateral negotiations once trade is liberalized at a regional level and non-members can also benefit from it, while the long-term credibility of the system is critically important when the economic situation is bad. In short, an FTA's friendliness to outsiders and to the system are closely related, yet different, issues. When an FTA is friendly to the multilateral trading system as well as its non-members, we can say such an FTA is truly WTO-friendly in a strict sense.

Moreover, it is also important to emphasize that the concepts of WTO consistency and WTO friendliness are related but different from one another. Rules set by WTO Agreements that should be satisfied by FTAs are usually implicitly based on economic theory. Thus, FTAs are expected to be WTO-friendly, by becoming WTO-consistent. But the two are not entirely the same — harmonious relations can be achieved only when an FTA is intentionally designed to be outward-oriented by its members; just because an FTA is legally consistent with WTO rules does not mean that it is outward-oriented. In other words, FTAs that satisfy the conditions set by WTO Agreements could be very exclusive in various senses. These would be cases of WTO-consistent, but WTO-non-friendly FTAs (Figure 1.2).[10]

The distinctions between WTO consistency and WTO friendliness, and the two types of WTO friendliness, are useful for analyzing regionalism and multilateralism in the field of trade. In other words, we should consider the appropriate relationship between FTAs and the WTO from several angles, including legal, economic, and political. These are not mutually exclusive, rather, they are closely interrelated. More precisely, the emphasis of the three angles is different, though all of them are useful in examining the appropriate relationship between FTAs and the WTO. In summary, only an FTA that is consistent with WTO rules and friendly to the WTO system in the long run and brings positive economic effects to non-members can be called WTO-compatible.

1.2   Overarching Research Question of the Study

This study examines the appropriate relationship between the WTO and FTAs by analyzing various aspects of the WTO compatibility of FTAs. Above all, it is critically important to recognize that WTO Agreements set disciplines that should be satisfied by regional initiatives. The assessment of FTAs' legal consistency with WTO rules is relatively straightforward, because conditions are explicitly set by WTO Agreements. For example, conditions to be met by regional agreements (covering trade in goods)

---

[10]While it is difficult to reach unanimous consensus about the consistency or inconsistency of an FTA with WTO rules, conceptually, there is a case of a WTO-inconsistent, but WTO-friendly FTA. For example, an FTA that is not notified to the WTO (WTO-inconsistent) may have a positive economic impact on non-members and may contribute to multilateral negotiations on trade liberalization. However, in reality, instances of WTO-inconsistent, but WTO-friendly FTAs seem to be rare.

are stipulated in the General Agreement on Tariffs and Trade (GATT) Article XXIV. However, there is always debate among international trade lawyers on whether FTAs satisfy conditions or not, and on what is the exact meaning of such conditions. Moreover, to satisfy the conditions in GATT Article XXIV alone is not sufficient for FTAs covering goods to be considered "open." In fact, Panagariya (1998, p. 503) argues that consistency with Article XXIV can serve as a necessary, but not sufficient, condition for an arrangement to be open; if this condition were sufficient, it is difficult to argue that regionalism in the 1960s was closed while that in the 1990s was open. Furthermore, the strength of discipline depends on issue areas. In some areas (e.g., goods) there are strong disciplines on regionalism, but in other areas (e.g., services), the multilateral discipline on regionalism is relatively weak. There are also areas where there is no discipline at all, such as economic cooperation. Thus, while the legal analysis provides us with a good start for discussions of WTO compatibility, it is necessary to go beyond that.

Accordingly, irrespective of its WTO consistency, we should also conduct a pragmatic assessment of an FTA — i.e., whether an FTA is WTO-friendly or not. For this purpose, this study proposes a general framework to assess the WTO friendliness of FTAs in terms of both system friendliness and non-member friendliness. First, in terms of system friendliness, the membership rules of an FTA are critically important in assessing its openness. It is interesting to note that Bhagwati, who originally used the term "building blocks or stumbling blocks," suggests that it is necessary to examine the nature of FTAs in a dynamic time-path sense from two angles: (i) acceleration of multilateral trade negotiations (multilateral freeing of trade) and (ii) membership expansion of an FTA (Bhagwati, 1991; Bhagwati and Panagariya, 1996). Whether signing an FTA accelerates the multilateral negotiation process is a difficult empirical question to be tested, but assessing the membership policy and membership fluctuation of an FTA is a relatively straightforward task. Second, in terms of non-member friendliness, while we conceptually know that an FTA has trade and welfare impacts on non-members, the method to assess an FTA's openness or exclusiveness, which is the critical determinant of friendliness *vis-à-vis* non-members, is underdeveloped. Thus, this study proposes a cluster of sequential tree-type questions to assess the type and degree of the openness of FTAs. In other words, the general framework attempts to assess the openness of

FTAs, which is the determinant of the size of effects on non-members, rather than measuring the actual effects on non-members brought about by FTAs. In short, the general framework for analyzing the WTO friendliness of FTAs involves both systemic and technical questions about FTAs, while legal analysis of FTAs in terms of their WTO consistency is conducted separately as a pre-requisite for WTO friendliness.

The general analytical framework can assess the WTO friendliness of FTAs that cover various issue areas and is not limited to trade or tariffs. However, the emphasis of analysis of WTO friendliness of FTAs depends on issue areas. In other words, in assessing WTO friendliness, the focal question among the tree-type questions is not always the same. This study examines the WTO compatibility of regionalism in four issue areas: (i) trade in goods, (ii) trade facilitation, (iii) trade in services, and (iv) economic cooperation (capacity building in particular). These four issue areas are usually included in FTAs as their important components.

- Trade in goods, namely tariffs on goods trade, is still extremely important in considering the WTO compatibility of FTAs. In fact, the past debates on WTO compatibility are based on trade in goods either explicitly or implicitly. A tariff is very unique in considering the exclusiveness of FTAs, because rendering discriminatory treatment is exceptionally easy for a tariff — i.e., preferential tariff treatment.

- Non-tariff issues are becoming critically important, which is usually called trade facilitation as opposed to trade liberalization. Tariffs are becoming less and less important in the trade picture, especially in Asia.[11] Some argue that the fundamental focus of FTAs in Asia is on trade facilitation, rather than tariff reduction (Pomfret, 2011). However, it is important to note that trade facilitation is still an issue related to goods trade.

- Trade in services, which came under the jurisdiction of the WTO after the Uruguay Round, is becoming increasingly important. From a legal perspective, international services trade law based on the General Agreement on Trade in Services (GATS) is a different animal from GATT. Thus, a regional services agreement should be notified to the

---

[11] The average most favored nation (MFN) tariff is very low; more than half of the world's and Asia's trade is conducted under zero MFN (WTO, 2011).

WTO Secretariat separately from the notification for an FTA covering goods. The nature of services liberalization at the regional level is very different from that of goods trade. Thus, careful examination is necessary when we analyze the WTO compatibility of regional services agreements.

• Economic cooperation is an important issue in considering the appropriate relationship between regionalism and multilateralism. Economic cooperation, in particular, the capacity building of developing FTA partners, is usually emphasized as an important component of FTAs. While the WTO's engagement on developmental issues is weak in terms of legal obligations, this important problem can be well addressed by regional initiatives.

This book is structured as follows. The following chapter proposes a general analytical framework to assess the WTO friendliness of FTAs. Using this general framework, we can assess the degree of WTO friendliness of various trade-related regional integration schemes. I believe that the analysis based on tree-type questions in the general framework compliments the legal analysis of the WTO consistency of FTAs. The next four chapters (Chapters 3–6) will empirically assess the WTO compatibility of regional initiatives with respect to (i) trade in goods, (ii) trade facilitation, (iii) trade in services, and (iv) economic cooperation (capacity building). The four empirical chapters share a consistent organizational structure. For each type of regional initiative listed above, the empirical chapters will examine the relevant features of multilateral governance of regionalism by considering how such governance differs from the multilateral governance of regionalism in trade in goods, namely the conditions stipulated in GATT Article XXIV. The empirical chapters then analyze the WTO friendliness of regional initiatives using the general framework introduced in Chapter 2. In the final part of each empirical chapter, we will consider the policy issues, especially questions of how to make regional cooperation under FTAs more WTO-compatible and WTO-friendly. The final chapter summarizes the counter-intuitive policy implications of empirical chapters.

Analytical Framework for WTO Friendliness of FTAs

How to Check If They Are Real "Friends" of WTO?

2.1 Introduction

This chapter tackles two principal tasks. The first is to review an enormous amount of literature that discusses the WTO compatibility of FTAs from various angles. There are two groups of literature. The first group is the so-called open regionalism literature, which developed in the 1980s and 1990s before the rise of trade regionalism in Asia. The authors of open regionalism literature freely suggested various possible options to enhance the openness (reduce the exclusiveness) of regionalism, partly because their thinking was not constrained by actual FTAs that take a specific form. However, the majority of the literature places emphasis on preferential tariffs in formulating the concept. The second-generation literature on the relationship between regionalism and multilateralism flourished after the proliferation of FTAs in Asia. These studies consider how to make the existing FTAs friendly to the WTO system and non-members. Because regional agreements now cover not only goods but also other issues, they also consider the relation between regionalism and multilateralism in the non-goods fields. The second task of this chapter is to establish a general analytical framework to assess the WTO friendliness of FTAs. It is designed to assess the openness of regional initiatives in various issue areas. The framework includes both system-level questions, which mainly deal with FTA's friendliness to the system, and technical-level questions, which mainly deal with an FTA's friendliness to non-members. In particular, the framework contains a cluster of tree-type technical questions that identify the nature and the degree of the second type of WTO friendliness of FTAs.

Accordingly, this chapter is structured as follows. Section 2.2 reviews an extensive list of options to render regionalism open, as proposed in early open regionalism literature. Section 2.3 reviews the more recent literature that discusses methods to enhance the harmony between the WTO and existing FTAs. Based on both early and recent literature on regionalism–multilateralism issues, Section 2.4 proposes a general analytical framework for the WTO friendliness of FTAs, which contains system-level questions as well as a cluster of technical-level, tree-type questions. Using the framework proposed, we will also conduct a preliminary assessment of the openness of regional initiatives in various issue areas and attempt to identify which specific question in tree-type questions is critical in assessing the openness of regionalism in each field. Section 2.5 summarizes the main discussion of this chapter.

2.2   First-generation Literature: Open Regionalism

Open regionalism was believed to be a fundamental feature of economic regionalism in Asia. Proponents of open regionalism have attempted to challenge the widespread belief outside Asia that regional economic cooperation works only if it discriminates against outsiders (Drysdale, Elek, and Soesastro, 1998, p. 104), as they believe that regionalism can be pursued without any detriment to outsiders (Elek, 1992). This unique term describes various contrasting aspects of regional integration in Asia; there is no need to consider open regionalism to be an oxymoron.[1]

Open regionalism was a particularly popular concept among scholars and policy-makers in the 1980s and 1990s, when economic interdependence among the Asia-Pacific economies deepened significantly. Although some have started to question the validity of this concept due to the recent trend of signing FTAs in Asia, its essence seems to still be useful in considering the harmonious relationship between economic regionalism

---

[1] Srinivasan (1996) considers open regionalism to be an oxymoron, or at least not a fruitful concept, but it is important to note that his definition of regionalism is FTAs. He argues that the extension of FTA preferences should be on a most favored nation (MFN) basis so that such a policy is consistent with WTO rules, but the extension of FTA preferences to all countries simply means that an FTA is redundant. However, if regionalism is defended broadly, such as a form of regional cooperation, then open regionalism is not necessarily an oxymoron (Garnaut, 1996, p. 1).

and the multilateral trading system as well as practical guidelines to reduce the negative sides of economic regionalism. Open regionalism is not only a theoretical issue but also a practical and operational perspective regarding regional cooperation in Asia. It has been progressively given clearer operational meaning over time as the process of cooperation in Asia has evolved (Drysdale, Elek, and Soesastro, 1998, p. 103), and it is safe to consider that such a process of development still continues. In a sense, open regionalism is a spirit or philosophy (Capie and Evans, 2002, p. 183), not a particular set of policies. What we need is its contemporary interpretation given the renewed policy relevance of the concept.

The primary reason why the openness of regionalism was emphasized in the Asia-Pacific was that economic integration in the region had been achieved on a market-driven basis, rather than a legal basis (Hormats, 1994). In analyzing such private-sector-led or market-driven integration, emphasis is usually placed on the private economic activities that network the region,[2] such as production networks (Katzenstein and Shiraishi, 1997).[3] By making a distinction between market-driven integration and international-law-driven integration, many scholars argued that *de facto* integration in Asia has been significant but *de jure* integration has not been (Hurrell, 1995; Wyatt-Walter, 1995). However, open regionalism does not simply mean economic integration without a legal framework for integration. One of the reasons why Asian countries avoid legalization of trade relations is that Asian countries were unable to create FTAs that meet the conditions stipulated in GATT Article XXIV (Elek, 1995). Thus, open regionalism was achieved not by the fulfillment of trade agreements that go beyond GATT Article XXIV but rather due to the inability to sign a trade agreement satisfying GATT Article XXIV. This can be called weak open regionalism. However, given that there are already a large number of FTAs in Asia, a more positive way to make regionalism open is necessary.

---

[2] Other than production networks, policy networks in the region are also emphasized in the discussion on Asian regionalism. See, for example, Harris (1994).

[3] Some point out the closed nature of market-driven economic integration in Asia, which is dominated by Japanese multinational corporations. While private-sector-led economic activities have been considered as the basis of open regional integration as opposed to legal integration, the nature of private-sector-led integration varies, especially between those of Japanese multinational corporations and corporations run by overseas Chinese.

Open regionalism has been the central question of Asia-Pacific Economic Cooperation (APEC) since it was launched in 1989. While the term has not been defined officially, several projects under APEC contributed to the materialization of the idea.[4] An early attempt at conceptualizing the embryonic idea of open regionalism was made by the Eminent Persons' Group of APEC in the 1990s. The Osaka Action Plan in 1995 elaborated on the fundamental nature of open regionalism, although the proposal did not define it, stipulating that "the outcome of trade and investment liberalization in the Asia-Pacific region will be the actual reduction of barriers not only among APEC economies but also between APEC and non-APEC economies" (APEC, 1995). The Action Plan emphasized the importance of the voluntary nature of trade liberalization.

Bergsten (1997) provides a comprehensive list of possible definitions or interpretations of open regionalism. According to him, there are five variants of open regionalism that are widely used by scholars and policy-makers in the Asia-Pacific. These include (i) open membership, (ii) unilateral most favored nation (MFN) liberalization, (iii) extension of FTA preferences to outsiders, (iv) multilateral liberalization, and (v) trade facilitation. It is useful to review these five types of open regionalism together with related literature. Those five variations of open regionalism are not mutually exclusive, and regionalism that is truly open may entail more than one feature. Detailed descriptions of policy options regarding the second, third, and fourth types of open regionalism, which are closely interrelated, are provided in Table 2.1 below.

Open membership. Interestingly, many economists tend to reach the conclusion that issues regarding openness of regionalism can be solved if a regional framework has an open membership policy, which is a highly political issue, rather than an economic issue.[5] This argument can be applied

---

[4]Even before the launch of APEC, the idea of open regionalism had already been introduced. According to Drysdale, Elek, and Soesastro (1998, p. 106), the elements of open regionalism were set out in the 1980s at the Pacific Economic Cooperation Council (PECC).

[5]There is a rich accumulation of literature on membership in the field of political science. Many political scientists attempt to explain why the control of membership is important and why regionalism tends to be exclusive. On the general theories on the control of membership of regional institutions, see Kelley (2010). On the politics of membership in Asian institutions, see Wesley (1997) and Hamanaka (2009).

not only to the accession to an FTA but also to the accession to any type of regional intergovernmental collaboration framework. The significance of open membership can be easily understood intuitively, because the problems associated with the negative externalities of regionalism (e.g., trade diversion) can be directly solved by the accession of adversely affected outsiders. Moreover, members of regionalism do not have an incentive to enjoy some benefit at the expense of outsiders if there is a possibility of accession, because such a benefit is not sustainable when outsiders actually join in.[6]

Theorists argued that an effective way to ensure that regional trade frameworks eventually lead to multilateral trade is to encourage them to adopt an open membership policy (Cooper, 1993, p. 455). Moreover, Baldwin's influential theory of the domino effect, which predicts that non-members will eventually decide to join an FTA, is also implicitly based on the open membership assumption. His premise is that an event that triggers closer integration within an existing bloc harms the profits of non-member exporters, therefore stimulating them to boost their pro-membership political activity *vis-à-vis* their governments. In addition, the enlargement of the bloc in terms of membership further harms non-member exporters since they now face a disadvantage in a greater number of markets, and this further incentivizes them to join the FTA. As a result, membership of the FTA continues to expand (Baldwin, 1993). With this path, regionalism is expected to contribute to global trade as it expands membership. As Panagariya (1998, pp. 23–24) argues, however, one important issue overlooked by Baldwin and others is that incumbent members have an incentive to block the participation of new members. It does not translate that accession can be achieved merely because non-members have an incentive to join.[7] Even if membership is open to anyone, the associated fee would be very expensive (Bhagwati, 1995, p. 13).[8]

---

[6]Many political scientists argue that cooperation among states becomes possible when they gain some benefit at the expense of outsiders. For example, see Keohane (1984, p. 79).

[7]Moreover, from a political perspective, regionalism is often motivated by a country's desire to assume exclusive influence in the region by excluding rival states; trade regionalism is not an exception (Hamanaka, 2009).

[8]The relevant problem here is a side-payment. For example, for Mexico to join the North American Free Trade Agreement (NAFTA), it needed to accept labor and environmental standards largely set by the US.

Bergsten himself acknowledges that implementation of open membership policy seems to be very difficult in reality and argues that no regional agreement has ever taken such a course, because a regional organization eventually becomes a global organization if membership continues to expand. Ironically, the difficulty in expanding membership even within a limited geographical area, which is also a controversial issue, is especially true in the case of Asia, even more than in Europe and North America. This is partly because the geographical boundaries of the region are significantly more ambiguous in Asia than in either Europe or North America.[9] In fact, both the EU and NAFTA have accession clauses, and the former actually expanded its membership.[10] Despite its advocacy of open regionalism, APEC experienced a membership moratorium twice.[11]

Unilateral MFN liberalization. Unilateral MFN reduction means that tariffs are reduced unilaterally under each country's own initiative (based on self-interest) and the lowered tariff is applicable to all other WTO Members (or even all countries in the world[12]) without any distinction (see the "Unilateral MFN Liberalization" column in Table 2.1). Unilateral MFN liberalization is usually an unconditional policy adopted by each country (Bergsten, 1997). Because this policy is based on each country's independent calculation of its self-interest, the accurate way to call this type of liberalization is as independent unilateral MFN liberalization (Elek, 1995, p. 10). Many economists consider that this is the only pure and faithful definition of open regionalism (Bergsten, 1997, p. 553), because no new

---

[9]In contrast, Haggard (1997, p. 45) argues that regionalism in the Americas compared with Asian regionalism is less open in terms of accepting new members. See also Pempel (2005).

[10]While NAFTA has an accession clause, no country has applied for membership. However, several countries, including Singapore, showed interest in participating in NAFTA. See Bergsten (1994, p. 24).

[11]The APEC Leaders agreed to introduce the first three-year moratorium at the 1993 Seattle APEC Summit. Soon after the end of this moratorium, three members (Russia, Peru, and Vietnam) obtained APEC membership in 1997. In the same year, APEC decided to precede with a 10-year moratorium in order to deepen the cooperation among existing members. At the 2007 APEC Summit, the moratorium was extended until 2010. See Kim (2008).

[12]Conceptually, unilateral MFN tariff reduction and unilateral tariff reduction are different. The former approach means that tariffs applicable to WTO Members are reduced, which implies that the tariff level for non-WTO members is unchanged. The latter means that tariffs applicable to all countries in the world are reduced. However, unless otherwise specified, this study does not distinguish the two types of tariff reduction.

Table 2.1   Varieties of open regionalism

Type of open regionalism	Conditional or unconditional	Independent or concerted, and type of condition	Description
Unilateral MFN Liberalization	Unconditional unilateral MFN liberalization	Independent unconditional unilateral MFN liberalization	I will cut MFN, irrespective of what others will do.
		Concerted unconditional unilateral MFN liberalization	We will cut MFN, irrespective of what others will do.
	Conditional unilateral MFN liberalization	Reciprocally conditional unilateral MFN liberalization	I will cut MFN, if you will cut MFN.
		Multilaterally conditional unilateral MFN liberalization (multilateral negotiations)	I will cut MFN, if others will cut MFN.
Unilateral Extension of Preferences	Unconditional unilateral extension of preferences	Independent unconditional unilateral extension of preferences	I will extend preferences to all, irrespective what others will do.
		Concerted unconditional unilateral extension of preferences (concerted efforts among FTA members)	We will extend preferences to all, irrespective what others will do.
	Conditional unilateral extension of preferences	Reciprocally conditional unilateral extension of preferences	I will extend preferences to all, if you will extend special preferences to all.
		Multilaterally conditional unilateral extension of preferences (multilateral negotiations)	I will extend preferences to all, if others will extend preferences to all.
Exclusive Extension of Preferences	Unconditional exclusive extension of preferences	NA	NA
	Conditional exclusive extension of preferences	(Reciprocally) conditional exclusive extension of preferences (new FTA)	I will extend preferences to you, if you will extend preferences to me.

Source: Author's compilation

preference or discrimination would be created. The theoretical root of this unilateral action of trade liberalization is the "prisoners' delight" thesis, as opposed to "prisoners' dilemma" proposed by Garnaut (1994).[13]

In the open regionalism literature, particular emphasis is placed on concerted unilateral MFN reduction (Garnaut, 1996; Drysdale, Vines, and House, 1998). While the MFN tariff reduction should be based on the autonomous decision of each country, which is essentially an independent action rather than a joint action, it can be achieved well if regional economies pursue this policy in a concerted manner. It should be noted that concerted actions and reciprocal actions are not exactly the same. Commitment to unilateral trade liberalization in one's own self-interest should not be regarded as concession for exchange although their collective outcome is mutually re-enforcing. In fact, for example, Yamazawa (1992) argues that APEC should become an open economic association that relies on unilateral actions rather than negotiations. It is argued that concerted unilateralism was an answer to the tension between advocates of pure unilateralism, who favored non-discrimination, and those who favored reciprocity (Ravenhill, 2001, p. 141). It can be said that concerted is a weak form of reciprocity.

The most fundamental problem of unilateralism in trade liberalization is that countries that participate in (concerted) unilateral actions lose bargaining power over non-members' trade liberalization. Unilateral liberalization may have its own economic benefits for the majority of Asia-Pacific economies, but this does not mean that other countries also follow unilateral liberalization. More concretely, APEC members' concerted unilateral trade liberalization may be achieved by their voluntary actions based on each country's own economic interests, but this would lead to APEC countries' inability to influence the attitude toward liberalization of

---

[13] It seems that this thesis is effective and correct, given that the tariff levels of most Asia-Pacific economies dropped significantly in the 1980s and 1990s without regional agreements. Some argue that the prisoner's delight thesis is problematic because it contradicts governments' actual resistance to cooperative approaches (Ravenhill, 2001, p. 40), emphasizing that the economically optimum choice is not always achieved due to political economy obstacles. Thus, for them, the idea of prisoners' delight payoffs, which are based on neo-classical economic assumptions, is wrong. However, it is plausible to consider that soft institutions like APEC that emphasize peer pressure and experience sharing are useful in achieving an economically beneficial equilibrium of prisoners' delight that overcomes political economy problems.

a non-APEC country. Accordingly, some countries in the Asia-Pacific, and especially countries in North America, prefer reciprocity of trade liberalization over unilateral liberalization (Drysdale, Elek, and Soesastro, 1998, p. 108). As suggested by the early formation of NAFTA, its members' preference for regionalism is based on reciprocity, wherein concessions are given only to members who are ready to exchange concessions; this can be called normal regionalism.

While Bergsten emphasizes unconditional unilateral MFN liberalization in arguing for open regionalism, unilateral MFN liberalization can also be achieved in a conditional manner as well (Funabashi, 1995, p. 123). A first possibility is reciprocally conditional MFN liberalization. In this scenario, two or more countries jointly (not solely) cut MFN tariffs, which is also applicable to other countries. Presume that two countries are interested in each other's markets, but they do not want to unilaterally cut tariffs alone. Under such circumstances, the two countries may agree to cut MFN tariffs together, because each of them can benefit significantly by the other's move. This scenario is similar to the idea of a "K-group" in the international relations literature.[14] A second possibility is multilaterally conditional unilateral MFN liberalization. In this case, MFN tariffs being cut is conditional upon other countries' (not a specific country) MFN cut. This is almost the same as multilateralism or multilateral negotiations on trade liberalization.

Extension of FTA preferences. The third type of open regionalism according to Bergsten is the extension of preferential treatment, which was initially exclusive for FTA partners, to all other countries.[15] Thus, the question here is how to make an FTA open, given that it has already been signed.

---

[14] A group of like-minded countries collaborate and supply international public goods — in this case, a liberal open trade regime — even if the public goods are free-ridden by others. Snidal (1985) argues that a group of like-minded countries (K-group) provide public goods based on their own self-interest, and thus those goods should be rather called private goods though outsiders can also enjoy the benefits by free-riding. See also Russett (1985).

[15] Bergsten (1998) uses the term "conditional MFN extension." However, this term is confusing because MFN refers to the most favored nation status, which should be given to all countries without condition according to GATT Article I. What Bergsten actually means is that FTA concessions, which are more preferential than MFN, can be extended to non-members only when certain conditions are met. These can be achieved by the reduction of MFN to the same level as FTA concessions. In an earlier work, he uses the term "temporarily conditional MFN" (Bergsten, 1994, p. 24).

The preferences can be easily extended on an exclusive basis (see the "Exclusive Extension of Preferences" column in Table 2.1). Bergsten emphasizes the importance of exclusive extension of FTA preferences, because in his view, countries need to sign an FTA (as opposed to unilateral tariff reductions) in order to avoid free-rider problems, and thus the extension of any regional preferences should also avoid free-rider problems. This option implicitly assumes the formation of a new FTA or customs union (Funabashi, 1995, p. 124; Park, 2002) because WTO members are not allowed to give better treatment than MFN to selected countries without the formation of FTAs or customs unions. Thus, the extension should be conditional[16] as well as reciprocal,[17] which means that the extension is conditional to a potential partner's reciprocal offer of concession. According to Bergsten, during the Seattle APEC Summit in 1993 and an informal summit in 1996, some APEC members were inclined to form an APEC FTA, wherein preferential treatment could be exchanged between APEC members and non-members on a reciprocal basis, in order to put pressure on Europe to seriously engage in multilateral negotiations, although it did not happen (Bergsten, 1996, p. 554). The idea of the linkage between the Association of Southeast Asian Nations (ASEAN) Free Trade Area (AFTA) and NAFTA in the mid-1990s is another example of "reciprocal exclusive extension of FTA preferences" (Haas, 1994, p. 844). Although some may question if a reciprocal exclusive extension should be included in open regionalism, the policy of extending FTA preferences can be said to be more open than a policy where FTA members as a group refuse to extend preferences or an FTA does not allow its members to sign a separate FTA with a potential partner under each country's own initiative.[18]

---

[16]The idea of unconditional exclusive extension is impossible because FTAs request all member countries to reduce tariffs in a reciprocal manner.

[17]A multilaterally conditional exclusive extension is practically impossible.

[18]The non-prohibition of member countries' own FTA policy was considered as an important element of open regionalism in the 1990s. This point was emphasized by the US, partly because North American countries signed NAFTA, although they are also members of APEC. The US Council of Economic Advisors (1995) stated that "open regionalism...requires that a plurilateral agreement not constrain members from pursuing additional liberalization either with non-members on a reciprocal basis or unilaterally." See Srinivasan (1996, p. 16).

However, it is important to understand that the extension of preferences can also be achieved on a unilateral basis (Funabashi, 1995; Park, 2002), though Bergsten does not carefully examine this possibility (see the "Unilateral Extension of Preferences" column in Table 2.1). The unilateral extension has both unconditional and conditional cases. First, the policy of unconditional unilateral extension of preferences has two possibilities.[19] Each member of an FTA[20] may decide to extend the FTA preferences to others irrespective of their policy, which would represent the independent unconditional unilateral extension of FTA preferences. Alternatively, a group of countries — in the case of both customs unions and FTAs — may decide to jointly extend the regional preferences to others irrespective of their policy: a concerted unconditional unilateral extension of regional preferences. In the recent literature, some call the policy of unconditional unilateral extension of regional preferences — mainly, independent unconditional unilateral extension — the policy of "multilateralization of regionalism" (WTO, 2011; Baldwin and Low, 2009b).[21] Second, the policy of conditional unilateral extension also has two possibilities. The first subcategory is reciprocally conditional unilateral extension of FTA preferences. In this case, the situation is similar to a K-group because a group of like-minded countries jointly extend FTA preferences to all other countries. Alternatively, the unilateral extension of preferences can be multilaterally conditional, not reciprocally. This case, which can be called multilaterally conditional unilateral extension of FTA preferences, is the same as multilateralism.

Commitment to multilateral liberalization. The fourth type of open regionalism outlined by Bergstein is multilateral liberalization. Countries

---

[19]The difference between unconditional unilateral extension of preferences and unconditional unilateral MFN liberalization mentioned above is that the former is the action after signing and FTA or establishing a customs unions, while the latter is the policy that does not entail the formation of a free trade area or customs union. However, it is also true that unconditional unilateral extension of regional preferences is usually implemented by means of unconditional unilateral MFN liberalization because the unilateral extension usually takes the form of a unilateral MFN cut.

[20]In the case of a customs union, this option is impossible because the external tariffs of a customs union should be harmonized.

[21]For example, WTO (2011, p. 15) defines multilateralizing regionalism as "extending existing preferential arrangements in a nondiscriminatory manner to additional parties."

that have membership in a regional initiative continue to engage in the trade liberalization negotiations at the multilateral (WTO) level. If FTA members lose interest in multilateral negotiations, which is known as attention diversion (Kruger, 1995), such regionalism is no longer open. This type of open regionalism also assumes that countries already have WTO Membership. This route of open regionalism can be reinforced by unilateral MFN reduction. This is because the primary concern of multilateral negotiations is reduction in the MFN bound tariff rate, while unilateral MFN reduction is a cut of the MFN applied tariff rate. The two specific types of open regionalism mentioned above — multilaterally conditional unilateral MFN liberalization and multilaterally conditional unilateral extension of FTA preferences — also fall under the category of multilateralism.

Trade facilitation. The final interpretation of open regionalism is an emphasis on trade facilitation measures. The inclusion of trade facilitation issues in regional cooperation is believed to be important because many trade facilitation measures do not translate to preferential treatment (Bergsten, 1997, p. 557). Garnaut (1996, p. 7) argues that trade facilitation can provide benefits to participants without any steps being taken to exclude outsiders from enjoying the benefits. Examples of trade facilitation that benefit non-members, according to Bergsten (1996), include customs reform and mutual recognition of standards among others. However, there is a possibility that some trade facilitation measures bring intended or unintended discrimination to non-members.

Finally, it is also interesting to understand the policy-makers' view on open regionalism when the issue is seriously discussed by scholars. As mentioned above, open regionalism is a policy orientation, rather than a theory, and its operational meaning developed over time as policy-makers' thinking on the issue developed. For example, Renato Ruggiero, the inaugural Director-General of the WTO said

> The second interpretation of open regionalism is the one I hear from a number of governments who are members of APEC or MERCOSUR. In this scenario, the **gradual** elimination of internal barriers to trade within a regional grouping will be implemented at **more or less** the same rate and on the same timetable as the lowering of barriers towards non-members. This would mean that regional liberalization would be generally consistent not only with the rules of the WTO but also — and this is very important — with the MFN principle (Ruggiero, 1996). (Underline supplied)

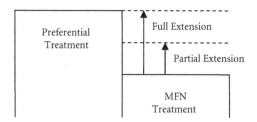

Figure 2.1   Types of extensions of preferences

Source: Author's illustration

It is important to note that the level and timing of reducing tariffs to non-members are "more or less" the same, not exactly the same, as those to members. The first important point is the level of extension (of FTA preferences) given to non-members. The extension of FTA preferences is not an all-or-nothing proposition. A partial extension, as opposed to a full extension, of FTA preferences is possible (Figure 2.1). When a country, for example, imposes a 20% MFN tariff on a particular product prior to signing an FTA, the partial extension could mean eliminating the said tariff for partners upon FTA entry and also reducing the MFN tariff to 10%. The second important point is the timing of unilateral MFN reduction. It is not assumed that FTA preferences are multilateralized soon after an FTA is concluded. Some time lag between regional and multilateral liberalization may be observed. Because the reduction of barriers for intra-FTA trade is gradual under many FTAs, rather than a one-off event, the reduction of MFN tariffs may also become gradual. For example, a gradual preferential tariff cut achieved under an FTA would lead to a gradual MFN cut after a certain period.

Although the early open regionalism literature includes fairly comprehensive policy options to outward-looking regionalism, one distinctive weakness regarding its analytical focus can be pointed out. The early open regionalism debate is dominated by trade in goods specialists. They always have FTAs, and more specifically GATT Article XXIV-based FTAs, in mind. The extreme position argues that open regionalism is an oxymoron because it defines regionalism as "discriminatory tariff treatment exclusive to partners" (Srinivasan, 1996). However, such a debate is of little use, especially for FTAs recently signed, because tariff is no longer the central issue of trade regionalism.

2.3   Second-generation Literature

Since 2000, FTAs have proliferated in Asia (Pomfret, 2011). The third wave of trade regionalism surged with Asia at the forefront, unlike the first[22] and second[23] waves of trade regionalism in the 1960s and 1970s and the 1980s and 1990s, that were led by countries in Europe and North America, respectively.[24] The proposal of the ASEAN–China FTA (ACFTA) in 2001 was the trigger of the third wave of trade regionalism (Baldwin and Carpenter, 2011). Since then, FTAs have proliferated in Asia partly as a result of the so-called domino effect. Because of the lack of operational accession rules in Asia, the domino effect manifested itself not through non-members joining an existing agreement as suggested might happen by Baldwin (1993), but rather through the signing or proposing of new FTAs.

It is important to take into account two new important environments that were created at the multilateral level by the early 2000s when FTAs started to proliferate in Asia. The first environmental change was the expansion of issue coverage of the multilateral trading system. Under

---

[22]There have been three waves of trade regionalism, although the time span of each wave of regionalism slightly varies across researchers (Bhagwati, 1993; Mansfield and Milner, 1999; Carpenter, 2009; Baldwin and Carpenter, 2011). The first wave of regionalism occurred in the 1960s and 1970s, with Europe at the forefront. The European Community was formed in 1958 and the European Free Trade Association (EFTA) came into force in 1960. At the same time, there were many regional cooperation schemes in the developing world, such as Central American Common Market (CACM), which was formed in 1961, and the Caribbean Community and Common Market (CARICOM), formed in 1973.

[23]The second wave of regionalism occurred in the 1990s, which was initiated primarily in the Americas. After the debt crisis of the 1980s, many Latin American countries started to adopt more liberal economic policies. One notable example is NAFTA, formed in 1994, which includes Canada, Mexico, and the US. There are also many bilateral FTAs in Latin America as well, such as the Costa Rica–Mexico FTA signed in 1995.

[24]Although there was no surge of trade regionalism in Asia during the second wave of regionalism in the 1980s and 1990s, since open regionalism was the dominant norm of trade policy in Asia, financial regionalism was active in Asia, especially after the 1997–1998 Asian financial crisis. Thus, just because trade regionalism is absent, we should not consider that Asian countries abstain from engaging in regional economic cooperation initiatives. It is important to note that many studies on financial regionalism in Asia point out that Asian financial regionalism has not been particularly open and Asian countries tend to have exclusive arrangement unlike in the case of trade (Hamanaka, 2011a; Pempel, 2006; Solingen, 2005). See also Higgott and Stubbs (1995) on exclusive regional groupings in general.

the new WTO system after the Uruguay Round, several new agreements expected to reduce non-tariff barriers were introduced. In this regard, technical barriers to trade (TBT) and sanitary and phytosanitary measures (SPS) are of particular importance. Some parts of customs procedures were also expected to be facilitated by the introduction of a Customs Valuation Agreement. A critically important issue that is newly covered by the WTO in considering trade regionalism is trade in services. The General Agreement on Trade in Services (GATS) Article V on Economic Integration, a dedicated article on services regionalism, can be regarded as a counterpart of GATT Article XXIV, which stipulates the conditions to be satisfied by goods trade regionalism. Under the initiative of Aid for Trade, which was initiated through the Hong Kong Declaration in 2005, a renewed emphasis was placed on capacity building for trade policy-making. WTO Members realized that aid could reinforce trade, going beyond the past discussions on "trade not aid,"[25] and "aid and trade."[26]

The second environmental change was the expansion of WTO Membership, as evidenced in additional Asian countries' accession to the WTO. Several Asian countries obtained WTO Membership during the 1990s and 2000s only after a long negotiation period.[27] For many countries, including developing countries in Asia, WTO Membership seems to be a kind of precondition for engaging in trade regionalism policies such as FTAs. This is because countries cannot enjoy the MFN status without WTO Membership. Needless to say, GATT Article I guarantees MFN treatment for WTO Members only. Thus, it is reasonable for countries to first pursue a WTO Membership to enjoy MFN tariffs before pursuing preferential tariff under FTAs. For example, it is widely said that one of the reasons why China was skeptical of unilateral MFN reduction under the APEC framework was that the country feared the possibility that such unilateral MFN reductions among APEC economies would not be enjoyed by China since it was not a WTO Member in the 1990s (Funabashi, 1995, p. 123).

---

[25]"Trade not aid" was the basic foreign economic policy of the Eisenhower administration in the US in the 1950s (Bowie and Immerman, 1998, p. 210).

[26]For the evolution of the idea of "aid for trade," including "aid and trade," see UNCTAD (2008).

[27]China joined the WTO in 2001 after 15 years of negotiations. Vietnam joined in 2007 after 12 years of negotiations.

It was also discussed in the 1990s that China's lack of WTO Membership was one of the main obstacles to envisioning any FTAs in Asia (Funabashi, 1995, p. 123; Drysdale and Elek, 1996, p. 169). In fact, some Asian countries were reluctant to engage in FTAs until they had WTO Membership, but their FTA policies become very proactive only after their accession to the WTO.[28] In this context, the argument developed by some scholars that Asia was a "vacuum area" in terms of FTA activities until around 2000, with the notable exception of AFTA,[29] seems to be slightly misleading; it was not only FTA membership but also WTO Membership that was absent in much of Asia.

As FTAs have flourished since 2000, studies on FTAs have also flourished. In particular, understanding how to reduce the adverse impacts of the proliferation of FTAs was the focal point of much analysis during the 2000s. The spread of FTAs was expected to lead to the spaghetti (or noodle) bowl problem. While there are many common aspects between the two, the second-generation literature can be classified into two groups: (i) multilateralizing regionalism literature, and (ii) new open regionalism literature. The former is originally based on Richard Baldwin's work, while the later is closely related to the first-generation literature on open regionalism.

2.3.1   *Multilateralizing regionalism literature*

Authors of multilateralizing regionalism literature,[30] consider the multi-lateralization of regionalism as the preferred approach to overcoming the negative effects of the proliferation of FTAs. Multilateralization of regionalism is defined as "the extension of existing preferential arrange-ments in a non-discriminatory manner to additional parties, or a fusion of distinct [F]TAs" (WTO, 2011, p. 190).

At the system-level, multilateralizing regionalism literature concludes that the tension between regionalism and multilateralism can be mitigated

---

[28]China's FTA activities became extremely proactive once it attained WTO Membership (Gao, 2008). In the year it obtained WTO membership, it became a member of the Asia-Pacific Trade Agreement (APTA) and officially proposed the ASEAN–China FTA (ACFTA).

[29]For example, see Chirathivat and Mallikamas (2004).

[30]See the edited volume by Baldwin and Low (2009a), which include a large number of papers on the topic of multilateralizing regionalism. See also UNESCAP (2005) for early discussions on multilateralizing regionalism.

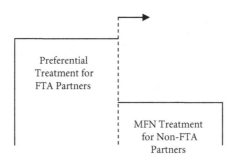

Figure 2.2   Expansion of beneficiaries: membership expansion
Source: Author's illustration

by two possible policies (Baldwin and Low, 2009b). The first method is the geographical extension of FTAs, such as was the case with EU enlargement. This approach significantly expands the number of countries that can enjoy the benefits of an FTA (Figure 2.2). Second, it proposes the replacement of existing agreements with a new agreement that extends to new members. In the Asian context, there is an argument that the consolidation of existing FTAs into a single region-wide FTA is necessary to solve the Asian noodle bowl problem. Such an idea is rather radical because it assumes the suspension of existing agreements.[31]

Technical-level policies to multilateralize regionalism are discussed in the multilateralizing regionalism literature. Baldwin (2006) and Baldwin, Evenett, and Low (2009) offer the most comprehensive recent studies that identify the methods to multilateralize regionalism.[32] The first method suggested by the authors is related to the extension of regional preferences (Figure 2.3 (a)). The extension of regional preferences can be achieved by either the inclusion of *de jure* MFN provisions with respect to a particular policy in FTAs or a *de facto* extension of regional preferences. In the former case, a particular provision in FTAs guarantees the same favorable treatment for both members and non-members. The latter, on the other hand, is not legally stipulated. If the extension is achieved on the *de facto* basis, there is

---

[31] For a critical review on the consolidation of FTAs in Asia, see Hamanaka (2012a). For a review of arguments consolidating FTAs in Asia, see Chia (2010) and Zhang and Shen (2011).
[32] See also papers in Baldwin and Low (2009a).

(a) Full-extension of Preferential Treatment

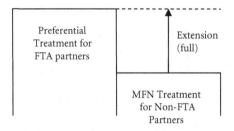

(b) Leveling the Preferential Treatment (third-party MFN)

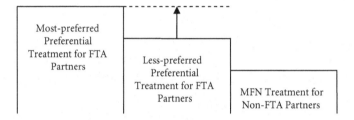

(c) Expansion of Beneficiaries in Terms of Products

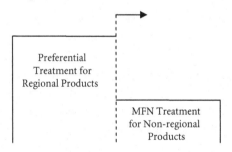

Figure 2.3   Technical-level methods to multilateralize regionalism
Source: Author's illustration

no legal back-up for the extension. The ultimate outcomes brought about by the expansion of membership (Figure 2.2) and extension of preferential treatment (Figure 2.3 (a)) are similar, because all countries and products are able to enjoy the regional preferential treatment in due course.

The second method suggested by the authors is the inclusion of third-party MFN clause (Figure 2.3 (b)). This means that the treatment of a certain contracting party of an FTA will not be preferred over the treatment of other contracting parties under different FTAs. If a new FTA includes more preferential treatment, the same treatment is extended to the partner of former FTAs that have a third-party MFN clause. Thus, with a third-party MFN, FTA partners under different FTAs are treated in the same manner (Pauwelyn, 2009). This method contributes in preventing the realization of differentiated treatment across FTA partners, not discriminatory treatment between members and non-members. The third method is the inclusion of provisions in FTAs that prevent actions allowed under WTO Agreements that result in discriminatory treatment.

In considering the discriminatory effects of FTAs, emphasis is placed on rules of origin (ROOs) — not limited to trade in goods but also extending to other issue areas — because they define the imports that can enjoy preferential access. Relaxing ROOs is another technical-level method to multilateralize regionalism. It is an effective way to expand the beneficiaries of the FTA in terms of products when the beneficiaries of the FTA in terms of countries, namely membership, are already given (Figure 2.3 (c)). While membership expansion (Figure 2.2) is the way to expand the beneficiaries of an FTA at the country level (membership level), the relaxing of ROOs is the way to expand beneficiaries in terms of products and services. The weaker the restrictiveness of ROOs, the less discriminatory their effects become. Baldwin, Evenett, and Low (2009) argue, for example, that the mutual recognition of standards (e.g., TBT) usually do not have the concept of origin. Thus, if there is mutual recognition of conformity assessment between the US and EU, and a certain US laboratory is registered under the mutual recognition agreement, then this laboratory can be used even by, for example, Canadian firms that wish to export their products to the EU (Baldwin, Evenett, and Low, 2009, p. 116). They argue that less discriminatory effects are brought about by FTAs in areas other than goods and tariffs, because ROOs in those issue areas are usually weak or "leaky" (for the detailed discussions on the exclusiveness of trade facilitation measures including mutual recognition, see Chapter 4, Section 4.5).

The most important contribution made by Baldwin, Evenett, and Low (2009) is that their analysis is not only limited to goods trade (tariffs) but also include non-tariff issues, such as services trade, government procurement, competition policy, TBT, and trade remedies. The factors that affect the openness of FTAs in the fields discussed in this literature

Table 2.2   Measures to reduce negative effects of regionalism

Issue areas	Factors affecting openness
Trade in Goods Liberalization	— Zero MFN (extension of FTA zero rate) to eliminate FTA preferences — Less restrictive ROOs
Trade in Services Liberalization	— GATS-plus commitments under regional services agreements — Extension of preferential treatment to non-members at the actual regulation level (whether unilateral liberalization is discriminatory) — Less restrictive ROOs — Third-party MFN
Competition Policy	— Non-discriminatory by nature (automatic multilateralization)
Investment Performance Requirement	— The same treatment of foreign investor from non-members
Technical Barriers to Trade	— Weak or no ROOs regarding the origin of products to be tested (automatic multilateralization) — Some measures under FTAs (e.g., transparency) are non-discriminatory by nature (automatic multilateralization

Source: Baldwin, Evenett, and Low (2009)

are summarized in Table 2.2. It can be observed that the extension of preferential treatment under FTAs to non-parties is an important factor in determining the level of openness. The multilateralizing regionalism literature emphasizes that the extension of preferential treatment is automatic in many issue areas because measures cannot be exclusive from the beginning (see Question 0 in Section 2.4). The said authors contend that many non-tariff measures under FTAs cannot have exclusivity in terms of implementation of obligations under FTAs (especially in the case of competition policy and transparency). Non-members can therefore enjoy the benefits of these measures. However, they do acknowledge that FTAs create preferential treatment in some issue areas. Market access-related problems are a typical example of where discriminatory treatment is possible ("Yes" to Question 0 in Section 2.4), and actual preference is usually given to FTA partners ("Yes" to Questions 1 and 2 in Section 2.4). The question then is whether to extend the same treatment to other parties by policy (Question 3 in Figure 2.4). In the case of tariffs, the said authors encourage multilateralizing the FTA tariff preferences to include all countries. In their view, zero MFN is the most optimal approach to achieving the multilateralization of regionalism because this eliminates any preferences given to FTA partners (Baldwin, Evenett, and Low, 2009, p. 84).

It seems that some authors of the multilateralizing regionalism literature have not fully considered the rich accumulation of open regionalism literature. There are some gaps between the multilateralizing regionalism literature and the early open regionalism literature. The authors of the former have been overwhelmed by the rapid proliferation of FTAs and either suggested extreme policy options at the system-level or analyze very technical issues to reduce the negative effects of FTAs (such as ROOs), unlike those of the latter who discussed ideas on how to achieve open regionalism and make the region (Asia and elsewhere) more outward-looking in general. This difference exists perhaps because the former group is constrained by FTAs that take a specific form, but authors of open regionalism literature were able to freely consider the issue in a situation where an FTA was unlikely. It is important to note, however, that many policy options suggested by open regionalism literature include the question of how to mitigate the tension between regionalism and multilateralism.

At the system-level, it is a puzzle why the majority of recent multilateralizing regionalism literature emphasizes the replacement of existing FTAs with a single FTA with wider membership as a solution to the spaghetti (or noodle) bowl problem (Baldwin and Low, 2009b, p. 1). In the Asian context, some argue that the consolidation of FTAs is necessary to overcome the noodle bowl problem. However, this is rather a radical proposal because the replacement is likely to entail the suspension of existing agreements. For example, given that many FTAs are already in place, many scholars argue that the consolidation approach is harmful if it entails the suspension of existing agreements since a newly created wider membership agreement is likely to be more restrictive than existing bilateral agreements that would be suspended.[33] It is also a big puzzle why Baldwin and Low (2009b) emphasize *actual* membership expansion (especially the European

---

[33] For example, see Hamanaka (2012a).

style of expansion[34]), not the *possibility* of accession. Open accession policy contributes to open regionalism, but whether an FTA's membership actually expands is a different question. Moreover, membership expansion based on discretionary decisions by incumbents does not seem to contribute to the openness of regionalism.

At the technical level, the recent multilateralizing regionalism literature seldom elaborates on the various options of extension of regional preferences — conditional and unconditional, individual and concerted, full and partial, immediate and tame-lag — which were already identified in the early open regionalism literature. It simply considers that the margin of preference can be eliminated if a member of an FTA fully extends regional preferences. Although the early open regionalism literature emphasizes MFN liberalization (lowering MFN tariffs, not eliminating MFN tariffs) as an effective tool of open regionalism, the recent multilateralizing regionalism literature seems to suggest an extreme policy which is an "unconditional full extension of preferential rate under FTA to all WTO Members" or zero MFN tariff (Baldwin, Evenett, and Low, 2009, p. 84).[35] They seem to consider immediate full extension of preferences as a preferable method of extension, and their central question focuses on whether regional liberalization leads to immediate unilateral liberalization as opposed to unilateral policy reform that contributes to trade liberalization in the long-term.

2.3.2   New open regionalism literature

There are many authors who attempt to offer prescriptions for the noodle bowl syndrome that are in line with early open regionalism literature and thus can be called "new" open regionalism literature. These studies set an analytical focus either on specific FTAs, or on the proliferation of FTAs as a whole, and consider how to make regional trade initiatives open. Thus, their

---

[34]The membership policy of the EU is not particularly open because only European countries are eligible for EU membership (De Bardeleben, 2005, p. 4). Open membership irrespective of geography (the spatial extension of regionalism) seems to be more open than geographical extension.

[35]The zero MFN argument is understandable because it is the only method to *eliminate* discriminatory treatment. However, from the perspective of policy implementation, lowering MFN to *mitigate* the discriminatory effects (in the occasion of the formation of an FTA) seems to be more reasonable, but it still contributes to open regionalism.

argument is not limited to the technical details of the design of each FTA, which is the point emphasized by the multilateralizing regionalism literature, but it also covers policy options to link Asian economies with global trade through various trade initiatives. They analyze various types of open membership policies, considering that openness of membership continues to be a critically important perspective of solving the problems caused by the proliferation of FTAs. In addition, similar to early open regionalism literature, they regard regionalism not only as a device of trade liberalization but also as a vehicle to achieve an outward-looking perspective of trade policy.

Ross Garnaut gives a plausible and realistic policy prescription in solving the problems associated with the proliferation of FTAs that is in line with the early open regionalism literature (Garnaut, 2004, 2005; Garnaut and Vines, 2007). His proposal is the creation of an Open Trading Agreement (OTA), which any country can join. This proposal is related to the (reciprocally) conditional exclusive extension of FTA preferences in the early open regionalism literature because only members can receive preferential treatment (Table 2.1). However, it places more emphasis on open accession policy. Membership in an OTA is available to any country that adheres to the agreement's rules. There are only three conditions to be a member of an OTA. First, members should offer at least the same preferences as the preferences in their (most favorable) existing FTA. Second, members should accept any new members on the same terms as they treat other incumbents, provided new applicants also satisfy these three conditions. Third, members should accept common ROOs of the OTA. The second condition is of particular importance because this implies that the accession of new members should not be subject to case-by-case negotiations. Any party that extends FTA preferences, accepts the ROOs of the OTA, and is willing to accept new members can automatically join the OTA. In addition, this proposal does not request the suspension of existing agreements, unlike the multilateralizing regionalism literature.

In the APEC context, Scollay (2004) argues that a "pathfinder" agreement offers a solution on how to achieve an agreement that is truly open in terms of membership. A pathfinder initiation is agreed to by all APEC members, but only a subset of all members joins in the initial stage. This proposal does not suggest the creation of an agreement among a small number of like-minded countries in APEC to which other APEC members can join during any subsequent stages as latecomers. Future participants can influence the modality of the pathfinder agreement and they are not regarded as latecomers expected to follow rules made only by incumbents. The common issue highlighted by Garnaut and Scollay is the establishment of an overarching trade agreement in the region that employs an open membership policy to avoid the incumbent–latecomer problem.

Park (2005) and Park and Lee (2009) also argue that APEC members should pursue an "opening regionalism" policy rather than "open regionalism", given the proliferation of FTAs in Asia. He proposes that APEC should form an FTA first and later APEC as a group should sign an FTA with other parties, and these two steps would lead to non-members' ultimate accession to the APEC FTA. (This proposal is also in line with the reciprocal conditional extension of preferences in the early open regionalism literature.) In similar fashion, Menon (2007, 2009) also considers policies to alleviate the noodle bowl problem in line with early open regionalism literature. He analyzes FTAs in Asia with some emphasis on membership and accession issues and with a clear distinction between a bilateral trade agreement (BTA) and a plurilateral trade agreement (PTA). Bilateral agreements between a member of a PTA (or a PTA as a group) and a non-member country seeking to join the PTA are important because they are "PTA facilitation BTAs." In particular, as far as a PTA is outward-looking, PTA facilitation BTAs contribute to open regionalism, leading to the territorial expansion of the PTA by eventually accepting non-members.[36] The common issue emphasized in these studies is the effective use of (existing) outward-looking plurilateral agreements that evolve into a wider membership agreement in the future.

Some recent studies also consider the technical method in overcoming the proliferation of FTAs in line with early open regionalism literature. In addition to the consolidation of FTAs, which is rather difficult to implement (Hamanaka, 2012a), there are three useful ways to solve the problem (Menon, 2009). The first option is the extension of FTA preferences

---

[36]Lloyd (2002) suggests that a "connecting FTA," which links two plurilateral FTAs such as the EU and MERCOSUR, contributes to global free trade. Menon's "PTA facilitation BTAs" are FTAs that link a plurilateral FTA and non-members, instead of two plurilateral FTAs. Lloyd emphasizes the membership expansion of existing agreements that contribute to global free trade.

to non-members on an MFN basis.[37] This proposal is equivalent to the unconditional unilateral extension of FTA preferences in the early open regionalism literature and is the core argument of multilateralizing region-alism literature. However, some emphasis is placed on the partial extension of FTA preferences that are achieved gradually as well as those achieved with some time lag, given the dynamic nature of regional liberalization.[38] The second option is the gradual reduction of MFN through harmonization among FTA members. In line with early open regionalism literature, this proposal underscores the significance of a concerted effort to reduce tariffs for non-members. While the early open regionalism literature emphasized concerted efforts to reduce MFN tariffs wherein there is no FTA, Menon (2009) argues that a concerted effort is necessary to harmonize MFN tariffs among members of existing FTAs. This option that requires FTA members to reduce their MFN through harmonization is a much more realistic policy for reducing preferences than achieving zero MFN tariffs. The harmoniza-tion of MFN as a means to reduce MFN is reasonable because harmonized MFN reduces the risk of trade deflection, similar to the case of a customs union.[39] The third option is the dilution of ROOs, which is identical to the suggestion made in the multilateralizing regionalism literature. More products can be enjoyed with a preferential access by this option, thereby reducing discriminatory effects.

The contribution of recent literature that discusses the regionalism–multilateralism problem in an environment of proliferating FTAs in Asia can be summarized as follows. The multilateralizing regionalism litera-ture is important because it discusses regionalism–multilateralism issues in various ways beyond goods and tariffs. It offers solid technical solu-tions to the problems associated with the technical design of FTAs such as ROOs. However, the suggestions in this group of literature sometimes seem to be radical. At the system level, the proposal to solve the spaghetti

---

[37] If one country grants different FTA rates to different partners under different FTAs, the equalization of FTA rates is required.

[38] Menon (2005) considers ASEAN countries accelerating the pace of multilateralizing regional preferences to all countries at the same time that ASEAN trade liberalization accelerated as a good example of open regionalism, because regional and global trade liberalization are synchronized.

[39] However, the reduction of MFN through harmonization does not necessarily requests members to form customs unions (Estevadeordal, Harris, and Suominen, 2008).

bowl problem is to replace existing FTAs with a new one that has wider membership. They also emphasize the actual expansion of membership (which may be achieved in a discretionary manner) rather than transparent and open accession policy that an FTA should have. At the technical level, it argues that reducing MFN to zero is the way to reduce the negative externality of FTAs. Finally, the central idea is whether regional liberalization leads to immediate unilateral liberalization rather than unilateral policy reform that contributes to trade liberalization in the long-term. In contrast, the new open regionalism literature proposes realistic solutions to the noodle bowl problem, parallel with the early open regionalism literature, although its analytical emphasis is largely concentrated on goods and tariffs. It considers how to best use existing agreements as building blocks for a multilateral and open regional trade system, and how to reduce MFN through concerted efforts in a progressive manner to reduce the negative effects of regionalism. This literature places analytical emphasis on an open membership policy of regionalism.

2.4   Analytical Framework for WTO Friendliness of FTAs

2.4.1   *Tree-type questions to examine the WTO friendliness of FTAs*

This section proposes an analytical framework to examine the WTO friendliness of FTAs or the openness of FTAs[40] that covers various issue areas in addition to tariff liberalization. The questions regarding the WTO friendliness of FTAs can be classified into two categories: (i) system-level and (ii) technical-level. System-level questions or methods attempt to eliminate the adverse effects of FTAs by eliminating the source of the problem. This is a meta-level solution because it eliminates the problem itself by changing the structure that causes the problem, rather than mitigating the problem. In contrast, technical-level questions or methods attempt to reduce the adverse effects of FTAs by changing the technical details of FTAs, or their parameters (e.g., scope of beneficiaries), when the structure is provided.

The questions to examine the WTO friendliness of FTAs are in line with existing literature reviewed in the previous sections. Open membership,

---

[40]As discussed in Chapter 1, an FTA's WTO friendliness and its openness are used interchangeably.

which is a critical question for both early and recent open regionalism studies, is the central question of system-level analysis. As to the technical-level, the nature and size of preferences, and the method of extending preferences, are the core analytical perspectives of this framework, which are also emphasized in the existing studies. The system-level and technical-level questions used in this study to examine the WTO friendliness of FTAs are summarized below.

System-level Question: Does an FTA accept outsiders? Membership expansion, which is the core element of open regionalism, solves many problems associated with the closed aspects that any regional integration schemes entail. From the standpoint of non-members, whether there is a chance to become a member is critical in assessing the openness or exclusiveness of a regional cooperation scheme. Clear and open accession rules are important, especially when an FTA brings large adverse effects to outsiders. Because an FTA is dynamic and it evolves over time, it is safe to consider that its adverse effects on non-members also evolve over time (Baldwin, 1993). When the adverse effects of an FTA cannot be solved at the technical-level, it is always useful to consider this system-level solution.

If the insiders and outsiders cannot be changed, then we need to consider technical solutions to make FTAs friendly to non-members. Technical-level methods attempt to mitigate the negative side of FTAs by changing the parameters of an FTA, which determine the level and nature of openness of FTAs. However, examining the size and nature of preferences in fields other than tariffs is not straightforward. We will borrow some ideas from recent studies such as Fink and Jansen (2007) and Hamanaka, Tafgar, and Lazaro (2010) that distinguish among various types of preferential treatment, as well as various means of extending preferential treatment to non-members that are suitable when analyzing non-tariff issues. In particular, the difference between legal preference and actual preference, as well as that between a *de jure* and a *de facto* extension, is especially important. The set of tree-type questions to identify the nature and size of preferences, and the method of extending preferences, are summarized in Figure 2.4.

Technical-level Question 0: Is a special measure for partners under an FTA preferential or exclusive by nature? The first issue to consider is the nature of measures under FTAs in terms of their exclusiveness. If measures are non-exclusive by nature, then no actual preferences can be given to the

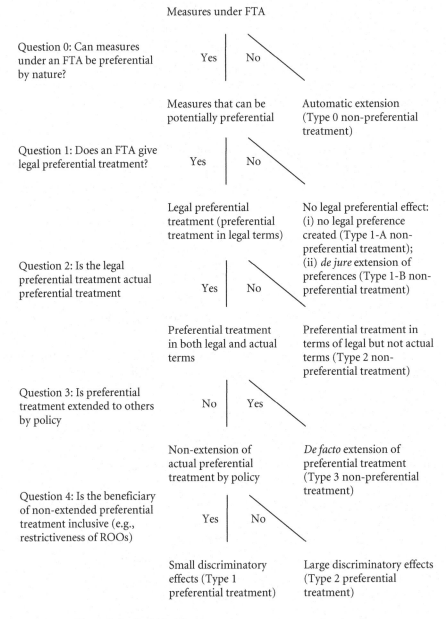

Figure 2.4   Technical-level questions on openness of regionalism

Source: Author's illustration

partner even if legal stipulations in an FTA appear to give some preference. In other words, if the measures are non-exclusive by nature, there is no discriminatory effect from the beginning. This is referred to as "Question 0" because it is the question on the nature of measures, not a policy question to be addressed by policy-makers.

Technical-level Question 1: Does an FTA give legal preferential treatment to partners (does an FTA have exclusive WTO-plus elements)? If measures can be preferential or exclusive, the next question is whether an FTA gives preference to partners, which is a technical question on the design of the legal stipulations of an FTA. Here the central question is whether an FTA has so-called WTO-plus elements. Given that regionalism is evolving, we need to carefully examine WTO-plus elements, since they may evolve over time. It is not relevant to consider that a project on trade regionalism is a one-off event and WTO-plus elements entailed by trade regionalism are static.

There are two scenarios that lead to FTAs without legal preferential effects: (i) if an FTA does not create preferential treatment (Type 1-A non-preferential treatment in Figure 2.4); and (ii) if an FTA includes a stipulation on non-discriminatory preferential treatment that is granted to both members and non-members, which can be called *de jure* extension of preferences (Type 1-B non-preferential treatment).[41] In the former case, no WTO-plus element is included in an FTA. In the latter case (*de jure* extension of preferences), the WTO-plus elements are applicable to non-members in legal terms (non-exclusive WTO-plus elements). If an FTA does not create legal preferences for partners, one may question the utility of such an FTA. However, under both scenarios, there is no adverse effect on outsiders. In contrast, if an FTA includes the stipulation of preferential

---

[41]There are issue areas wherein an FTA usually does not mention the treatment of non-members (e.g., express shipment for imports from members should be introduced). For example, tariff treatment of non-members is seldom mentioned in an FTA. In this case, *de jure* extension is ruled out. However, in some issue areas, treatment of non-members can be mentioned in an FTA. In this case, *de jure* extension becomes possible. *De jure* extension has two possibilities. First, explicit *de jure* extension, wherein the provision directly mentions the treatment of non-members (e.g., express shipment for imports from members and non-members should be introduced). The second possibility is implicit *de jure* extension. In this case, the provision mentions the favorable treatment in a general manner without specifying the scope of beneficiaries (e.g., express shipment should be introduced).

treatment for partners that is better than the treatment legally granted to other WTO Members, such an FTA has legal preferential effects. In this case, the FTA has exclusive WTO-plus elements in legal terms.

Accordingly, we should not simply assume that the inclusion of WTO-plus elements in FTAs makes them a building block for multilateralism. Rather, WTO-plus elements of FTAs could be the source of concern because of their possible discriminatory effects. We should examine whether the beneficiaries of WTO-plus preferences are exclusive or not in legal terms. As we discussed, if WTO-plus elements are extended to non-members on the *de jure* basis, such an FTA does not even create preferential effects in legal terms. If an FTA has WTO-plus elements that are not extended on a *de jure* basis and it gives legal preferential treatment exclusive to FTA partners (exclusive WTO-plus elements), we should carefully examine possible negative external effects inherent in such an FTA without prejudging it as a contributor to the multilateral trading system. In short, it is the WTO-plus elements that make FTAs non-WTO-friendly (Table 2.3).

Technical-level Question 2: Is the legal preferential treatment actual preferential treatment (are exclusive WTO-plus elements unilateral policy-plus)? Even if an FTA creates legal preferential treatment, this does not mean that the FTA brings actual preferential treatment. This is because the level of legal preferential treatment may be lower than the level of unilateral liberalization available to anyone. We should examine the unilateralism-plus elements of FTAs (as opposed to multilateralism-plus elements) to understand the real value of preferential treatment. In other words, a legal stipulation on preferential treatment in an agreement

Table 2.3   WTO-plus FTAs and discriminatory effects

Types	Effects
No WTO-plus elements (Type 1-A non-preferential treatment)	Without legal preferential effects
WTO-plus elements, but non-members also enjoy the WTO-plus benefits (*de jure* extension of legal preference; Type 1-B non-preferential treatment)	Without legal preferential effects
WTO-plus elements exclusive to members ("Yes" to Question 1)	With legal preferential effects

Source: Author's compilation

could be less preferential than actual policy. For example, before signing an FTA, a country has a 10% MFN bound rate and zero MFN applied rate for a certain product. Then, when the country later signs an FTA and the preferential tariff rate becomes 5%, we can say that there is preferential treatment in legal terms (because a 5% preferential tariff rate is lower than a 10% MFN bound tariff rate), but there is no actual preferential treatment (because zero MFN applied tariff rate is lower than a 5% preferential tariff rate). Thus, whether an FTA brings actual preferential treatment depends on the level of unilateral liberalization. If the level of unilateral liberalization is substantially high, there are two possible consequences. First, there may not be a large enough incentive to sign an FTA with such a country, because actual preferences cannot be made. This is the point emphasized in the early open regionalism literature. Second, even if an agreement is signed, such an FTA does not create significant actual preferential treatment (Hamanaka, 2013a).

In the case of tariffs, legal preferential treatment usually means actual preferential treatment, because an MFN applied tariff rate and an MFN bound tariff rate are usually at a similar level. The distinction between Questions 1 and 2 in Figure 2.4 is not that critical in this case. The above example, which creates legal preferential treatment but no actual preferential treatment, is an unusual case because it assumes a high MFN bound tariff rate (10%) and a low MFN applied tariff rate (zero). However, in many policy areas such as services, the distinction between Questions 1 and 2 is critically important. This is because there is a large policy space between a multilaterally committed level of liberalization and the actual level of liberalization that usually takes the form of unilateral liberalization. In other words, in fields other than goods, legal preferential treatment without actual preferential treatment is common (Type 2 non-preferential treatment in Figure 2.4).

Technical-level Question 3: Is actual preferential treatment extended by policy on a *de facto* basis? If an FTA has exclusive WTO-plus elements, which have actual preferential effects, there is a need to reduce their negative effects on outsiders. The extension of preferential treatment that is originally exclusive to FTA partners to all parties by policy is one effective technical method to eliminate or reduce the adverse effects. The same treatment between members and non-members can be achieved on a *de facto* basis by the policy application, even if different treatment continues to exist in legal terms (Type 3 non-preferential treatment in Figure 2.4).

Because trade liberalization at the regional level is often conducted in a gradual manner, the question is not limited to whether exclusive WTO-plus elements are extended or multilateralized at a particular point in time. The extension can also be gradual in two ways. First, there is a possibility that there is some time lag between liberalization at the regional level and the extension of preferences to others. Second, the extension can be a partial extension, not a full extension. In short, given the evolutionary nature of liberalization at the regional level, the extension or multilateralization of FTA preferences can be progressive.

Moreover, we should carefully consider the form that the extension of FTA preferences takes. We usually emphasize the direct linkage between the improved treatment of partners under an FTA and the possible improved treatment of non-members when the FTA is signed, and tend to regard the immediate extension of actual preferential treatment as the only way to achieve an extension. However, given the nature that legal preferential treatment under an FTA evolves over time, the real question should be "whether actual preferential treatment induces policy reforms that gradually improve market access to all parties" rather than "whether actual preferential treatment immediately leads to non-discriminatory market access to all parties." Thus, a narrow focus on the extension of preferential treatment may be misleading in some cases, considering the treatment of outsiders as well as insiders. The reform-inducing effect of an FTA is critically important in considering the enhanced treatment for both FTA members and non-members (for a detailed discussion on reform-inducing effects, see Chapter 5, Section 5.6).

Technical-level Question 4: Are the beneficiaries of non-extended preferential treatment limited? If preferential treatment under an FTA is not extended to outsiders, either *de jure* or *de facto*, then the FTA cannot avoid offering preferential treatment to partners only, which is likely to have some adverse effects on outsiders. The final technical question is how to expand the beneficiaries of an FTA when the membership is given. The restrictiveness of ROOs is critical because they determine the products that are qualified for the preferential access. In other words, weak or leaky ROOs expand the beneficiaries of an FTA at the product level. Aside from

ROOs, which are the main determinants, there may be other issues that are decisive to the scope of the beneficiaries of FTA such as the definition of local residents.

2.4.2   Focal question for each issue area: beyond tariffs

This book considers the relationship between regionalism and multilateralism from several issue areas: (i) trade in goods liberalization (tariff liberalization), (ii) trade facilitation, (iii) trade in services, and (iv) economic cooperation. Existing studies emphasize Question 1 (preferential tariff cuts under an FTA) and Question 4 (ROOs of an FTA) in examining the external effects of FTAs, which are usually based on GATT Article XXIV. Such a narrow focus does not tell us the whole story of external effects of recent FTAs that go beyond tariff liberalization. While a detailed empirical study is beyond the scope of this chapter, it is useful to briefly review how different the analytical angle of non-tariff issues is from trade in goods regionalism, and how unique the necessary approaches should be in discussing open regionalism in fields other than goods. The significance of both system- and technical-level questions introduced in the earlier section varies depending on the issue area in question.

Trade in goods. The principal problem of proliferation of FTAs in Asia after 2000 is that the majority of intra-Asian, South–South FTAs are based on the Enabling Clause, not GATT Article XXIV. Thus, the GATT Article XXIV-centric open regionalism debate is not relevant in Asia. The products to be liberalized under Enabling Clause-based FTAs can be highly selective, unlike GATT Article XXIV-based FTAs, and the liberalization project takes a fairly long time to be implemented. Thus, Enabling Clause-based FTAs are believed to have more serious adverse effects on non-members than GATT Article XXIV (Park and Park, 2011). However, given that the formation of Enabling Clause-based FTAs by developing countries is allowed under the WTO legal system, it is fruitless to argue how serious the negative economic effects of such FTAs are and whether the use of the Enabling Clause should be avoided. Moreover, expecting developing country FTA members to multilateralize their FTA preferences would be too optimistic as a solution of negative effects of Enabling Clause-based FTAs. Thus, the technical method to make Enabling Clause-based FTAs open does not seem to work, given the flexibility allowed for them. The key angle in considering the openness of Enabling Clause-based FTAs relates to system-level (meta-level) questions, rather than technical-level questions, of open regionalism, namely open membership policy.

Trade facilitation. As tariffs become lower and lower, more attention is given to non-tariff issues, especially trade facilitation measures. Regional trade initiatives usually cover not only trade liberalization but also regional schemes to facilitate trade. Almost all existing literature suggests that multilateralism-plus trade facilitation measures achieved at the regional level seldom have discriminatory effects on non-members on the grounds that their implementation is usually conducted on a non-discriminatory basis. Thus, the more pronounced the inclusion of trade facilitation measures in an FTA, the greater the degree of multilateralization of the FTA. It is, however, critically important to note that many of them simply assume that the majority of trade facilitation measures at a regional level are non-exclusive at the onset, which should be examined as the first question of the openness of regionalism, as mentioned above. Thus, the analytical focus of the openness of regional trade facilitation measures should be on whether trade facilitation measures can be preferential (Question 0 in Figure 2.4) and whether an FTA entails multilateralism-plus preferential trade facilitation measures that are exclusive to members (Question 1 in Figure 2.4).

Services trade. Services trade is very different from goods trade because it is directly related to domestic regulatory issues. The difference between the two is especially prominent in the case of liberalization at the regional level. While the regional goods agreement assumes that substantially all internal trade should be liberalized in a timely manner, a regional services agreement assumes that the liberalization of services trade is gradual and evolving. Interestingly, many studies on regional services agreements assert that regional services commitments in Asia do not have much multilateralism-plus elements. This is mainly because they overlook the fact that commitments under regional services agreements evolve over time. And if commitments under regional services agreements, in fact, have gradually increasing multilateralism-plus elements, then we need to consider if they produce new market access and if such new market access is available only to FTA members. However, more importantly, given that services liberalization is gradual in nature, whether a regional commitment, which may be implemented on a preferential basis, leads to long-term reform of the services industry is a fundamental question in considering the open-ness of services agreement. What we need to consider is not only whether regional commitments create new immediate market access, which may be non-discriminatory, but also whether regional commitments induce future reform of services regulations, which usually takes the form of unilateral liberalization (Question 3 in Figure 2.4).[42]

Economic cooperation. Emphasis has been placed on the significance of economic development and cooperation, and technical assistance or capacity building in particular, as a method to achieve open regionalism, especially in the APEC context (Yamazawa, 2006). This is not only because capacity building contributes to trade liberalization but also because capacity building projects expand the beneficiaries of regional coopera-tion in various ways. However, despite the recent proliferation of FTAs, the contribution of FTAs to the capacity building of developing countries through technical assistance has not been carefully studied. It is impor-tant to consider whether FTAs bring technical assistance projects. If so, it is expected that this would contribute to the openness of regionalism in various ways. First, it is very likely that technical assistance projects under regional initiatives can directly benefit non-members. Both partners and non-partners engaged in trade can benefit from the enhanced capacity resulting from reformed trade policies brought about by FTAs. As far as capacity building is concerned, we say that the answer to Question 0 (whether measures under FTAs can be preferential in nature) is likely to be "No." However, whether FTAs actually include *de jure* capacity building obligation should be carefully examined (Question 1 in Figure 2.4).

2.4.3　*Analytical assumption: evolutionary regionalism*

In analyzing the WTO friendliness of FTAs, this study places special emphasis on the dynamic nature of trade regionalism. The openness of Asian trade regionalism should be understood in line with more nuanced concepts regarding regionalism such as "gradualism" and "incrementalism" (Acharya, 1997; Zhang, 2009). It is not surprising that regionalism in

---

[42]It is widely pointed out that regionalism is a vehicle of not only liberalization but also reform (Drysdale, 2006).

Asia has a developmental nature, which can be called "developmental regionalism" (Nesadurai, 2003; Dent, 2008), because the fundamental goal of economic liberalization cooperation is not liberalization *per se,* but rather the economic development of the participating countries. Thus, regionalism in Asia, including trade regionalism, such as through an FTA, is evolving in terms of liberalization levels and commitments over time. Even though FTAs are legal frameworks, it is wrong to assume that they are static in nature.

Although the fact that schemes for economic integration are evolving should not be surprising, this is often overlooked in the academic debate on the regionalism–multilateralism problem. One critical weakness shared by many existing studies is that there are either no or little dynamic perspectives of regional initiatives. The focus of the debate is usually limited to the impact of one-off events such as the timely elimination of internal tariffs under the newly created FTA.[43] Thus, the discussions tend to center on whether or not to extend FTA preferences to other countries, or whether or not to achieve zero MFN at a particular time.

Perhaps one of the reasons why gradualism is not emphasized in the existing literature is that trade in goods regionalism, especially an FTA based on GATT Article XXIV, is still the basis of their argument. It is undeniable that the goods-centric discussion on trade regionalism lacks a dynamic perspective. GATT Article XXIV stipulates that substantially all the trade between partners should be eliminated in a timely manner. Thus, the creation of GATT Article XXIV-based FTAs can be said to be a one-off event where the decision on all-or-nothing should be made. Gradualism is ruled out from the beginning partly because of the condition set by GATT Article XXIV. However, such an argument is not necessarily applicable to issues other than goods trade and even to trade in goods integration if that is not based on GATT Article XXIV.

In fields other than goods, the dynamic perspective is more important in considering the overall effects of regional initiatives. For example, in the case of services, the scope of liberalization is not limited to so-called border issues because domestic regulatory issues are also included in the

---

[43]There is economic literature that discusses the dynamic aspects of FTAs, but it comprises the analysis of dynamic aspects of one-off events, namely the formation of FTAs.

liberalization negotiations. The timely elimination of domestic regulations is not expected. It is important to realize that a services agreement can be a trigger of not only liberalization but also domestic reform, which leads to a more effective regulatory framework in a gradual manner. Moreover, for many (developing) countries in Asia, the capacity of conducting reform policies is underdeveloped. FTAs may then contribute to capacity development in various ways, including technical assistance. In summary, the dynamic perspective of analyzing trade regionalism or FTAs is important because regionalism can be reform-inducing and capacity-enhancing. While the analytical framework for the WTO friendliness of FTAs assesses the openness of FTAs at a particular point in time, the actual examination of the WTO friendliness should involve a dynamic perspective that incorporates time-factors.

2.5 Summary

As we have seen in this chapter, there is a rich accumulation of literature on open regionalism. It is correct to argue that open regionalism has gradually taken on a more clear operational meaning over time. Authors of early open regionalism literature in the 1990s freely considered various options to maintain open regionalism without constraints because there were no FTAs at that time. In fact, their proposals included open membership, unilateral MFN liberalization without forming an FTA, various forms of extending FTA preferences, a commitment to multilateralism, and regional projects for trade facilitation. Despite comprehensive proposals to maintain openness of regionalism in Asia, one critical weakness that has been identified was that these proposals implicitly or explicitly have tariff treatment of trade in goods under FTAs, which is based on the GATT Article XXIV in mind in formulating their argument. Recent multilateralizing regionalism literature expands the focus of analysis and includes issues other than goods, such as services, trade facilitation, competition policy, and investment. It attempts to solve the negative externalities of FTAs by addressing technical aspects of FTAs, such as ROOs, and identify the distinction of *de jure* and *de facto* liberalization. However, under the environment where the proliferation of FTAs is given, the argument in the multilateralizing regionalism literature tends to be constrained by the experience to date of FTA implementation and is not necessarily based on the rich accumulation of early literature on open regionalism. Moreover, the system-level argument of this literature is rather unrealistic in saying that the replacement of existing bilateral FTAs with new wider membership agreements can solve the Asian noodle bowl problem. Recent new open regionalism literature suggests another way to maintain open regionalism in Asia that is aligned with early open regionalism literature, with some emphasis on the membership issue. Its authors focus on how to make new agreements open and how to formulate existing agreements such that they serve as building blocks of open regionalism in Asia. Garnaut's proposal on an OTA is an excellent example.

This chapter has identified several key questions that are useful in assessing the openness of regionalism, which include both system-level and technical-level methods. At the system-level, open membership policy is critical in maintaining the openness of regionalism. In addition, a set of technical-level questions is proposed in this chapter, which will be the basis of the empirical assessment in the following chapters. Those technical-level questions are useful in assessing the openness of regionalism. The questions include:

- System-level question: Does an FTA adopt an open membership policy?
- Technical-level question 0: Are measures under an FTA preferential in nature?
- Technical-level question 1: Does an FTA give preferential treatment to partners in legal terms?
- Technical-level question 2: Is the *de jure* preferential treatment actual preferential treatment?
- Technical-level question 3: Is actual preferential treatment extended to others by policy?
- Technical-level question 4: Are the beneficiaries of non-extended actual preferential treatment limited?

In the case of goods and tariffs, there is no doubt that tariff treatment can be preferential ("Yes" to Question 0) and actual discriminatory tariff treatment is likely to be brought about by GATT Article XXIV-based FTA ("Yes" to Questions 1 and 2) because GATT Article XXIV requests members to eliminate tariffs on substantially all intra-regional trade. Thus, existing studies tend to focus on the question of whether preferential treatment is extended to non-members (Question 3) as a method to reduce the negative externalities of FTAs. However, the majority of recently signed FTAs in Asia are based on the Enabling Clause, which does not require the elimination of tariffs on substantially all trade. Moreover, expecting the extension of preference under Enabling Clause-based FTA is unrealistic because they are developing countries. Thus, technical-level questions that assess the openness of tariff treatment under regionalism are not sufficient. Accordingly, we need to consider system-level questions of open regionalism, namely the open membership problem.

Having trade in goods in mind in considering open regionalism is only a part of the whole story. In the case of trade facilitation, many assume that regional trade facilitation measures are not discriminatory in nature and thus the inclusion of trade facilitation measures in an FTA contributes to its openness. This means that many consider the answer to Question 0 (whether treatment under an FTA can be preferential by nature) to be "No" as far as trade facilitation is concerned. However, it is important to carefully examine the discriminatory elements of various regional trade facilitation measures rather than simply assume that trade facilitation is non-discriminatory. In the case of services, many consider that regional services commitments are poor in quality (no multilateralism-plus elements) and therefore do not have much impact. In other words, many consider the answer to Question 1 to be "No" with regard to regional services agreements. As a result, they tend to overlook both the discriminatory and non-discriminatory effects of regional services agreement. Aside from immediate market access created by regional services agreements, services regulatory reforms induced by commitments are also important in considering the effects of regional services agreements. In the case of technical assistance, it has not yet been thoroughly assessed whether FTAs entail multilateralism-plus technical assistance. It is important to examine whether an FTA brings technical assistance and if such technical assistance brought about by FTAs contributes to utility of non-members.

CHAPTER 3

Free Trade Agreements in Goods

Is Trade Bilateralism in Asia Consistent with WTO Rules and Norms?

3.1 Introduction

Most favored nation (MFN) treatment is the most important principle of the multilateral trading system. In fact, the first Article of the General Agreement on Tariffs and Trade (GATT) is the "General Most-Favored-Nation Treatment" article (GATT Article I). It means that tariffs and other advantages given to one country with regard to trade must be given to all World Trade Organization (WTO) Members without any conditions. The prohibition of differentiated treatment across countries is the very essence of MFN treatment. The other important principle of GATT is national treatment, which is the prohibition of discrimination between domestic and foreign products.

It is widely known that a free trade agreement (FTA)[1] is a legitimate deviation from the MFN principle. As long as the conditions stipulated in WTO Agreements are satisfied, WTO Members are allowed to be contracting parties of any FTA. However, WTO Members have several options with regard to the choice of legal provisions in forming FTAs. In the case of trade in goods, GATT Article XXIV and the Enabling Clause are the two main considerations.[2] Though there are some commonalities, the conditions

---

[1]This chapter uses the term "free trade agreement (FTA)" to refer to trade agreement in goods based on either GATT Article XXIV or the Enabling Clause. These agreements are also sometimes called regional trade agreements or preferential trade agreements. GATT Article XXIV uses the term FTA in reference to a "free trade area," while the Enabling Clause uses the term "regional agreement." In this chapter, FTAs include customs unions unless otherwise stated.

[2]Another possible option is to use the GATT Article XXV waiver.

that need to be satisfied by each type of FTA are not identical and have different policy implications.

While many studies discuss the systemic implications of the proliferation of FTAs in Asia on the multilateral trading system, few studies distinguish between FTAs based on either GATT Article XXIV or the Enabling Clause. In arguing how to make FTAs compatible with WTO, many studies seem to presume that FTAs are based primarily on GATT Article XXIV, but such an assumption is not valid, at least in Asia.[3] It is a puzzle as to why the regionalism–multilateralism debate surrounding the goods trade still centers on the conditions stipulated in GATT Article XXIV, given the multitude of FTAs in Asia signed since 2000 that are based on the Enabling Clause. In general, trade economists tend to overlook the legal differences between the two types of agreements and focus only on the substance of FTAs, despite the fact that the requirements that need to be met by each type of FTA, according to the WTO, are different.[4] Trade lawyers tend to overstate potential inconsistencies between WTO rules and each existing FTA on a case-by-case basis, rather than considering the systemic implications of those provisions.

This chapter looks into FTAs in Asia, with a special reference to the Enabling Clause, and considers the implications of the proliferation of Enabling Clause-based FTAs in Asia to the openness of Asian regionalism. The systemic implications of FTAs based on either the Enabling Clause or GATT Article XXIV are very different, as we will see later. While FTAs suddenly started to proliferate in Asia after 2000 (Pomfret, 2011), the choice of the primary legal provision used in forming FTAs before and after 2000 was also very different. Moreover, the way in which the Enabling Clause is used in forming FTAs in Asia has been very different from the regions other than Asia.

In this chapter, the Asian region is limited to the two subregions of wider Asia: (i) East Asia, which includes Southeast Asia and North East Asia; and (ii) South Asia.[5] In other words, the Central Asian members of the former Commonwealth of Independent States (CIS) and the Persian Gulf region

---

[3] See for example, Lim (2007).
[4] One notable exception is Park and Park (2011).
[5] Such a narrow focus is common in analyzing FTAs in Asia. For example, see Plummer (2007).

(West Asia, or the Middle East) are not included. This distinction is due primarily to the state of FTAs in Central Asia and the Persian Gulf, which is very different from that of East and South Asia, as we will see later. Furthermore, the terms "FTAs in Asia" and "Asian FTAs" refer to FTAs that involve at least one Asian economy. Thus, cross-regional FTAs that include Asian economies as well as non-Asian countries, such as the Japan–Mexico Economic Partnership Agreement (EPA), are regarded as Asian FTAs. We use the terms "FTAs within Asia" and "intra-Asian FTAs" to refer to FTAs whose contracting parties are exclusively Asian economies, and the terms "FTAs outside Asia" and "non-Asian FTAs" to refer to FTAs that do not include any Asian countries.

The structure of this chapter is as follows. Section 3.2 discusses the differences between the two legal provisions that are used in forming FTAs: GATT Article XXIV and the Enabling Clause. Section 3.3 presents the analytical framework for the openness of FTAs, in particular, Enabling Clause-based FTAs. Section 3.4 discusses the status of Enabling Clause-based FTAs in the world and identifies their common features outside Asia. The anatomy of Enabling Clause-based FTAs in Asia is examined in the Section 3.5, in particular, how they differ from those outside Asia. Section 3.6 considers the policy implications of the proliferation of Enabling Clause-based FTAs on the nature of trade regionalism in Asia, especially open regionalism. Section 3.7 summarizes the main discussion of this chapter.

3.2 Difference in Multilateral Principles of Regionalism: GATT Article XXIV versus Enabling Clause

3.2.1 *Historical background of GATT Article XXIV and Enabling Clause*

First, it is important to know the historical context surrounding the negotiations of GATT Article XXIV. The proposed International Trade Organization (ITO) and, subsequently, the GATT, were first negotiated in the 1940s, prior to the advent of economic debates on FTAs and customs unions. Joseph Viner's pioneer work on trade regionalism, *The Customs Union Issues*, which included one of the first theoretical analyses on trade creation and trade diversion, was published in 1950. It is not an exaggeration to suggest that trade diplomats at that time engaged in the negotiations to establish GATT without having a concrete idea of the economic implications and consequences of Article XXIV (Davey, 2011; Mathis, 2002, p. 103).

There are two main reasons why the GATT system allows regionalism within the multilateral trade system. First, when the GATT was negotiated, there were already several existing or proposed customs unions. For example, Benelux — comprising Belgium, the Netherlands, and Luxembourg — was proposed and established in the 1940s. Because customs unions received exemption from MFN norm long before the GATT was created, the GATT system needed to accommodate them (Mathis, 2002). Second, while it is widely argued that the US was concerned with the establishment of a multilateral system (Ruggie, 1992) that built on the norms of non-discrimination, indivisibility, and reciprocity (Caporaso, 1992), the US also understood the political realities of regionalism during the post-war period. The US considered trade regionalism important because (Western) European integration was deemed critical for world peace and US security during the Cold War (Bhagwati, 1991). Also, the US was of the view that Britain and other developing countries would lose interest in multilateral trading systems if regionalism was not allowed. In fact, GATT Article I:2 explicitly exempts in perpetuity (i.e., "grandfathers") from the MFN requirement those preferential trade agreements existing at the time the GATT came into effect, including the British Imperial Preferences and Benelux. However, other customs unions were expected to be created in the future and effectively governed by GATT Article XXIV.

While it is understandable that GATT negotiators decided to allow regionalism under the multilateral trade system as an exception, one critical puzzle is why GATT Article XXIV allows not only customs unions but also FTAs. Several customs unions existed before GATT, but no FTAs (Chase, 2005, p. 24). Thus, the principal concern was how to reconcile existing customs unions, such as Benelux, and other customs unions that would be created in the near future with the GATT system. As the title of Viner's book suggests, at that time, the primary concern of policy-makers and economists regarding trade regionalism was customs unions, which were dominant, and not FTAs. It is therefore puzzling why GATT Article XXIV allows the future creation of FTAs.

There are two main factors that explain the inclusion of FTAs in GATT Article XXIV. First, there was, in fact, an argument that supported the idea of including FTAs in GATT Article XXIV as a deviation from the MFN principle. Introducing an exception for FTAs was important for developing countries that might go on to form FTAs, especially since maintaining the delicate balance between developed and developing countries was necessary at the negotiations at Geneva (Mathis, 2002, p. 42; WTO, 2007). It was developing countries, not developed countries, that were expected to be signatories of FTAs. Second, and more importantly, the original proposal of the US for the International Trade Organization (ITO), which ultimately led to the GATT, included an exception for customs unions only (Davey, 2011; Chase, 2005). A recent study[6] finds that the US insisted upon the inclusion of FTAs in Article XXIV only later, because it started to secretly pursue a possible US–Canada FTA (Chase, 2005).[7] Thus, it was mainly an individual and self-interested political decision, rather than an economic philosophy based on trade theory, that led the US to favor the inclusion of FTAs in GATT Article XXIV.

Meanwhile, the original text of the GATT did not allow preferences in favor of developing countries, except in the case of FTAs based on GATT Article XXIV that required the elimination of trade barriers for "substantially all the trade" between members. Under GATT Article XXIV, developed and developing countries are treated equally. Because there was no system that encouraged trade integration cooperation among developing countries,[8] the granting of trade preferences to developing

---

[6]It was widely considered in past literature that "the United States initially opposed preferential agreements when negotiating a post-war trade organization, but was quite willing to have the GATT articles permit customs unions. When the issue of free trade agreements was raised, the United States accepted them as well, reportedly without any significant deliberation, on the grounds that free trade agreements would be a first step toward a customs union" (Krueger, 1997, p. 170).

[7]However, the plan did not ultimately materialize. It has been said that Canada rejected the proposal (Smith, 1988, p. 39).

[8]When Part IV of the GATT on Trade and Development was negotiated in 1964, many developing countries suggested the amendment of GATT Article I so that trade preferences for developing countries would be allowed. However, such an attempt was unsuccessful (Tangermann, 2002).

countries, by both developed countries and developing countries, required a waiver based on GATT Article XXV. In fact, when the Generalized System of Preferences (GSP) was adopted at the United Nations Conference on Trade and Development (UNCTAD) in 1970, a waiver was used (Tangermann, 2002).

As a result of the Tokyo Round of negotiations, which sought a more permanent legal solution for trade preferences for developing countries as one of its objectives, the Enabling Clause, which is formally called "Differential and More Favorable Treatment, Reciprocity, and Fuller Participation of Developing Countries — Decision of 28 November 1979," was agreed upon. The Enabling Clause was adopted in the context of the New International Economic Order (NIEO) that sought to improve the position, in the global economy, of the so-called Third-World countries relative to developed countries.[9] The Enabling Clause allows WTO Members to grant differential and more favorable treatment to developing countries without granting the same treatment to all other WTO Members. The first paragraph of the Enabling Clause states that "notwithstanding the provisions of Article I of the General Agreement, contracting parties may accord differential and more favorable treatment to developing countries, without according such treatment to other contracting parties." This provision provides another channel for the deviation from the MFN principle of the GATT and WTO, with emphasis on the developmental aspects of developing countries.[10]

The specific situations wherein the Enabling Clause can be applied are identified in Paragraph 2, which has four subparagraphs. As we will discuss later, there has been a debate over whether the four measures are exhaustive or not. These measures include:

(i) preferential tariff treatment accorded by developed contracting parties to products originating in developing countries in accordance with the GSP (Paragraph 2 (a));
(ii) differential and more favorable treatment with respect to the provisions of the GATT concerning non-tariff measures (Paragraph 2 (b));

---

[9] For example, see Schreuer (1990, p. 77).
[10] Before the adoption of the Enabling Clause, a waiver was used to form preferential agreements.

(iii) regional or global arrangements among less-developed contracting parties for the mutual reduction or elimination of tariffs, and for the mutual reduction or elimination of non-tariff measures on products imported from one another (Paragraph 2 (c)); and

(iv) special treatment for the least developed countries (LDCs) among the developing countries in the context of any general or specific measures in favor of developing countries (Paragraph 2 (d)).

FTAs among developing countries can be formed based on the Enabling Clause, using the provision in Paragraph 2 (c). The Enabling Clause, which is less demanding than GATT Article XXIV, is an alternative avenue for developing countries to sign FTAs, as we will see in detail later.

The historical background of provisions regarding the formation of FTAs has important contemporary implications; the proliferation of FTAs tends to happen when clauses are used in a way the drafters did not expect (Hamanaka, 2012b). So far, there have been three waves of regionalism (Baldwin and Carpenter, 2011; Mansfield and Milner, 1999). The first wave of regionalism surged in Europe in the 1960s, but most agreements at that time were plurilateral customs unions based on GATT Article XXIV, such as the European Community (EC).[11] Thus, GATT Article XXIV was used in an expected way during the first wave. The second wave occurred in 1980s and 1990s, with the Americas at the forefront. The agreements signed were usually FTAs, not customs unions, such as the North America Free Trade Agreement (NAFTA) and the Southern Common Market (MER-COSUR). Thus, GATT Article XXIV was first used in an unexpected way. In fact, Fiorentine, Verdeja, and Toqueboeuf (2006) suggest that the landscape of FTAs would have been very different if GATT Article XXIV covered only customs unions. Meanwhile, many South–South FTAs based on the Enabling Clause were also concluded during this period, but the way in which the Enabling Clause was used was consistent with the idea of NIEO. What about the third wave of regionalism, which was primarily driven by a surge of new Enabling Clause-based FTAs after 2000? We will attempt to answer this question in the empirical sections below.

---

[11] There were also so-called South–South customs unions in 1961, such as the Central America Common Market (CACM).

3.2.2   Conditions for forming FTAs: GATT Article XXIV and Enabling Clause

Several conditions — both substantive and procedural — must be met by GATT Article XXIV-based FTAs, including customs unions, if they are to be regarded as being WTO-consistent.[12] The first substantive requirement to be satisfied by FTAs refers to the treatment of internal trade, namely trade within an FTA (Table 3.1). GATT Article XXIV:8 (a) stipulates that duties and other restrictive regulations of commerce (ORRCs) shall be eliminated

Table 3.1   Substantive requirements under GATT Article XXIV and the Enabling Clause

		GATT Article XXIV	Enabling Clause
	Treatment	Elimination	Reduction
Barriers to internal trade	Coverage	Substantially all the trade	No stipulation
Treatment of barriers to external trade (neutrality to non-members)		Trade barriers for non-members shall not be higher than those prior to the formation of FTAs (including customs unions).	Trade barriers for non-members shall be designed to facilitate internal trade, not to raise barriers for trade with non-parties.
		Obligation to conduct ex ante and ex post level of barriers	No obligation to conduct ex ante and ex post level of barriers
Time framework		Within 10 years	No obligation

Source: Author's compilation

---

[12]GATT Article XXIV covers free trade areas and customs unions. (Note that GATT Article XXIV uses free trade areas and not free trade agreements). A free trade area is a preferential agreement wherein tariff rates among members are zero, although external tariffs may be set at different rates by different members of an agreement. A customs union is an arrangement in which there are zero duties between members on imported goods and a common external tariff (Krueger, 1997). Free trade areas and customs unions are similar in the sense that internal tariffs should be eliminated (internal requirement). The difference between free trade areas and customs unions is the members' treatment of external tariffs (external requirement). As stated already, in this chapter, free trade agreements (FTAs) include both free trade areas and customs unions.

with respect to "substantially all the trade." The important term in this provision is "eliminate." In the case of FTAs based on GATT Article XXIV, the elimination of tariffs and other barriers is required, unlike the case of Enabling Clause-based FTAs, where the "reduction" of tariffs and other barriers is sufficient. In the case of tariffs, elimination means the abolishment of tariffs (Gobbi, Estrella, and Horlick, 2006, p. 137), while reduction means lowering the level of tariffs. Nevertheless, the concept of substantially all the trade has not been thoroughly defined, and the ambiguity in its interpretation still remains. Despite the adoption of the Understanding on the Interpretation of Article XXIV to clarify stipulation 8 (a) in GATT Article XXIV when the WTO was established in 1994, this clarification still does not provide a clear definition of the term. It is unclear if this refers to FTA trade in substantially all product sectors, or substantial trade in all product sectors combined (Onguglo, 2005).

In general, there are two ways to assess substantial coverage: through either (i) quantitative or (ii) qualitative approaches (WTO, 2002). The qualitative approach assesses substantially all the trade in a sector-by-sector analysis. Under this approach, no major sector of economic activity should be excluded from coverage under FTAs or customs unions. For example, many FTAs signed by developed countries in the past have excluded agricultural sectors or certain components of it. Proponents of this approach insist that such FTAs do not conform to substantially all the trade portion. On the other hand, the quantitative approach emphasizes horizontal trade coverage, which does not consider the coverage of specific sectors. In this case, the coverage is calculated quantitatively in a holistic manner. One option in calculating the coverage is to use the number of tariff lines whose tariffs have been eliminated. Another option, which is more popular among some WTO Members, is to calculate the coverage using actual trade volume. The majority of WTO Members are of the view that a combination of the quantitative and qualitative approaches is desirable. However, there are divergent views on the actual level of the quantitatively derived coverage that satisfy the term substantially all the trade. Some developed Members of the WTO are of the view that at least 90% of trade volume should be covered (the European Union (EU) and Japan), while others insist that at least 95% should be covered (Australia). The definition of "major sector" in the case of the qualitative approach is still far from having reached a consensus.

The second substantive condition for forming GATT Article XXIV-based FTAs or customs unions relates to the treatment of external trade, namely duties and other barriers to trade with non-members. GATT Article XXIV:5(a) stipulates that duties and other regulations of commerce applicable to non-members shall not be higher or more restrictive than those in effect prior to the formation of FTAs or customs unions. This provision is especially important in the case of customs unions, because contracting parties need to agree upon a common external tariff for each product, which could be higher than the lowest tariff previously applied by the customs union's members. It is understood that tariffs and non-tariff barriers applied to non-members should not be higher than the pre-union average. While the weighted average can easily be calculated in the case of tariffs and charges, it is difficult to quantify non-tariff barriers, and thus, some case-by-case examination may be required (Paragraph 2 in the Understanding on the Interpretation of GATT Article XXIV). In the case of FTAs, because there is no need to have a common external tariff, the possibility of higher tariffs and other trade barriers for non-members appears not to be large.[13]

The third substantive requirement of forming FTAs relates to the time frame for completing the project. According to GATT XXIV:5(c), agreements on FTAs or customs union shall include a plan and schedule for their formation within a reasonable length of time. While this provision is unclear about the exact time span, the Understanding on the Interpretation of GATT Article XXIV (Paragraph 3) stipulates that a reasonable length of time should not exceed 10 years. When 10 years is insufficient, members of FTAs or customs unions shall provide a full explanation to other WTO members of why a longer period is necessary. The timely completion of the interim agreement and formation of the final FTA is a critical requirement; otherwise agreements covering only selected sectors continue to exist on the ground that they are interim agreements.

Enabling Clause-based FTAs should also satisfy some conditions, though they are less demanding than those under GATT Article XXIV. First, tariffs and other regulations should be reduced, as stipulated in

---

[13] However, as Krueger (1997, p. 177) argues, the rules of origin can act as additional trade barriers for non-members.

Paragraph 2. Unlike FTAs based on GATT Article XXIV, wherein the elimination of tariffs and other regulations is required, reduction is already sufficient in the case of the Enabling Clause.[14] Second, FTAs shall be designed to facilitate and promote the trade of developing countries and not raise barriers or create undue difficulties for trade involving any other contracting parties (Paragraph 3(a)). However, there is no obligation to compare the *ex ante* and *ex post* levels of protection, unlike in GATT Article XXIV. Relating to this, it is required that FTAs based on the Enabling Clause shall not become an impediment to the reduction or elimination of tariffs and other regulations based on MFN treatment (Paragraph 3(b)), although this is hardly an operational criteria. It is important to note that the Enabling Clause makes no mention of the coverage of trade under FTAs and that there is no time limitation for completing the integration scheme.

WTO Members also have an obligation to report their FTAs to the WTO (Table 3.2). Participants in a prospective FTA shall promptly notify other WTO Members and make available to them such information regarding the proposed agreement (GATT Article XXIV: 7(a)). All proposed GATT Article XXIV-based FTAs shall be examined by a working party (Understanding on the Interpretation of GATT Article XXIV, Paragraph 7), unlike the case of the Enabling Clause-based FTA, where only consultation is required. The working party shall produce a report and submit it to the Council of Trade in Goods (CTG), which will make the final decision on the conformity of the agreement to GATT Article XXIV. However, in reality, a decision on conformity to GATT Article XXIV based on a consensus has seldom been made.[15] Because of this consensus requirement, members of an FTA are able to reject a majority recommendation. Thus, the process of conformity assessment of GATT Article XXIV-based FTAs has not been fruitful and can be said to be "self-declaratory" (Mathis, 2002, p. 82). In December 2006, a Decision on the Transparency Mechanism for Regional Trade Agreements was adopted at the General Council. It was agreed that the Committee on Regional Trade Agreements (CRTA) shall be the forum in which to examine GATT Article XXIV-based FTAs and

---

[14]The reduction of tariffs and other regulations should be mutual.
[15]The only agreement in which consistency with GATT Article XXIV was concluded by the working party is the customs union between the Czech Republic and Slovakia.

Table 3.2   Procedural requirements under GATT Article XXIV and the Enabling Clause

		GATT Article XXIV	Enabling Clause
Review of FTAs	Forum	CTG/CRTA	CTD
	Modality	Examination	Consultation
Data submission	Data to be submitted	All data should be submitted (special consideration for GATT Article XXIV-based FTAs between developing countries)	Special considerations given in terms of data availability
	Data submission timeline	10 weeks (20 weeks in the case of GATT Article XXIV-based FTAs between developing countries)	20 weeks

Source: Author's compilation.

that the WTO Secretariat shall prepare a factual presentation of a notified FTA for the purpose of examination of each FTA among members.[16] The data to be submitted by the contracting parties of FTAs to the WTO were also clarified in this decision. Basically, the contracting parties of a GATT Article XXIV-based FTA should submit detailed data on tariff rates, both FTA and MFN rates, and trade volume as well as other important information regarding the FTA (Table 3.3). The data should be submitted the WTO within 10 weeks.[17] It is expected that the examination of GATT Article XXIV-based FTAs will be more effective in future.[18]

Just like the case of GATT Article XXIV, Enabling Clause-based FTAs also have some WTO reporting requirements, though these are not as demanding. Members of Enabling Clause-based FTAs should notify the Committee on Trade and Development (CTD), and the CTD may establish a working party to conduct consultations on, rather than the examination

---

[16] See the WTO Document WT/L/671, Transparency Mechanism for Regional Trade Agreements.

[17] However, special consideration is given with regard to the data to be submitted, as well as the data submission timeline, when a GATT Article XXIV-based FTA involves only developing countries. For a detailed discussion on this issue, see Section 3.7.

[18] On the preliminary assessment of the recent achievements of CRTA, see Crawford and Lim (2011).

Table 3.3   Data submission requirements for FTAs

Tariff concessions under the FTA

A full listing of each party's preferential duties applied in the year of entry into force of the FTA

A full listing of each party's preferential duties to be applied over the transition period if the FTA is to be implemented in stages

MFN duty rates

A full tariff listing of each FTA party's MFN duties applied in the year of entry into force of the agreement

A full tariff listing of each FTA party's MFN duties applied in the year preceding the entry into force of the agreement

Other data, where applicable

Preferential margins
Tariff rate quotas
Seasonal restrictions
Special safeguards
Ad valorem equivalents for non–*ad valorem* duties, if available

Product-Specific Preferential Rules of Origin as Defined in the FTA

Import statistics (the most recent three years)

The value of each party's imports from each of the other parties
The value of each party's imports from the rest of the world, broken down by country of origin

Source: Author's compilation based on WTO Document WT/L/671.

of, an FTA in light of the relevant provisions in the Enabling Clause. It is argued that "a certain level" of transparency is the only obligation imposed on Enabling Clause-based FTAs (WTO, 2007, p. 305; Onguglo, 2005). While the recent Decision at the General Council stipulates that GATT Article XXIV-based FTAs should be examined at CRTA, the consultation on Enabling Clause-based FTAs will continue to be conducted by CTD, not CRTA.

The difference between GATT Article XXIV and the Enabling Clause in terms of the conditions to be satisfied in forming FTAs is summarized as follows. The legal requirements of the two types of FTAs look similar but are actually very different. First, in the case of internal trade

(trade within an FTA), while the elimination of tariffs on substantially all internal trade is required in the case of GATT Article XXIV, the reduction of tariffs is enough in the case of Enabling Clause. There is no requirement on products coverage of tariff reduction for Enabling Clause-based FTAs. Second, as to trade barrier to non-members, in the case of GATT Article XXIV, there is an obligation to compare *ex ante* and *ex post* levels of protection to non-members. However, there is no such requirement in the case of the Enabling Clause. Third, GATT Article XXIV-based FTAs should be completed within 10 years, while there is no time limit in the case of the Enabling Clause. Finally, GATT Article XXIV-based FTAs shall be notified and examined by the WTO based on the detailed data submitted by the contracting parties, while notification and consultation is sufficient in the case of the Enabling Clause. In short, the level of multilateral governance for Enabling Clause-based FTAs is much lower than for GATT Article XXIV-based FTAs.[19]

3.2.3   *Developmental levels and legal choices*

WTO Members are allowed to sign FTAs that cover trade in goods based on either GATT Article XXIV or the Enabling Clause.[20] Such a situation is in sharp contrast to an agreement covering trade in services in which only the General Agreement on Trade in Services (GATS) Article V can be used. (The use of the Enabling Clause in forming services agreement is impossible, irrespective of developmental level.) While we tend to focus our argument on GATT Article XXIV when discussing the relationship between regionalism and the multilateral trading system, it is important to note that FTAs can also be formed based on the Enabling Clause, as long as all members included in the FTA are developing countries (Table 3.4). In fact, there are many existing Enabling Clause-based FTAs in the world, particularly in Asia.

---

[19]However, note that the lower discipline is applied to a GATT Article XXIV-based FTA if it involves only developing countries with regard to the date of submission. See Section 7 for more detail on this issue.

[20]When all contracting parties of FTAs or customs unions are non-members of the WTO, such an integration scheme is not subject to WTO disciplines. When an FTA or customs union includes WTO Members and non-members, such an agreement should be based on either GATT Article XXIV or the Enabling Clause.

Table 3.4   Usage of GATT Article XXIV and the Enabling Clause

	Use of GATT Article XXIV	Use of Enabling Clause
FTA including only developed countries	possible	impossible
FTA including both developed and developing countries	possible	impossible
FTA including only developing countries	possible	possible

Source: Author's compilation.

Whether the Enabling Clause can be used for the formation of FTAs between developing and developed countries is an important question. International trade lawyers have argued that there are three ways to interpret the legal implications of the Enabling Clause on FTAs between developed and developing countries (Irish, 2008). The first possible interpretation is that the list of measures permissible under the Enabling Clause spelled out in Paragraph 2 is non-exhaustive (see above), and that forming a mixed FTA based on the Enabling Clause is possible. The second interpretation is that the list is exhaustive and that the Enabling Clause is applicable to FTAs comprising only developing countries because Enabling Clause Paragraph 2(c) covers such agreements only. In this case, the Enabling Clause cannot be invoked in mixed FTAs. The third interpretation is that a mixed agreement between developed and developing countries is possible through a combination of GATT Article XXIV, which allows discrimination among members and non-members, and Enabling Clause Paragraphs 2(a) and 2(b), which justify non-reciprocal treatment among members in terms of trade negotiations. In practice, however, it seems that the dominant view among practitioners as well as some WTO staff is that the Enabling Clause cannot be used for a mixed FTA. In fact, many practitioners, including WTO staff, openly argue that mixed FTAs should be based on GATT Article XXIV.[21]

While GATT Article XXIV presumes that FTAs are formed between developed countries, it is important to note that any WTO member can sign an FTA using GATT Article XXIV. FTAs between developing countries and those between developed and developing countries can also be formed,

---

[21]See presentation by Roberto Fiorentin. Available at http://www.hss.ed.ac.uk/ila/pp/Notification_and_Review.ppt

based on GATT Article XXIV. Thus, while developing countries can use the Enabling Clause when they jointly form FTAs, this does not mean that FTAs between these countries must be formed based on the Enabling Clause. The use of the Enabling Clause is optional and not mandatory for developing countries when signing FTAs among themselves. In contrast, it is imperative that FTAs between developed countries be based on GATT Article XXIV and not on the Enabling Clause.

It is worth considering the GATT Article XXIV-based FTAs that are formed between developed and developing countries. The question here is whether non-reciprocal preferential access for the products of developing country partners is acceptable in the case of GATT Article XXIV-based FTAs. In the *Bananas II* case, the relevancy of the special trading preferences granted to bananas from the African, Caribbean, and Pacific Group of States (ACP) by the European Community (EC) under the Lomé Convention was disputed. The EC was of the view that non-reciprocal treatment under GATT Article XXIV-based FTAs is possible because GATT Article XXXVI:8 states that "developed contracting parties do not expect reciprocity for commitments made by them in trade negotiations to reduce or remove tariffs and other barriers to the trade of less-developed contracting parties." The panel's view was that GATT Article XXXVI:8 is not applicable to FTAs based on GATT XXIV because such is not listed in the Interpretative Note of Article XXVI:8. Also, if such was justifiable based on GATT XXXVI:8, there would have been no need for GATT Members to adopt a scheme for GSP (Irish, 2008). Thus, if FTAs are formed based on GATT Article XXIV, all contracting parties' measures should be compatible to the three conditions stipulated in the Article, irrespective of developmental level (Fiorentino, Verdeja, and Toqueboeuf, 2007). In fact, in order to maintain the trading preference of ACP countries, the EC eventually requested a waiver based on GATT Article XXV, which was granted in 1994.

Finally, the relation between the two provisions in forming FTAs is unclear. There is uncertainty if the two provisions are mutually exclusive in terms of the notification to the WTO in the case of FTAs formed by developing countries. It seems that the WTO Secretariat expects members to choose between them when signing agreements. However, in reality, member countries of some FTAs submit notifications under both GATT Article XXIV and the Enabling Clause for the same FTA.

The legal choice of forming FTAs can be summarized as follows. While GATT Article XXIV presumes that FTAs are formed between developed countries and the Enabling Clause presumes that FTAs are formed between developing countries, in reality, there are many mixed FTAs that involve both developed and developing countries. Mixed agreements cannot be based on the Enabling Clause and should be based on GATT Article XXIV, while reciprocal arrangements between developed and developing Members are necessary. In addition, FTAs between developing countries can be based on GATT Article XXIV as the use of the Enabling Clause is optional.

3.3 Analytical Framework for Assessing the Openness of Enabling Clause-based FTAs

This chapter places special emphasis on Enabling Clause-based FTAs in considering the openness of trade regionalism in Asia, with the primary concern of the analysis being the legal stands of each FTA in Asia. It attempts to identify common institutional features of Enabling Clause-based FTAs in Asia in comparison with those in other regions. However, the analysis is not limited to the question of which clause is used by each FTA, and we will also examine the tendency of each developing country in Asia to use either GATT Article XXIV or the Enabling Clause. Whether developing Asian countries' legal choice when forming FTAs is consistent or not is an important question in considering the implications of the legal basis of FTAs in Asia.

In considering the openness of Enabling Clause-based FTAs, we need to consider not only technical-level but also system-level questions. This is because, using the Enabling Clause, developing countries are allowed to form FTAs among themselves that do not satisfy the conditions stipulated in GATT Article XXIV, and thus technical-level methods to minimize the negative externalities of Enabling Clause-based FTAs — such as insubstantial coverage and large preferential margins — are limited. While we can always recommend that the contracting parties of Enabling Clause-based FTAs should make efforts to satisfy the conditions in GATT Article XXIV to reduce externalities (UNCTAD-JRTRO, 2008, p. 53; Plummer, 2007), there is no mechanism that guarantees this will happen. Despite the fact that many empirical studies find that Enabling Clause-based FTAs are not economically ideal (Park and Park, 2011; Rajapatirana, 1994), the matter of fact is that developing countries are entitled to pursue them. Thus, rather than contemplating detailed techniques that make FTAs open, the system-level approach to securing the open aspect of regionalism is useful, especially in the cases of FTAs based on the Enabling Clause.

The open accession policy is the core of the system-level method to make regionalism open. When the technical details of FTAs that may entail some negative external effects — such as insubstantial coverage and large preferential margins — are already present, accepting new members is an effective way to solve these negative externalities of regional cooperation and keep trade regionalism open. Several institutional features that we will discuss below are closely related to an open accession policy and the expansiveness of an agreement in general.

Number of participants. The number of participating members is critical in considering the openness or exclusiveness of an agreement. International relations scholars have argued that agreements between two parties and those among three or more parties are critically different in nature. A bilateral agreement is an agreement between two parties that is based on specific reciprocities, wherein the simultaneous balancing of specific *quid-pro-quos* by each party is required (Ruggie, 1992). It is premised on the assumption of a specific exchange between the two in each dyadic relationship. Thus, bilateralism is regarded as exclusive by definition (Capie and Evans, 2002, p. 39). Krauss and Pempel (2004, p. 5) summarize bilateralism as being when "two countries cede particular privileges to one another that they do not give to other countries." Note, however, that the degree of bilateralism depends on the design of each agreement. As Brian Job discusses, there is "expansive bilateralism," which contributes to cooperation among a wider membership (Capie and Evans, 2002, p. 40). In fact, in the case of trade, Menon (2009) argues that a bilateral agreement between a member of a plurilateral agreement and a non-member that seeks membership in the plurilateral agreement may have good external effects, calling such an agreement a "plurilateral-agreement-facilitating bilateral agreement." Nevertheless, it is undeniable that bilateralism tends to be non-expansive because it tries to address the specific needs and concerns of the two members. In fact, even if a bilateral agreement has an accession clause, a country that is interested in membership tends to suggest the establishment of a new agreement, rather than simply joining an existing bilateral agreement. For example, the idea of a Pacific Three (P3) agreement involving Singapore, New Zealand, and Chile was launched in the early 2000s, when they decided to negotiate a new agreement, despite the fact that there was already a bilateral FTA between New Zealand and Singapore that included an accession clause.[22] This episode implies that bilateral agreements are designed to serve the specific needs of members and the level of "diffuse reciprocity," which will be discussed in more detail below, tends to be low by nature.

Ruggie (1992, p. 571) defines multilateralism as an "institutional form which coordinates relations among three or more states on the basis of generalized principles of conduct, that is, principles which specify appropriate conduct for a class of actions, without regard to the particularistic interests of the parties or the strategic exigencies that may exist in any specific occurrence."[23] He argues that an agreement that simply has more than three members may not be worth calling multilateral and insists that Nazi pre-war trade and monetary arrangements were bilateral in nature, although the number of the concerned parties was large. What is called "diffuse reciprocity" is the key to multilateralism, which means that an arrangement is expected to yield rough equivalence of benefits over time, unlike specific reciprocity. Although, in theory, multilateral agreements can be used to refer to non-global arrangement among parties of three or more, we will used the term plurilateral (rather than multilateral) FTA to refer to an FTA among three or more parties for two reasons. First, the term multilateralism is usually used to refer to a multilateral arrangement at the global level — such as the WTO — and thus the use of the term "multilateral FTA" would be confusing from a practical perspective. Second, agreements among three or more parties do not always entail multilateralism in Ruggie's sense. Whether an agreement of three or more parties entails a generic nature, versus a specific nature, is an empirical question. Thus, it is inappropriate to automatically assume that agreements

---

[22] The Pacific Four (P4) agreement, including Brunei Darussalam, was ultimately signed in 2006 and is known formally as the Trans-Pacific Partnership Agreement (TPP). For details, see Hamanaka (2012a).

[23] Keohane (1990) also discusses the nature of multilateralism. However, he defines multilateralism in a nominal manner as institutions with three or more members.

among three or more parties are expansive agreements and that, therefore, plurilateral is better than multilateral when referring to non-bilateral agreements.

Labeling an agreement. Relating to the above argument on the number of participants is the name or label of an agreement, which is equally important when considering the expansiveness of agreements. Some agreements spell out the participants in the name of the agreement, while other agreements use a geographical label. The latter case tends to be more open to the accession of other countries in the region. Bilateral agreements usually take the name of the two members and this makes it difficult for non-members to join. In fact, the FTA between Singapore and New Zealand mentioned above, which Chile ultimately decided not to participate in, proposing instead a new agreement among the three, is called the New Zealand–Singapore FTA. In contrast, plurilateral agreements tend to use a geographical label. This may facilitate the participation of regional countries. However, the use of a particular geographical label may prevent non-regional countries from participating, because a geographical label implies which countries are inside versus outside and, as a consequence, which are welcome and which are not (Hamanaka, 2009). For example, while Singapore was once interested in membership in NAFTA, it finally decided not to join for a simple reason: Singaporeans did not regard themselves as North Americans (Haas, 1994; Bergsten, 1994, p. 25).

Vision and ultimate output. The vision of an FTA in terms of the comprehensiveness of the ultimate output of the agreement is important in assessing the openness of cooperation, at least from a regional perspective. While examining the vision *per se* is a difficult task, the form an FTA takes implies a vision of the agreement that members intend to achieve over the long-run in terms of comprehensiveness. Trade agreements sometimes take the form of customs unions, and, moreover, they sometimes mention an ultimate goal of regional cooperation beyond trade integration (e.g., monetary union). Agreements sometimes take the form of a partial scope agreement (PSA). In these cases, the sectoral coverage is very limited, and we can argue that the agreement attempts to serve the specific needs of contracting countries. The membership that the agreement intends to achieve in the long-run also relates to the comprehensiveness of an agreement. In short, whether or not the agreement envisages itself evolving into a (sub)region-wide cooperative agreement with comprehensive issue coverage is the question.

Accession clause. An accession clause is the fundamental institutional parameter in considering the open membership policy of regional projects. There are four types of agreements with regard to the accession of new members (Fon and Parisi, 2005).[24] The first possibility is that the FTA does not have any accession clause (closed agreement). Note, however, that this scenario does not exclude the possibility of accession, which may be achieved by amending the original agreement. Second, there is semi-closed type of agreement for which acceptance of a new member requires the unanimous approval of the current signatory states. A semi-open agreement is an agreement where acceptance of a new member depends on approval by a majority of the existing signatory states. Finally, there is a (truly) open agreement, in which all states that are willing to agree to the terms of treaty can join. In addition, whether accession criteria are clear or there is room for discretion is an important question. When incumbents have discretion, this becomes a source of influence and the agreement becomes less open (Findlay, 2003, p. 218; Kelley, 2010; Hamanaka, 2012a). However, the accession clause is one aspect of open membership, and the agreement can be non-expansive in terms of membership even if it has an accession clause.[25]

Thus, the empirical sections of this research analyze FTAs in terms of the (i) number of members (two versus three or more), (ii) name of the agreement, (iii) comprehensiveness of the agreement, and (iv) accession clause. A plurilateral agreement with a geographical label that has a liberal

---

[24] Fon and Parisi (2005) do not distinguish between closed and semi-closed agreements, and put them together under the classification of closed agreement. Although they define a closed agreement as an "agreement for which acceptance of a new member requires the unanimous approval of the current signatory states," they also consider that an agreement without an accession clause that ultimately accepts a new member by amending the original treaty should be classified as a closed agreement. Rather than assessing the openness regarding membership based on results, this study distinguishes between a (real) closed agreement without an accession clause (to which a new member may be accepted by amending the agreement) and a semi-closed agreement that requires unanimous approval for accession.

[25] For example, suppose a situation where a certain regional (bilateral or plurilateral) agreement excludes the agricultural sector because the member countries have a specific interest in protecting their respective agriculture sectors. Then, even if the membership of this regional agreement is open to anyone, such an agreement cannot be said to be fully open.

accession clause and envisages itself evolving into pan-regional cooperation can be said to be fairly open. In contrast, a bilateral agreement with a partial scope, a name that includes only two contracting countries, and without an accession clause can be deemed to be less expansive. Note, however, that I do not argue that plurilateral agreements always include geographical labels and accession clauses, and vice versa, with regard to bilateral agreements. Actual openness and exclusiveness depend on institutional design.[26]

3.4   Overview of FTAs around the World

3.4.1   *The universe of Enabling Clause-based FTAs*

As of December 2011, there were a total of 316 notifications of regional agreements in force that had been submitted to the GATT and WTO, counting goods and services notifications separately.[27] However, there are some regional agreements that have not been notified to the WTO, which is outside the scope of this analysis.[28]

Among the 316 notifications, 11 notifications relate to accession to existing regional agreements, although there were many instances where membership expansion was achieved without notifying the WTO.[29] The other 305 notifications were for the establishment of new regional

---

[26] For example, Findlay (2003) argues that plurilateral agreements in the field of services initiated by the US are not particularly open based on an examination of several institutional parameters.

[27] The number of FTAs has been determined using a notification basis. Thus, very recent FTAs that have not yet be notified to the WTO, such as the Korea–US FTA, are not included here.

[28] For more on FTAs that have not been notified to the WTO, see Hamanaka (2013b). In Asia, a notable example of a regional agreement not notified to the WTO is the ASEAN Framework Agreement on Trade in Services (AFAS), which covers the services trade rather than goods trade.

[29] Seven notifications were for accession to GATT Article XXIV-based FTAs: (i) EFTA Accession of Iceland, (ii) EC (9) Enlargement, (iii) EC (10) Enlargement, (iv) EC (12) Enlargement, (v) EC (15) Enlargement, (vi) EC (25) Enlargement, (vii) EC (27) Enlargement. Three notifications were for accession to GATS Article V-based Economic Integration Agreements (EIAs): (i) EC (15) Enlargement; (ii) EC (25) Enlargement; and (iii) EC (27) Enlargement. One notification was for accession to an Enabling Clause-based FTA: China's accession to the Asia-Pacific Trade Area (APTA).

agreements. Among them, there were 213 agreements (FTAs) covering trade in goods and 92 agreements on trade in services.

Among the 213 FTAs covering trade in goods, 179 FTAs have been notified under GATT Article XXIV and 34 under the Enabling Clause. It is interesting to note that three FTAs have been notified under both GATT Article XXIV and Enabling Clause: (i) ASEAN–Korea FTA, (ii) Gulf Cooperation Council (GCC); and (iii) India–Korea FTA. Thus, only about 16% of FTAs worldwide have been notified under the Enabling Clause.[30] Figure 3.1 provides a summary of the universe of FTAs, with different legal backgrounds.

Among the 34 Enabling Clause-based FTAs, 18 FTAs are located in Asia, and only 14 located outside Asia. (Two agreements do not have

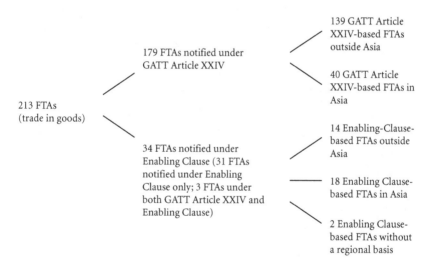

Figure 3.1　The universe of FTAs

Source: Author's compilation

---

[30] FTAs notified under both GATT Article XXIV and the Enabling Clause are counted as Enabling Clause-based FTAs, because the focus of this research is the use of the Enabling Clause and the possibility that these FTAs would not have been formed if there were no Enabling Clause.

regionally based membership). Thus, the majority of Enabling Clause-based FTAs signed worldwide are located in Asia. Among the 14 Enabling Clause-based FTAs located outside Asia, five are located in Africa, three in Latin America, three in the Pacific Islands region, and three in the Middle East.[31] Thus, Enabling Clause-based FTAs exist all over the world, and each region has several such FTAs, whose memberships overlap with one another.

Two FTAs based on the Enabling Clause do not have any regional basis. The first one is the Global System of Trade Preferences among Developing Countries (GSTP), which has more than 40 members from Africa, South America, West Asia, the Caribbean, Europe, East Asia, the Middle East, North America, and Central America. The second one is the Protocol on Trade Negotiations (PTN), which has 15 members from West Asia, South America, Africa, the Middle East, East Asia, North America, and Europe.

3.4.2   *Common features of Enabling Clause-based FTAs outside Asia*

As previously explained, the number of Enabling Clause-based FTAs outside Asia is very limited, at only 14. Because there are 134 GATT Article XXIV-based FTAs outside Asia, the share of Enabling Clause-based FTAs of those outside Asia is about 9%. Enabling Clause-based FTAs are a minor subcategory of FTAs outside Asia. Below is an exhaustive list of the 14 Enabling Clause-based FTAs outside Asia:

(i)   Southern Common Market (MERCOSUR)
(ii)   Pacific Island Countries Trade Agreement (PICTA)
(iii)   Egypt–Turkey FTA
(iv)   Economic Community of West African States (ECOWAS)
(v)   East African Community (EAC)
(vi)   Economic and Monetary Community of Central Africa (CEMAC)
(vii)   Latin American Integration Association (LAIA)
(viii)   South Pacific Regional Trade and Economic Cooperation Agreement (SPARTECA)
(ix)   West African Economic and Monetary Union (WAEMU)

---

[31] The Egypt–Turkey FTA is counted as a Middle Eastern FTA.

(x) Melanesian Spearhead Group Trade Agreement (MSGTA)
(xi) Andean Community (CAN)
(xii) Common Market for Eastern and Southern Africa (COMESA)
(xiii) Economic Cooperation Organization (ECO)/ECO Trade Agreement (ECOTA)[32]
(xiv) Gulf Cooperation Council (GCC)

It is interesting to note that non-Asian, Enabling Clause-based FTAs share several common features (Table 3.5). First, in terms of the size of membership, the majority of Enabling Clause-based FTAs outside Asia are plurilateral agreements. Signed in 2007, the Egypt–Turkey FTA is the only bilateral FTA based on the Enabling Clause outside Asia. All other such FTAs are plurilateral, and it seems that these FTAs eventually expect to include additional members from within their respective regions (see below for more details on their accession clauses). However, (sub)regional groupings are not mutually exclusive and they sometimes overlap with each other. For example, the African continent has five Enabling Clause-based FTAs: (i) ECOWAS, (ii) COMESA, (iii) CEMAC, (iv) WAEMU, and (v) EAC. Several of these FTAs have common members.

Related to this point is the fact that the names of these plurilateral FTAs usually include a geographical label rather than the names of the participating countries, which is common in the case of bilateral FTAs. The use of a geographical label makes it easy for non-members to join the group. The name of a subregion — such as West Africa or the South Pacific — is usually used as a geographical label.[33]

The second important common feature is that most plurilateral FTAs based on the Enabling Clause are customs unions and not FTAs in the narrow sense, while there are some FTAs that usually take the form of

---

[32] ECO was established in 1985 with three founding members: Iran, Pakistan, and Turkey. The preferential tariff protocol among the three ECO members was signed in May 1991, and an additional protocol was signed in February 1992. The agreement notified to the WTO was the trilateral preferential tariff agreement. Meanwhile, ECO expanded its membership in 1992 when seven additional members joined. The ECOTA agreement, which can be regarded as a successor to the early trilateral preferential tariff scheme, was signed by 10 members in 2003.

[33] There are several agreements that spell out the name of participating countries even though these are plurilateral agreements. One example is the El Salvador–Honduras–Chinese Taipei, Agreement.

Table 3.5   Exhaustive list of 14 Enabling Clause-based FTAs outside Asia

Agreements	Membership	Type	Date of entry into force
SPARTECA	Australia, Cook Islands, Fiji, Kiribati, Marshall Islands, Micronesia, Nauru, New Zealand, Niue, Papua New Guinea, Samoa, Solomon Islands, Tonga, Tuvalu, and Vanuatu	FTA (PSA)	01-Jan-1981
LAIA	Argentina, Venezuela, Bolivia, Brazil, Chile, Colombia, Cuba, Ecuador, Mexico, Paraguay, Peru, and Uruguay	FTA (PSA)	18-Mar-1981
CAN	Bolivia, Colombia, Ecuador, Peru, and (Venezuela)	CU	25-May-1988
MERCOSUR	Argentina, Brazil, Paraguay, and Uruguay	CU	29-Nov-1991
ECOTA	Afghanistan, Azerbaijan, Iran, Kazakhstan, Kyrgyz Republic, Pakistan, Tajikistan, Turkey, Turkmenistan, and Uzbekistan	FTA (PSA)	17-Feb-1992
ECOWAS	Benin, Burkina Faso, Cape Verde, Côte d'Ivoire, Gambia, Ghana, Guinea, Guinea Bissau, Liberia, Mali, Niger, Nigeria, Senegal, Sierra Leone, and Togo	CU	24-Jul-1993
MSGTA	Fiji, Papua New Guinea, Solomon Islands, and Vanuatu	FTA (PSA)	01-Jan-1994
COMESA	(Angola), Burundi, Comoros, Congo, D. R., Djibouti, Egypt, Eritrea, Ethiopia, Kenya, (Lesotho), Libya, Madagascar, Malawi, Mauritius, Rwanda, Seychelles, Sudan, Swaziland, (Tanzania), Uganda, Zambia, and Zimbabwe	CU	08-Dec-1994
CEMAC	Cameroon, Central African Republic, Chad, Congo, and Equatorial Guinea, Gabon	CU	24-Jun-1999
WAEMU	Benin, Burkina Faso, Côte d'Ivoire, Guinea Bissau, Mali, Niger, Senegal, and Togo	CU	01-Jan-2000
EAC	Burundi, Kenya, Rwanda, Tanzania, and Uganda	CU	07-Jul-2000
GCC	Bahrain, Saudi Arabia, Kuwait, Oman, Qatar, and United Arab Emirates	CU	01-Jan-2003

(Continued)

Table 3.5 (*Continued*)

Agreements	Membership	Type	Date of entry into force
PICTA	Cook Islands, Fiji, Kiribati, Micronesia, Nauru, Niue, Papua New Guinea, Samoa, Solomon Islands, Tonga, Tuvalu, and Vanuatu	FTA	13-Apr-2003
Egypt–Turkey	Egypt and Turkey	FTA	01-Mar-2007

Note: Original members of the agreement are underlined. Parentheses signify withdrawal from the agreement. While the WTO is of the position that the Melanesian Spearhead Group Trade Agreement has four original members, Fiji is not included as an original member because the treaty that established the Melanesian Spearhead Group Trade Agreement gives only Papua New Guinea, Solomon Islands, and Vanuatu as the original members. The group accepted Fiji in 1998

Source: Author's compilation based on the WTO FTA Database and various agreements

partial scope agreement (PSA). This means members not only liberalize internal trade but also harmonize external barriers. While the Enabling Clause does not distinguish between FTAs and customs unions, unlike GATT Article XXIV, and there is no obligation to harmonize external trade barriers among members of an Enabling Clause-based FTA, the reality is that developing countries outside Asia tend to sign Enabling Clause-based FTAs that include the harmonization of external trade barriers. Moreover, some of the Enabling Clause-based trade integration schemes outside Asia are part of more comprehensive projects of regional community building, including monetary integration, labor market integration, and even future political integration.[34]

Third, the majority of the 13 plurilateral Enabling Clause-based FTAs outside Asia include an accession clause. Based on available data, we confirmed that all non-Asian plurilateral FTAs based on the Enabling Clause include provisions on the accession of new members, except

---

[34] However, it should be noted that the visions of the framers of the agreement and its actual implementation of trade liberalization are often different. This is especially true in the case of FTAs in Africa. See Khadiagala (2011) for more details on unsuccessful trade integration cooperation in Africa.

GCC and ECOWAS.[35] Among the remaining 11 Enabling Clause-based plurilateral FTAs outside Asia, membership in three — SPARTECA, ECOTA, and MSGTA — requires accession to the umbrella institution. Being a member of the Pacific Island Forum (PIF), formerly known as the South Pacific Forum (SPF), is a prerequisite for SPARTECA membership (Article XIV of SPARTECA). However, membership in PIF is open to the territories of the Pacific Islands region (Article I of the Agreement Establishing the Pacific Island Forum). In the case of ECO, though the original trilateral preferential tariff protocol under ECO signed in 1991 was open to any developing country (Article IV of the 1991 Protocol), being a member of ECO is a prerequisite for membership in ECOTA, which was established in 2003 (Article 1 of ECOTA). The accession policy of ECO is liberal because it is open to any state enjoying geographical contiguity with ECO members and/or sharing the objectives and principles of ECO (Article XIII of Treaty of Izmir). Being a member of the Melanesian Spearhead Group (MSG) is a prerequisite for MSGTA membership (Article 16 of MSGTA). The accession procedure for MSG is unclear, though it accepted a new member, Fiji, in 1998.[36]

Other than the five cases mentioned above — GCC, ECOWAS, SPARTECA, ECOTA, and MSGTA — the eight plurilateral FTAs directly accept members based on the accession clause in their respective agreements.[37] The accession rules of those FTAs are expansive in nature in terms of membership policy, though the details of the accession procedure

---

[35] ECOWAS includes a provision on withdrawal (Article 91).

[36] Article I.3 of the Agreement Establishing the Melanesian Spearhead Group states "the Leaders' Summit may determine from time to time, the criteria for observers and associate members ... or whereby other governments, territories or organizations may be admitted to observer and associate membership of MSG."

[37] Conceptually, this can be classified into two groups: (i) direct accession to an FTA, and (ii) direct accession to a "package agreement" that includes an FTA. In the latter case, members cannot be a member of an FTA only, because the FTA is an inseparable part of the package agreement. For example, MERCOSUR falls under the first category since this agreement mainly covers only trade, while COMESA falls under the second category because it covers a wide range of issues including a customs union. However, distinguishing between the two is difficult in reality because some FTAs have comprehensive coverage, which can be regarded as a package agreement.

are often determined and assessed by subsidiary bodies such as a council. All have clear stipulations on application eligibility, which contributes to the transparency and openness of the agreement. In many cases, the provision states "the agreement shall be open to the accession of the rest of" the countries in a particular region (or even any country). Some FTAs consider geographical proximity and economic interdependence as the critical elements of eligibility, which implies that nearby countries affected by the FTA are allowed to join the agreement (e.g., COMESA and EAC). In terms of the procedures of approval made by incumbents, some agreements (e.g., COMESA) adopt an open accession principle, but other agreements (e.g., CAN) make a decision on whether to accept new members by voting (semi-open). There are agreements (e.g., CEMAC[38]) that require unanimous concurrence to accept new members. The accession rules of each FTA are summarized in Table 3.6.

Below are illustrative examples of accession clauses in agreements from three regions (Africa, the Pacific Islands, and South America).

MERCOSUR

CHAPTER IV: Accession

Article 20

This Treaty shall be open to accession, through negotiation, by other countries members of the Latin American Integration Association[39]; their applications may be considered by the States Parties once this Treaty has been in force for five years.

Notwithstanding the above, applications made by countries members of the Latin American Integration Association who do not belong to subregional integration schemes or an extraregional association may be considered before the date specified.

Approval of applications shall require the unanimous decision of the States Parties.

---

[38]While CEMAC uses "Central Africa" in its name, membership is, in fact, open to any African country.

[39]The membership of LAIA is also open to non-members.

Table 3.6   Accession rules of Non-Asian Enabling Clause-based FTAs

Agreements	Countries who may apply	Accession procedures	Article
LAIA	Open to accession by all Latin American countries	Accession shall be adopted by the Council of Foreign Ministers, which requires two-thirds majority vote	Article 43 and 58 (of the Montevideo Treaty)
CAN	Open to accession of the rest of Latin American countries	Affirmative vote of the absolute majority	Article 151 (of the Cartagena Agreement)
MERCOSUR	Open to accession of other members of LAIA	Unanimous decision of members	Article 20
COMESA	Open to immediate neighbors of a member state	Automatic accession provided that terms and conditions are met	Article 1 and Article 194
CEMAC	Open to any other African states	Unanimous agreement of the members	Article 6
WAEMU	Open to all West African states	Agreement between member states and the applicant state	Article 103
EAC	Geographical proximity to and inter-dependence with members	Approval given by members	Article 3
PICTA	Open to any state, territory or self-governing entity	Unanimous agreement by members	Article 27

Source: Author's compilation.

PICTA

Article 27: Accession by Other States, Territories or Self-Governing Entities

1. By unanimous agreement the Parties may permit any State, Territory or Self-Governing Entity not listed in Paragraph 1 of Article 26 to accede to this Agreement.

2. The terms of such accession shall be negotiated between the Parties and the State, Territory or Self-Governing Entity desiring to accede to this Agreement pursuant to Paragraph 1 of this Article.

CEMAC

Article 6

Any other African state, sharing the same ideals as those which the founding members declare solemnly committed, may apply for membership in the Economic and Monetary Community of Central Africa.

This membership not be made until unanimous agreement of the founding members. Any subsequent accession of a new state will be subject to the unanimous agreement of members of the Community.

Fourth, most Enabling Clause-based FTAs have a relatively long history. Among the 14 such FTAs outside Asia, 3 came into force in the 1980s and 6 in the 1990s. Only four entered into force after 2000. Thus, we can say there is no recent proliferation of Enabling Clause-based FTAs outside Asia. This is mainly because most subregions in the world already have Enabling Clause-based FTAs that have an accession clause and non-members can simply join those existing FTAs, rather than establish a new such FTA. In fact, since most of these FTAs have been in effect for a long period, existing agreements experience fluctuations in membership across time. Among the 13 plurilateral FTAs outside Asia based on the Enabling Clause, four underwent membership expansion while two experienced a withdrawal of members.

Interestingly, it is rare that a developing country outside Asia signs both GATT Article XXIV-based and Enabling Clause-based FTAs. Usually, a developing country outside Asia signs more than one FTA of the same kind, either Enabling Clause-based or GATT Article XXIV-based. For example, Fiji has membership in three FTAs based on the Enabling Clause: (i) South Pacific Regional Trade and Economic Cooperation (SPARTECA), (ii) Melanesia Spearhead Group Trade Agreement (MSGTA), and (iii) Pacific Island Countries Trade Agreement (PICTA). Likewise, Kenya is a member of the Common Market for Eastern and Southern Africa (COMESA) and East African Community (EAC).[40]

There are also cases of non-Asian developing countries signing several FTAs based solely on GATT Article XXIV. For example, the Central America Common Market (CACM) is based on GATT Article XXIV,[41] and all other FTAs signed by members of CACM are also based on GATT Article XXIV.[42] Although some countries sign both Enabling Clause-based and

---

[40]What is unique about Africa is that some countries have membership in multiple customs unions, which is theoretically very difficult (Krueger, 1997). This is perhaps because the nature of an Enabling Clause-based customs union is very different from a GATT Article XXIV-based customs union, and the former does not function well economically. (For a discussion on dysfunctional economic integration schemes in Africa, see Khadiagala, 2011).

[41]However, some are of the view that members of those agreements are perceived to be able to renege on MFN obligations (Ng and Yeats, 2003).

GATT Article XXIV-based FTAs, their choice of legal provision is fairly consistent — all plurilateral agreements that have (sub)regional member-ship are based on the Enabling Clause, while all bilateral agreements are based on GATT Article XXIV.[43] Thus, outside Asia, developing countries consistently decide to use only one of the two provisions, either the Enabling Clause or GATT Article XXIV.

In summary, the Enabling Clause is used outside of Asia as the legal basis for forming plurilateral (not bilateral) FTAs with the objective of achieving deeper integration (including customs unions) in future, and subsequently covering all countries in a (sub)region. Most Enabling Clause-based FTAs have been in effect for a long period and have managed to expand their respective memberships using accession clauses. As a result, proliferation of Enabling Clause-based FTAs outside of Asia has not occurred in recent years. Finally, among non-Asian developing countries, the choice of a legal provision in forming FTAs is fairly consistent.

3.5   Empirical Study of Enabling Clause-based FTAs in Asia

3.5.1   *Use of the Enabling Clause by developing Asian countries*

As we have seen, in Asia, there are a total of 18 Enabling Clause-based FTAs (Table 3.7), and a total of 40 FTAs based on GATT Article XXIV (Table 3.8). As stated already, FTAs that involve at least one Asian country are regarded as Asian FTAs, including cross-regional FTAs in which the contracting parties include both Asian and non-Asian countries. (For a discussion of cross-regional agreements, see Katada and Solis, 2011).

The worldwide share of Enabling Clause-based FTAs is only 16%, as we have already confirmed. However, simply considering these FTAs to be a minor subcategory in the universe of FTAs is not accurate. If we compare Asian and non-Asian FTAs, the composition of various types of FTAs is very different (Figure 3.1). In Asia, there are 18 Enabling Clause-based FTAs and 40 GATT Article XXIV-based FTAs, and thus the share of Enabling Clause-based FTAs is as high as 31%. As we saw, outside Asia, the share of Enabling Clause-based FTAs is as low as 9%. We can conclude that the number of such FTAs is significant only in Asia.

---

[42] CACM includes Costa Rica, El Salvador, Guatemala, Honduras, and Nicaragua.
[43] For example, many Latin American countries.

Table 3.7   Enabling Clause-based FTAs in Asia

Agreements	Membership	Type	Entry into force
Asia-Pacific Trade Agreement (APTA)	Bangladesh, China, <u>India</u>, <u>Korea</u>, <u>Lao PDR</u>, <u>Sri Lanka</u>	FTA (PSA)	17-Jun-1976
Lao PDR–Thailand	Bilateral (intraregional)	FTA (PSA)	20-Jun-1991
ASEAN Free Trade Area (AFTA)	<u>Brunei Darussalam</u>, Cambodia, <u>Indonesia</u>, Lao PDR, <u>Malaysia</u>, Myanmar, <u>Philippines</u>, <u>Singapore</u>, <u>Thailand</u>, Viet Nam	FTA	28-Jan-1992
South Asian Preferential Trade Arrangement (SAPTA)	Bangladesh, <u>Bhutan</u>, <u>India</u>, <u>Maldives</u>, <u>Nepal</u>, <u>Pakistan</u>, <u>Sri Lanka</u>	FTA (PSA)	07-Dec-1995
India–Sri Lanka	Bilateral (intraregional)	FTA	15-Dec-2001
India–Afghanistan	Bilateral (intraregional)	FTA (PSA)	13-May-2003
ASEAN–China	Bilateral (intraregional)	FTA (PSA)	01-Jan-2005
Pakistan–Sri Lanka	Bilateral (intraregional)	FTA	12-Jun-2005
South Asian Free Trade Agreement (SAFTA)	Bangladesh, <u>Bhutan</u>, <u>India</u>, <u>Maldives</u>, <u>Nepal</u>, <u>Pakistan</u>, <u>Sri Lanka</u>	FTA	01-Jan-2006
India–Bhutan	Bilateral (intraregional)	FTA	29-Jul-2006
Chile–India	Bilateral (cross-regional)	FTA (PSA)	17-Aug-2007
Pakistan–Malaysia	Bilateral (intraregional)	FTA	01-Jan-2008
MERCOSUR–India	Bilateral (cross-regional)	FTA (PSA)	01-Jun-2009
India–Nepal	Bilateral (intraregional)	FTA (PSA)	27-Oct-2009
ASEAN–India	Bilateral (intraregional)	FTA	01-Jan-2010
ASEAN–Korea	Bilateral (intraregional)	FTA	01-Jan-2010
India–Korea	Bilateral (intraregional)	FTA	01-Jan-2010
India–Malaysia	Bilateral (intraregional)	FTA	01-Jul-2011

Notes: In the case of plurilateral FTAs (e.g., APTA, AFTA, SAPTA, and SAFTA), original members are underlined
Source: Author's compilation based on WTO RTA Database

Table 3.8   GATT Article XXIV-based FTAs in Asia

Agreements	Membership	Entry into force
New Zealand–Singapore	Bilateral (cross-regional)	01-Jan-2001
Japan–Singapore	Bilateral (intraregional)	30-Nov-2002
EFTA–Singapore	Bilateral (cross-regional)	01-Jan-2003
Singapore–Australia	Bilateral (cross-regional)	28-Jul-2003
China–Macau	Bilateral (intraregional)	01-Jan-2004
China–Hong Kong	Bilateral (intraregional)	01-Jan-2004
US–Singapore	Bilateral (cross-regional)	01-Jan-2004
Korea–Chile	Bilateral (cross-regional)	01-Apr-2004
Thailand–Australia	Bilateral (cross-regional)	01-Jan-2005
Japan–Mexico	Bilateral (cross-regional)	01-Apr-2005
Thailand–New Zealand	Bilateral (cross-regional)	01-Jul-2005
India–Singapore	Bilateral (intraregional)	01-Aug-2005
Jordan–Singapore	Bilateral (cross-regional)	22-Aug-2005
Korea–Singapore	Bilateral (intraregional)	02-Mar-2006
Trans-Pacific Strategic Economic Partnership	Brunei Darussalam, Chile, New Zealand, Singapore	28-May-2006
Guatemala–Chinese Taipei	Bilateral (cross-regional)	01-Jul-2006
Japan–Malaysia	Bilateral (intraregional)	13-Jul-2006
Panama–Singapore	Bilateral (cross-regional)	24-Jul-2006
EFTA–Korea	Bilateral (cross-regional)	01-Sep-2006
Chile–China	Bilateral (cross-regional)	01-Oct-2006
Pakistan–China	Bilateral (intraregional)	01-Jul-2007
Chile–Japan	Bilateral (cross-regional)	03-Sep-2007
Japan–Thailand	Bilateral (intraregional)	01-Nov-2007
Nicaragua–Chinese Taipei	Bilateral (cross-regional)	01-Jan-2008
Honduras–El Salvador–Chinese Taipei	Honduras; El Salvador; Chinese Taipei	01-Mar-2008
Japan–Indonesia	Bilateral (intraregional)	01-Jul-2008
Brunei Darussalam–Japan	Bilateral (intraregional)	31-Jul-2008
China–New Zealand	Bilateral (cross-regional)	01-Oct-2008
ASEAN–Japan	Bilateral (intraregional)	01-Dec-2008
Japan–Philippines	Bilateral (intraregional)	11-Dec-2008
China–Singapore	Bilateral (intraregional)	01-Jan-2009
Peru–Singapore	Bilateral (cross-regional)	01-Aug-2009
Japan–Switzerland	Bilateral (cross-regional)	01-Sep-2009
Japan–Vietnam	Bilateral (intraregional)	01-Oct-2009
ASEAN–Australia–New Zealand	ASEAN, Australia, New Zealand	01-Jan-2010

(Continued)

Table 3.8   (*Continued*)

Agreements	Membership	Entry into force
Peru–China	Bilateral (cross-regional)	01-Mar-2010
Hong Kong–New Zealand	Bilateral (cross-regional)	01-Jan-2011
EU–Korea	Bilateral (cross-regional)	01-Jul-2011
India–Japan	Bilateral (intraregional)	01-Aug-2011
Peru–Korea	Bilateral (cross-regional)	01-Aug-2011

Note: All agreements listed in this table are FTAs
Source: Author's compilation based on WTO RTA Database.

Table 3.9   Breakdown of FTAs in Asia

	Intraregional	Cross-Regional	Total
Plurilateral	4 FTAs in total	3 FTAs in total	7 FTAs in total
	– 0 GATT XXIV	– 3 GATT XXIV	– 3 GATT XXIV
	– 4 Enabling Clause	– 0 Enabling Clause	– 4 Enabling Clause
Bilateral	27 FTAs in total	24 FTAs in total	51 FTAs in total
	– 15 GATT XXIV	– 22 GATT XXIV	– 37 GATT XXIV
	– 12 Enabling Clause	– 2 Enabling Clause	– 14 Enabling Clause
Total	31 FTAs in total	27 FTAs in total	58 FTAs in total
	– 15 GATT XXIV	– 25 GATT XXIV	– 40 GATT XXIV
	– 16 Enabling Clause	– 2 Enabling Clause	– 18 Enabling Clause

Source: Author's compilation based on WTO RTA database.

If we distinguish between intraregional FTAs and cross-regional FTAs in Asia, very interesting observations can be made (Table 3.9). The share of Enabling Clause-based FTAs is considerably different between intraregional FTAs (all contracting parties are Asian economies) and cross-regional FTAs (contracting parties involve both Asian and non-Asian countries). Among the 58 FTAs in Asia, 31 are intraregional and 27 are cross-regional. Out of 31 intraregional FTAs, 16 are Enabling Clause-based and 15 are GATT Article XXIV-based. This means that more than half of intraregional FTAs in Asia are based on the Enabling Clause. The predominance of Enabling Clause-based FTAs is evident if the samples are limited to intra-Asian FTAs. Interestingly, there are only two cross-regional FTAs in Asia that are based on the Enabling Clause.

In addition, it is important to remember that, FTAs involving developed countries shall be based on GATT Article XXIV, not the Enabling Clause. In the case of Asia, FTAs including Japan shall be based on GATT Article XXIV. Of the 15 intraregional FTAs based on GATT Article XXIV in Asia, six involve Japan (Japan–Singapore, Japan–Malaysia, Japan–Thailand, Japan–Indonesia, ASEAN–Japan, and India–Japan). These six FTAs are thus ineligible to apply the Enabling Clause. Among the 25 intraregional South–South FTAs in Asia not involving Japan, 16 are based on the Enabling Clause. Thus, Enabling Clause is the dominant tool when signing South–South FTAs in Asia. This is in sharp contrast to the situation outside Asia, as described in the previous section.

Which Asian countries have signed the most intraregional Enabling Clause-based FTAs in Asia? In fact, almost all developing countries in Asia have signed them (Table 3.10), including China, India, Indonesia, Korea, Malaysia, Pakistan, Philippines, Sri Lanka, Thailand, Viet Nam, and ASEAN as a group. While the majority of FTAs signed by South Asian countries are based on the Enabling Clause, Southeast and Northeast Asian countries are also regular users of the Enabling Clause. Thus, we can say that heavy usage of the Enabling Clause is a common feature throughout Asia.

It is important to note that some contracting parties of Enabling Clause-based FTAs in Asia also sign GATT Article XXIV-based FTAs. Almost all developing countries in Asia, other than the least developed countries (LDCs) and the notable exception of Sri Lanka, have signed both types of FTAs.[44] For example, China has signed two Enabling Clause-based FTAs ([APTA] and the ASEAN–China FTA) and seven GATT Article XXIV-based FTAs (China–Macau; Chile–China; China–Hong Kong; China–Pakistan; China–Singapore; China–New Zealand; China–Peru). Moreover, some FTAs between developing countries are based on the Enabling Clause even when both contracting parties have signed GATT Article XXIV-based FTAs with another trading partner. For example, although both Malaysia and India have signed GATT Article XXIV-based FTAs with other parties (e.g., Japan–Malaysia EPA, India–Singapore EPA), the FTA between Malaysia and

---

[44] There are four LDCs in East and South Asia: Bangladesh, Bhutan, Cambodia, and Lao PDR. None of them have signed a GATT Article XXIV-based FTA. However, for example, the Japan–ASEAN EPA covers LDCs in ASEAN.

Table 3.10   FTAs signed by developing countries in Asia

	Enabling Clause-based FTAs	GATT Article XXIV-Based FTAs
China	APTA, ASEAN–China	China–Macau; China–Hong Kong; Chile–China; Pakistan–China; China–New Zealand; China–Singapore; Peru–China
Korea	APTA, ASEAN–Korea, Korea–India	Korea–Chile, Korea–Singapore, EFTA–Korea, EU–Korea, Peru–Korea
Malaysia	AFTA, ASEAN–China, Pakistan–Malaysia, ASEAN–India, ASEAN–Korea, India–Malaysia	Japan–Malaysia, ASEAN–Japan, ASEAN–Australia–New Zealand
Thailand	AFTA, ASEAN–China, ASEAN–India, ASEAN–Korea	Thailand–Australia, Thailand–New Zealand, Japan–Thailand, ASEAN–Japan, ASEAN–Australia–New Zealand
Indonesia	AFTA, ASEAN–China, ASEAN–India, ASEAN–Korea	Japan–Indonesia, ASEAN–Japan, ASEAN–Australia–New Zealand
Philippines	AFTA, ASEAN–China, ASEAN–India, ASEAN– Korea	ASEAN–Japan, Japan–Philippines, ASEAN–Australia–New Zealand
Singapore	AFTA, ASEAN–China, ASEAN–India, ASEAN–Korea	New Zealand–Singapore, Japan–Singapore, EFTA–Singapore, Singapore–Australia, US–Singapore, India–Singapore, Jordan–Singapore, Korea–Singapore, Trans-Pacific Strategic Economic Partnership, Panama–Singapore, ASEAN–Japan, China–Singapore, Peru–Singapore, ASEAN–Australia–New Zealand
Vietnam	AFTA, ASEAN–China, ASEAN–India, ASEAN–Korea	ASEAN–Japan, Japan–Vietnam, ASEAN–Australia–New Zealand

(Continued)

Table 3.10   *(Continued)*

	Enabling Clause-based FTAs	GATT Article XXIV–Based FTAs
India	APTA, SAPTA, SAFTA, India–Sri Lanka, India–Afghanistan, India–Bhutan, Chile–India, MERCOSUR–India, ASEAN–India, Korea–India, India–Malaysia	India–Singapore, India–Japan
Pakistan	SAPTA, SAFTA, Pakistan–Malaysia	Pakistan–China
Sri Lanka	APTA, SAPTA, SAFTA, India–Sri Lanka	None

Source: Author's compilation.

India is based on the Enabling Clause. Obviously, one of the reasons behind the parallel usage of the two legal provisions is that many developing countries in Asia sign FTAs with nearby developed countries such as Japan and Australia; therefore, these FTAs should be based on GATT Article XXIV. However, even we limit our analysis to South–South FTAs in Asia, the choice of legal provision is not as homogenous as is the case with non-Asian developing countries. For example, while the ASEAN–China and Malaysia–Pakistan FTAs are based on the Enabling Clause, the China–Pakistan FTA is based on GATT Article XXIV. This parallel usage of the two provisions could be one of the reasons why there are so many Enabling Clause-based FTAs in Asia.

3.5.2   *Bilateral Enabling Clause-based FTAs in Asia*

The most unique aspect of Enabling Clause-based FTAs in Asia is that the majority of them are bilateral FTAs.[45] Among the 16 (intraregional) Enabling Clause-based FTAs in Asia, 12 are bilateral. This is in sharp contrast to the situation outside Asia, where almost all such FTAs are plurilateral. As aforementioned, there is only one bilateral FTA based on the Enabling Clause outside Asia. As a result, almost all bilateral Enabling Clause-based FTAs are located in Asia. Two-thirds of such FTAs in Asia

---

[45]One of the parties of bilateral agreement can be a regional entity like ASEAN or MERCOSUR. These agreements are classified as bilateral by the WTO.

(12 out of 18) are intraregional as well as bilateral. Thus, the most distinctive feature of FTAs in Asia can be summarized as follows: Asia is home to many bilateral South–South FTAs that are based on the Enabling Clause.

As far as bilateral Asian FTAs based on the Enabling Clause are concerned, most of them are relatively new. Among the 14 bilateral Enabling Clause-based FTAs, only one was signed before 2000, four were signed between 2001 and 2005, and nine were signed between 2006 and 2011. Thus, we can say that bilateral Enabling Clause-based FTAs are the principal contributor to the recent proliferation of FTAs in Asia. As discussed, outside Asia, the number of new Enabling Clause-based FTAs has been limited, while GATT Article XXIV-based FTAs have proliferated. It is also important to note that the predominance of bilateral FTAs in Asia that are based on the Enabling Clause is a recent phenomenon, which became evident only after 2000.

All bilateral FTAs based on the Enabling Clause in Asia are FTAs, and none of them include a customs union. Sometimes, FTAs take the form of a partial scope agreement (PSA), with limited product coverage. At present, no bilateral Enabling Clause-based FTAs in Asia, except several agreements signed by Singapore, have an accession clause[46] (The exceptions involving Singapore being New Zealand–Singapore FTA Article 79, Australia–Singapore FTA Chapter 17 Article 4, Singapore–US FTA Article 21.6.) Furthermore, all bilateral Enabling Clause-based FTAs spell out the participating countries in the name of the agreement. As a result, none of them experienced a change in membership, whether the accession of a new member or the withdrawal of an existing one. In short, the nature of bilateral FTAs based on the Enabling Clause is not expansive, which is not surprising, since bilateralism is exclusive by definition.

3.5.3 *Plurilateral Enabling Clause-based FTAs in Asia*

In Asia, there are four plurilateral FTAs based on the Enabling Clause: (i) Asia-Pacific Trade Agreement (APTA), (ii) ASEAN Free Trade Area

---

[46]The number of bilateral FTAs that have an accession clause is limited outside Asia as well. Examples include Australia–US (Article 23.1), Australia–Chile (Article 23.2), Peru–US (Article 23.5), and the Closer Economic Relations (CER) Agreement between New Zealand and Australia (Article 24 in goods and Article 22 in services). See Lewis (2010).

(AFTA), (iii) South Asian Preferential Trade Arrangement (SAPTA), and (iv) South Asian Free Trade Agreement (SAFTA).

The fundamental features of plurilateral FTAs based on the Enabling Clause in Asia are similar to such FTAs outside Asia, albeit with a few differences. The period in which plurilateral Enabling Clause-based FTAs in Asia were signed is almost the same period that such FTAs were signed outside Asia. Except for SAFTA, which was signed in 2006, all plurilateral Enabling Clause-based FTAs in Asia were signed in the 1970s and 1990s. One interesting issue relating to this is that the first Enabling Clause-based FTA, APTA, was signed in Asia. In addition, there was only one bilateral Enabling Clause-based FTA in Asia before 2000. Prior to that year, the Enabling Clause was applied to FTAs in a similar manner in Asia as in other regions. Thus, Asian countries have also used the Enabling Clause as the basis for their regional cooperation projects.

All four of the plurilateral Enabling Clause-based FTAs in Asia mentioned above have a strong (sub)regional basis. Membership in these FTAs usually includes many countries in a (sub)region. A geographical label is also used in the name of these FTAs, specifically, the name of a subregion such as Southeast Asia or South Asia. Similar to Enabling Clause-based FTAs outside Asia, such FTAs in Asia also overlap with each other in terms of geographical scope and membership. For example, India has membership in both APTA and SAFTA.

However, there are some critical differences between Asian plurilateral Enabling Clause-based FTAs and similar non-Asian FTAs. First, with the notable exception of APTA, no plurilateral FTA in Asia based on the Enabling Clause includes an accession clause (APTA's accession clause is provided below for reference.)

APTA

Chapter VII — Accession and Withdrawal

Article 30 Accession to the Agreement

(i) After its entry into force, this Agreement shall be open for accession by any developing member country of ESCAP.

(ii) After due negotiations, the applicant country may accede to the Agreement by consensus. If consensus is not reached, however, the applicant country may accede to the Agreement if at least two thirds of the Participating States recommend its accession. If any of the

Participating States objects to such accession, however, the provisions
of the Agreement shall not apply as between that country and the
acceding country.

It seems that plurilateral FTAs in Asia, other than APTA, adopt relatively
exclusive membership policies. It may be the case that it is necessary for an
applicant to first be a member of, for example, ASEAN in order to become
an AFTA member, although this is not mentioned in the agreement.[47]
Thus, for non-members that are interested in AFTA membership, there
is no indication on how to become an AFTA member. Likewise, SAFTA
does not have an accession clause, though it has a clause on withdrawal of
membership (Article 21).[48]

Second, for plurilateral Enabling Clause-based FTAs in Asia, the creation
of future customs unions does not seem to be a possibility. It can be said
that the integration scheme of economies for Enabling Clause-based FTAs
in Asia is not as bold as those FTAs outside Asia, where customs unions,
not FTAs are common. Moreover, many of them are PSAs, in which only a
limited number of sectors are covered.

In summary, among plurilateral FTAs formed before 2000, Asian
developing countries used the Enabling Clause in a similar manner
as non-Asian countries, although Asian plurilateral FTAs based on the
Enabling Clause seldom had clear accession rules, unlike such non-Asian
FTAs. It was only after 2000 that Asian developing countries started to use
the Enabling Clause to form bilateral FTAs.

3.6 Policy Issues of Bilateral Enabling Clause-based FTAs

3.6.1 *Policy considerations: Three waves of FTAs and their WTO compatibility*

As discussed in Section 3.2, both GATT Article XXIV and the Enabling
Clause have interesting historical backgrounds, and it seems safe to argue

---

[47]Moreover, it is widely recognized that ASEAN adopts a relatively exclusive membership
policy. While the ASEAN Charter has an accession clause, it does not say to whom that the
membership is open. For an assessment of the membership policy of ASEAN, see Fon and
Parisi (2005, p. 3).
[48]Moreover, the South Asian Association for Regional Cooperation (SAARC) does not have
an accession clause.

that nowadays both provisions are used in a manner that drafters of these agreements did not expect, which itself is not a problem, but it does have several important implications to the multilateral trade system. The original draft of GATT Article XXIV included only the formation of customs unions, which already existed when the GATT treaty was negotiated in the 1940s. The later inclusion of FTAs into GATT Article XXIV was achieved partly because the US secretly intended to sign an FTA with Canada, though such a plan was never realized (Chase, 2005). However, the inclusion of FTAs in GATT Article XXIV did not have any immediate impact because the number of GATT Article XXIV-based FTAs had been limited. Meanwhile, the Enabling Clause was agreed upon in 1979 as a result of the Tokyo Round negotiations. It is important to note that the Enabling Clause was negotiated in the context of the New International Economic Order (NIEO) that seeks to improve the position in the world economy of third world countries relative to the developed countries.

So far, there have been three waves of trade regionalism (Baldwin and Carpenter, 2011; Mansfield and Milner, 1999) but the way in which the two provisions have been used in each of the three waves is quite distinct. It can be said that the number of agreements increased suddenly in the second and third waves of regionalism because of the new way of using these provisions in forming agreements.

The first wave of regionalism occurred in the 1960s and 1970s, with Europe at the forefront. The EC was formed in 1958 and the European Free Trade Association (EFTA) came into force in 1960. At the same time, regionalism also spread outside Europe. There are many regional cooperation schemes in the developing world such as Central American Common Market (CACM), which was formed in 1961, and Caribbean Community and Common Market, (CARICOM) formed in 1973. While there were some FTAs (mostly signed by EC), many important projects during the first wave of regionalism involved customs unions. The EC is a typical example, but one should note that agreements including only developing countries, such as CACM and CARICOM, are also customs unions. In short, during the first wave of regionalism, GATT Article XXIV was used in the manner expected by drafters of GATT.

The second wave of regionalism occurred in the 1980s and 1990s, which was initiated primarily in the Americas. After the debt crisis of the 1980s, many Latin American countries started to adopt more liberal economic policies. One notable example is NAFTA, formed in 1994, which includes the US, Canada, and Mexico and is based on GATT Article XXIV. There are many bilateral FTAs in Latin America that are based on GATT Article XXIV as well, such as the Costa Rica-Mexico FTA signed in 1995. A distinctive feature of the second wave is that most GATT Article XXIV-based agreements are FTAs and not customs unions. Although there is nothing wrong in forming FTAs based on GATT Article XXIV, the point is that it was only in the 1990s that WTO Members started to extensively use this provision to form FTAs, not customs unions, despite the fact that GATT Article XXIV covered FTAs from the onset. In other words, the predominance of FTAs over customs unions became evident only after the second wave of regionalism. As Fiorentine, Verdeja and Toqueboeuf (2006) suggests, the landscape of agreements would have been very different if GATT Article XXIV covered only customs unions. It is safe to consider that in drafting the GATT, it was not expected that FTAs and not customs unions would proliferate half a century later since the enforcement of the GATT.

In addition, during the second wave of trade regionalism, several plurilateral Enabling Clause-based RTAs were signed in many parts of the world. The Enabling Clause, which was agreed in 1979 as a result of the Tokyo Round, made it easier for developing countries to sign agreements comprising only of developing countries. But the majority of Enabling Clause-based agreements during the second wave were customs unions as in the analysis above. Moreover, most Enabling Clause-based agreements in the 1980s and 1990s were plurilateral agreements, which included several countries in the region, and the majority of them had accession clauses. The creation of those agreements was consistent to the very idea of the clause which was agreed in the context of the NIEO. Thus, we can say that the manner in which the Enabling Clause was used in the 1990s is to be expected.

The third wave of regionalism was triggered by the proposal of the ASEAN–China FTA in 2001, which is based on the Enabling Clause and not GATT Article XXIV (Baldwin and Carpenter, 2011). After this, agreements have proliferated in Asia partly due to so-called domino effects. As we have seen, nearly half of the intraregional bilateral agreements in Asia are based on the Enabling Clause. The proliferation of agreements in Asia is partly because of the use of the Enabling Clause in forming bilateral agreements, especially FTAs. What is interesting is that, outside Asia, the Enabling Clause is commonly used for subregional economic cooperation projects whose membership is composed of more than three countries. It is only in Asia that the Enabling Clause is used to form bilateral agreements. While many have noted that the distinctive feature of Asian trade regionalism is "bilateralism," little attention has been paid to the fact that these agreements are based on the Enabling Clause. Again, there is nothing wrong even if developing countries decide to form bilateral agreements using the Enabling Clause, but it seems that such usage of the Enabling Clause was not expected when it was agreed on in 1979. Two decades later, developing countries in Asia have found this provision convenient in creating bilateral FTAs.

3.6.2   Policy suggestions: Enhancing the WTO compatibility of Asian FTAs

The proliferation of Enabling Clause-based FTAs has important implications for Asian regionalism, whose nature has mainly been described as being open. The number of Enabling Clause-based FTAs is significant in Asia but not elsewhere. While there is no doubt that developing countries are entitled to sign Enabling Clause-based FTAs, it is another matter whether or not these FTAs are consistent with open regionalism. As weaker disciplines are required for signing Enabling Clause-based FTAs, it is very important to closely examine the openness of Enabling Clause-based FTAs. Because Asian developing countries use the Enabling Clause to form bilateral FTAs, unlike countries outside Asia, a central question is the openness of an FTA that is both bilateral and Enabling Clause-based, a combination popular in Asia since 2000. Has the nature of Asian regionalism been altered by the rise of bilateralism, especially bilateral Enabling Clause-based FTAs? Can we still say that Asian trade regionalism is open despite the fact that many bilateral Enabling Clause-based FTAs have been signed by Asian countries? How should bilateral Enabling Clause-based FTAs be made more open?

Open regionalism has three variations with regard to trade in goods liberalization (see Chapter 2, Section 2.2).[49] The first definition of open regionalism is "open membership," which suggests that any country that is

---

[49]Another possible definition of open regionalism is trade facilitation, which is not in the scope of this chapter (Bergsten, 1997).

willing to accept the rules of the institution can be invited to join (Soesas-tro, 2003). The second variation is the unilateral and unconditional reduc-tion of MFN tariffs. This is widely considered the truest interpretation of open regionalism, although it is difficult to be achieved in reality given the risk of free riding. This option is sometimes referred to as the unilateral "multilateralization" of preferential tariffs. The third type of open regional-ism is the commitment to global liberalization, which is mainly achieved at the multilateral negotiations of the WTO. These are not necessarily mutu-ally exclusive ideas. It is useful to analyze bilateral Enabling Clause-based FTAs in terms of open regionalism from three different angles that will be discussed in turn below.

First, in relation to the membership policy of FTAs, it seems safe to say that the manner in which the Enabling Clause is used in Asia is not as open as that outside Asia. Asian developing countries use the Enabling Clause to form bilateral FTAs. Outside Asia, the Enabling Clause is commonly used to form plurilateral FTAs under which all countries in the (sub)region are expected to join. As such, these plurilateral FTAs have an accession clause. Because weaker disciplines are required for signing Enabling Clause-based FTAs than GATT Article XXIV-based FTAs, there is always the risk of negative externalities for non-members. The potential adverse effects of weakly disciplined FTAs can be mitigated by the inclusion of an accession clause, with outsiders that are negatively affected by an agreement are able to become insiders. In short, bilateral Enabling Clause-based FTAs, which are popular in Asia, are less open than plurilateral Enabling Clause-based FTAs that have accession clauses, which are common outside Asia. The formation of bilateral FTAs based on the Enabling Clause that do not include an accession clause is not an ideal situation as far as the openness of FTAs is concerned.[50]

How should bilateral Enabling Clause-based FTAs be made more open? One way to solve this problem is to include an accession clause in FTAs so that they adhere to an open membership policy (Soesastro, 2003). In reality, however, this seems to be difficult to achieve (Bergsten, 1997). Another more viable solution is the effective use of APTA, which is based on the Enabling Clause. APTA is the oldest FTA in Asia and it is a plurilateral FTA. APTA has an accession clause through which all developing countries of

---

[50] This type of bilateral agreement cannot be said to be "expansive bilateralism" (Job, 1998).

ESCAP can obtain membership. Moreover, no country can exercise a veto over the accession process of other states, instead a two-thirds majority vote is used to confirm accession. As far as the membership policy is concerned, APTA can be deemed the most liberal agreement in the world. If APTA were used effectively, there would be no need for developing countries in Asia to sign bilateral FTAs based on the Enabling Clause. (It is important to note that the two giant economies in Asia — China and India — are both members of APTA.)

Second, on the relation between an FTA and the MFN rate, it is not easy to empirically examine whether Enabling Clause-based FTAs in Asia facilitate or prevent the unilateral MFN rate reduction of FTA members compared with GATT Article XXIV-based FTAs. In general, however, Enabling Clause-based FTAs seem to be less effective in achieving the unilateral reduction of the MFN rate than GATT Article XXIV-based FTAs. Many economics studies find that Enabling Clause-based FTAs are more trade distortive than GATT Article XXIV-based FTAs (Park and Park, 2011). In fact, after the establishment of many FTAs based on the Enabling Clause in the 1980s and 1990s, Latin American countries faced the risk of significant trade diversion (Rajapatirana, 1994).

There are at least two reasons for explaining why Enabling Clause-based FTAs do not generate sufficient incentives for MFN rate reduction. The first point relates to the direct force brought about by the signing of FTAs in reducing the MFN rate.[51] In the case of GATT Article XXIV-based FTAs, there is an obligation to conduct a comparison of *ex ante* and *ex post* levels of protection against non-members (GATT Article XXIV: 5(a)). Thus, the external tariffs of members of GATT Article XXIV-based FTAs tend to be lower. However, the Enabling Clause simply requires that FTAs not raise barriers to trade with non-members without conducting *ex ante* and *ex post* assessments. Thus, the external trade barriers of the group can even be higher after the implementation of Enabling Clause-based FTAs, which is contradictory to a unilateral MFN rate reduction. Another reason is that in the case of GATT Article XXIV-based FTAs, the protection of sensitive

---

[51] The treatment of not only internal tariffs within FTAs, but also external tariffs against non-members (namely MFN rates), are critical for FTAs to avoid being trade distortive. In terms of welfare effects, it also critical to determine if FTAs lead to an increase or decrease in external tariffs for non-members (El-Agraa, 2002).

sectors is basically prohibited due to the "substantially all the trade" rule (GATT Article XXIV: 8(a)). FTA members tend to fully liberalize a sector to all countries once it is opened to regional members. Thus, it is GATT Article XXIV-based FTAs that can create an incentive for the unilateral reduction of the MFN rate (GATT Article XXIV: 8(a)). In contrast, the signing of Enabling Clause-based FTAs may not lead to unilateral reductions of the MFN rate because the protection of sensitive sectors is possible (*Ibid.*). In short, the problem of Enabling Clause-based FTAs is not limited to their weaker requirements for trade liberalization *per se*. Rather, Enabling Clause-based FTAs do not create an incentive (or even create any disincentive) for unilateral MFN rate reduction among participating countries, unlike GATT Article XXIV-based FTAs.

How can Enabling Clause-based FTAs trigger unilateral MFN tariff reduction? It is not easy to achieve this goal. The only way to solve this problem completely is for FTAs between developing countries to be based on GATT Article XXIV, rather than the Enabling Clause (Park and Park, 2011; Rajapatirana, 1994). At the very least, when signing Enabling Clause-based FTAs, it is important for developing countries to bear in mind that FTAs should be designed to avoid (i) raising barriers to trade with non-members (Enabling Clause Paragraph 3(a)) and (ii) giving preferential treatment to FTA members that may supersede unilateral MFN rate reduction.

Third, in relation to the commitment to global liberalization through the multilateral negotiations of the WTO, it is still too early to make any definitive statement because the Doha Round negotiations have yet to be concluded. However, the future result of the Doha Round will be a good test to determine whether the commitment of Asian countries to global liberalization is real. In order for Asian countries to be called pursuers of open regionalism, the MFN bound rates after the Doha Round should be much lower than the current MFN applied rates. Moreover, the MFN bound rates should be significantly lowered for products that are covered by FTAs.

The policy prescription for making Asian trade regionalism more open can be summarized as follows. Enabling Clause-based FTAs do not seem to be as desirable as GATT Article XXIV-based FTAs in terms of the economic effects on third parties. Moreover, Enabling Clause-based FTAs are unlikely to lead to MFN reductions among member countries; this manner of achieving open regionalism — through the multilateralization of FTA tariff rates — seems to be difficult. If Enabling Clause-based FTAs inevitably entail large negative externalities, accepting negatively affected non-members to the group is an effective method to minimize the cost of FTAs. This is a more realistic way of achieving open regionalism.

3.7   Summary

We have witnessed the proliferation of FTAs in Asia since 2000. One of the critical (and often overlooked) features of these newly signed FTAs is that many of them are based on the Enabling Clause and not GATT Article XXIV. While many analysts implicitly assume that FTAs are based on GATT Article XXIV when discussing how to make FTAs multilateralism-friendly, such an assumption is not valid in the case of Asia. In fact, the heavy use of the Enabling Clause is one of the critical reasons behind the recent proliferation of FTAs in Asia.

It is important to note that the manner in which the Enabling Clause is used in Asia is very different from its use in other regions. Above all, the number of Enabling Clause-based FTAs is very limited outside Asia. If the Enabling Clause is used to form plurilateral FTAs among non-Asian developing countries, the agreements often take the form of customs unions. Moreover, Enabling Clause-based FTAs outside Asia usually have an accession clause, with the objective of developing into a (sub)region-wide trade or economic agreement. Because Enabling Clause-based FTAs inevitably entail negative effects for non-members, outside Asia, there are attempts to solve this problem by accepting a new member that would otherwise suffer from the FTA. In other words, Enabling Clause-based FTAs outside Asia attempt to minimize negative external effects by adhering to the principle of open membership. While developing countries outside Asia also sign bilateral FTAs, these are usually based on GATT Article XXIV, not the Enabling Clause; in these cases, members attempt to minimize the negative external effects by satisfying conditions similar to those required in North–North FTAs.

In contrast, Asian developing countries began using the Enabling Clause to form bilateral FTAs after 2000. The Enabling Clause is no longer used in the traditional way in Asia: small developing countries envisaging the creation of (sub)region-wide economic or trade cooperation. Currently, more than half of intra-Asian South–South FTAs are based on the Enabling Clause, and the majority of these are bilateral. The critical feature of FTAs in Asia is the predominance of bilateral agreements that are Enabling Clause-based. One should also note that bilateral FTAs based on the Enabling Clause exist only in Asia. It is important for Asian policymakers to realize that their innovative use of the Enabling Clause has led to the proliferation of FTAs in Asia, but this approach is far from optimum in terms of fostering an open platform of economic and trade cooperation in the region.

Enabling Clause-based FTAs may not be economically as desirable as those based on GATT Article XXIV, and they may also generate large negative externalities. FTAs based on the Enabling Clause tend to have trade-distorting effects and carry the risk of welfare deterioration for non-members because the requirements of Enabling Clause-based FTAs are much weaker than those of GATT Article XXIV. Moreover, Enabling Clause-based FTAs are unlikely to lead to MFN tariff reduction among member countries. Thus, it is too optimistic to expect that open regionalism through the multilateralization of preferential tariffs can be achieved as far as bilateral Enabling Clause-based FTAs are concerned. Although we should not forget that developing countries are legally entitled to sign Enabling Clause-based FTA among themselves, signing politically driven bilateral FTAs that have economically poor effects can be described as a "deviation from WTO norms" (Bergsten *et al.*, 2008, p. 16). This is especially so if bilateral FTAs are based on the Enabling Clause.

There are two ways to solve this problem. The first possible option is to pursue FTAs that are plurilateral, not bilateral, if the Enabling Clause is to be used. Such plurilateral FTAs should also have an accession clause. Because we cannot expect that Enabling Clause-based FTAs will have as few trade-distorting effects as GATT Article XXIV-based FTAs, and thus they may entail large negative externalities, there should be opportunities for affected developing country non-members to join such FTAs. In practical terms, Asian developing countries joining APTA would be a better option than signing a new bilateral South–South Enabling Clause-based FTA in Asia. The second possible solution is that if developing countries in Asia still want to pursue bilateral FTAs they should use GATT Article XXIV, not the Enabling Clause, in order to minimize negative externalities. Thus, countries in the region seeking open regionalism should pursue either plurilateral Enabling Clause-based FTAs or bilateral GATT Article XXIV-based FTAs, rather than bilateral Enabling Clause-based FTAs.

Appendix 3.1

GATT Article XXIV

Territorial Application — Frontier Traffic — Customs Unions
and Free-trade Areas

1. The provisions of this Agreement shall apply to the metropolitan customs territories of the contracting parties and to any other customs territories in respect of which this Agreement has been accepted under Article XXVI or is being applied under Article XXXIII or pursuant to the Protocol of Provisional Application. Each such customs territory shall, exclusively for the purposes of the territorial application of this Agreement, be treated as though it were a contracting party; *Provided* that the provisions of this paragraph shall not be construed to create any rights or obligations as between two or more customs territories in respect of which this Agreement has been accepted under Article XXVI or is being applied under Article XXXIII or pursuant to the Protocol of Provisional Application by a single contracting party.

2. For the purposes of this Agreement, a customs territory shall be understood to mean any territory with respect to which separate tariffs or other regulations of commerce are maintained for a substantial part of the trade of such territory with other territories.

3. The provisions of this Agreement shall not be construed to prevent:
   (*a*) Advantages accorded by any contracting party to adjacent countries in order to facilitate frontier traffic;
   (*b*) Advantages accorded to the trade with the Free Territory of Trieste by countries contiguous to that territory, provided that such advantages are not in conflict with the Treaties of Peace arising out of the Second World War.

4. The contracting parties recognize the desirability of increasing freedom of trade by the development, through voluntary agreements, of closer integration between the economies of the countries parties to such agreements. They also recognize that the purpose of a customs union or of a free-trade area should be to facilitate trade between the constituent territories and not to raise barriers to the trade of other contracting parties with such territories.

5. Accordingly, the provisions of this Agreement shall not prevent, as between the territories of contracting parties, the formation of a customs union or of a free-trade area or the adoption of an interim agreement necessary for the formation of a customs union or of a free-trade area; *Provided* that:

   (*a*) with respect to a customs union, or an interim agreement leading to a formation of a customs union, the duties and other regulations of commerce imposed at the institution of any such union or interim agreement in respect of trade with contracting parties not parties to such union or agreement shall not on the whole be higher or more restrictive than the general incidence of the duties and regulations of commerce applicable in the constituent territories prior to the formation of such union or the adoption of such interim agreement, as the case may be;

   (*b*) with respect to a free-trade area, or an interim agreement leading to the formation of a free-trade area, the duties and other regulations of commerce maintained in each of the constituent territories and applicable at the formation of such free-trade area or the adoption of such interim agreement to the trade of contracting parties not included in such area or not parties to such agreement shall not be higher or more restrictive than the corresponding duties and other regulations of commerce existing in the same constituent territories prior to the formation of the free-trade area, or interim agreement as the case may be; and

   (*c*) any interim agreement referred to in subparagraphs (*a*) and (*b*) shall include a plan and schedule for the formation of such a customs union or of such a free-trade area within a reasonable length of time.

6. If, in fulfilling the requirements of subparagraph 5 (*a*), a contracting party proposes to increase any rate of duty inconsistently with the provisions of Article II, the procedure set forth in Article XXVIII shall apply. In providing for compensatory adjustment, due account shall be taken of the compensation already afforded by the reduction brought about in the corresponding duty of the other constituents of the union.

7. (*a*) Any contracting party deciding to enter into a customs union or free-trade area, or an interim agreement leading to the formation

of such a union or area, shall promptly notify the CONTRACT-ING PARTIES and shall make available to them such information regarding the proposed union or area as will enable them to make such reports and recommendations to contracting parties as they may deem appropriate.

(b) If, after having studied the plan and schedule included in an interim agreement referred to in paragraph 5 in consultation with the parties to that agreement and taking due account of the information made available in accordance with the provisions of subparagraph (a), the CONTRACTING PARTIES find that such agreement is not likely to result in the formation of a customs union or of a free-trade area within the period contemplated by the parties to the agreement or that such period is not a reasonable one, the CONTRACTING PARTIES shall make recommendations to the parties to the agreement. The parties shall not maintain or put into force, as the case may be, such agreement if they are not prepared to modify it in accordance with these recommendations.

(c) Any substantial change in the plan or schedule referred to in paragraph 5 (c) shall be communicated to the CONTRACTING PARTIES, which may request the contracting parties concerned to consult with them if the change seems likely to jeopardize or delay unduly the formation of the customs union or of the free-trade area.

8. For the purposes of this Agreement:

(a) A customs union shall be understood to mean the substitution of a single customs territory for two or more customs territories, so that

(i) duties and other restrictive regulations of commerce (except, where necessary, those permitted under Articles XI, XII, XIII, XIV, XV and XX) are eliminated with respect to substantially all the trade between the constituent territories of the union or at least with respect to substantially all the trade in products originating in such territories, and,

(ii) subject to the provisions of paragraph 9, substantially the same duties and other regulations of commerce are applied by each of the members of the union to the trade of territories not included in the union;

(*b*) A free-trade area shall be understood to mean a group of two or more customs territories in which the duties and other restrictive regulations of commerce (except, where necessary, those permitted under Articles XI, XII, XIII, XIV, XV and XX) are eliminated on substantially all the trade between the constituent territories in products originating in such territories.

9. The preferences referred to in paragraph 2 of Article I shall not be affected by the formation of a customs union or of a free-trade area but may be eliminated or adjusted by means of negotiations with contracting parties affected.* This procedure of negotiations with affected contracting parties shall, in particular, apply to the elimination of preferences required to conform with the provisions of paragraph 8 (*a*)(i) and paragraph 8 (*b*).

10. The CONTRACTING PARTIES may by a two-thirds majority approve proposals which do not fully comply with the requirements of paragraphs 5 to 9 inclusive, provided that such proposals lead to the formation of a customs union or a free-trade area in the sense of this Article.

11. Taking into account the exceptional circumstances arising out of the establishment of India and Pakistan as independent States and recognizing the fact that they have long constituted an economic unit, the contracting parties agree that the provisions of this Agreement shall not prevent the two countries from entering into special arrangements with respect to the trade between them, pending the establishment of their mutual trade relations on a definitive basis.

12. Each contracting party shall take such reasonable measures as may be available to it to ensure observance of the provisions of this Agreement by the regional and local governments and authorities within its territories.

Appendix 3.2

UNDERSTANDING ON THE INTERPRETATION OF ARTICLE XXIV OF THE GENERAL AGREEMENT ON TARIFFS AND TRADE 1994

Members,

Having regard to the provisions of Article XXIV of GATT 1994;

Recognizing that customs unions and free trade areas have greatly increased in number and importance since the establishment of GATT 1947 and today cover a significant proportion of world trade;

Recognizing the contribution to the expansion of world trade that may be made by closer integration between the economies of the parties to such agreements;

Recognizing also that such contribution is increased if the elimination between the constituent territories of duties and other restrictive regulations of commerce extends to all trade, and diminished if any major sector of trade is excluded;

Reaffirming that the purpose of such agreements should be to facilitate trade between the constituent territories and not to raise barriers to the trade of other Members with such territories; and that in their formation or enlargement the parties to them should to the greatest possible extent avoid creating adverse effects on the trade of other Members;

Convinced also of the need to reinforce the effectiveness of the role of the Council for Trade in Goods in reviewing agreements notified under Article XXIV, by clarifying the criteria and procedures for the assessment of new or enlarged agreements, and improving the transparency of all Article XXIV agreements;

Recognizing the need for a common understanding of the obligations of Members under paragraph 12 of Article XXIV;

Hereby *agree* as follows:

1. Customs unions, free-trade areas, and interim agreements leading to the formation of a customs union or free-trade area, to be consistent with Article XXIV, must satisfy, *inter alia*, the provisions of paragraphs 5, 6, 7 and 8 of that Article.

Article XXIV: 5

2. The evaluation under paragraph 5(a) of Article XXIV of the general incidence of the duties and other regulations of commerce applicable before and after the formation of a customs union shall in respect of duties and charges be based upon an overall assessment of weighted average tariff rates and of customs duties collected. This assessment shall be based on import statistics for a previous representative period to be supplied by the customs union, on a tariff-line basis and in values and quantities, broken down by WTO country of origin. The Secretariat shall compute the weighted average tariff rates and customs duties collected in accordance with the methodology used in the assessment of tariff offers in the Uruguay Round of Multilateral Trade Negotiations. For this purpose, the duties and charges to be taken into consideration shall be the applied rates of duty. It is recognized that for the purpose of the overall assessment of the incidence of other regulations of commerce for which quantification and aggregation are difficult, the examination of individual measures, regulations, products covered and trade flows affected may be required.

3. The "reasonable length of time" referred to in paragraph 5(c) of Article XXIV should exceed 10 years only in exceptional cases. In cases where Members parties to an interim agreement believe that 10 years would be insufficient they shall provide a full explanation to the Council for Trade in Goods of the need for a longer period.

Article XXIV: 6

4. Paragraph 6 of Article XXIV establishes the procedure to be followed when a Member forming a customs union proposes to increase a bound rate of duty. In this regard Members reaffirm that the procedure set forth in Article XXVIII, as elaborated in the guidelines adopted on 10 November 1980 (BISD 27S/26–28) and in the Understanding on the Interpretation of Article XXVIII of GATT 1994, must be commenced before tariff concessions are modified or withdrawn upon the formation of a customs union or an interim agreement leading to the formation of a customs union.

5. These negotiations will be entered into in good faith with a view to achieving mutually satisfactory compensatory adjustment. In such

negotiations, as required by paragraph 6 of Article XXIV, due account shall be taken of reductions of duties on the same tariff line made by other constituents of the customs union upon its formation. Should such reductions not be sufficient to provide the necessary compensatory adjustment, the customs union would offer compensation, which may take the form of reductions of duties on other tariff lines. Such an offer shall be taken into consideration by the Members having negotiating rights in the binding being modified or withdrawn. Should the compensatory adjustment remain unacceptable, negotiations should be continued. Where, despite such efforts, agreement in negotiations on compensatory adjustment under Article XXVIII as elaborated by the Understanding on the Interpretation of Article XXVIII of GATT 1994 cannot be reached within a reasonable period from the initiation of negotiations, the customs union shall, nevertheless, be free to modify or withdraw the concessions; affected Members shall then be free to withdraw substantially equivalent concessions in accordance with Article XXVIII.

6. GATT 1994 imposes no obligation on Members benefiting from a reduction of duties consequent upon the formation of a customs union, or an interim agreement leading to the formation of a customs union, to provide compensatory adjustment to its constituents.

<u>Review of Customs Unions and Free-Trade Areas</u>

7. All notifications made under paragraph 7(a) of Article XXIV shall be examined by a working party in the light of the relevant provisions of GATT 1994 and of paragraph 1 of this Understanding. The working party shall submit a report to the Council for Trade in Goods on its findings in this regard. The Council for Trade in Goods may make such recommendations to Members as it deems appropriate.

8. In regard to interim agreements, the working party may in its report make appropriate recommendations on the proposed time-frame and on measures required to complete the formation of the customs union or free-trade area. It may if necessary provide for further review of the agreement.

9. Members parties to an interim agreement shall notify substantial changes in the plan and schedule included in that agreement to the

Council for Trade in Goods and, if so requested, the Council shall examine the changes.

10. Should an interim agreement notified under paragraph 7(a) of Article XXIV not include a plan and schedule, contrary to paragraph 5(c) of Article XXIV, the working party shall in its report recommend such a plan and schedule. The parties shall not maintain or put into force, as the case may be, such agreement if they are not prepared to modify it in accordance with these recommendations. Provision shall be made for subsequent review of the implementation of the recommendations.

11. Customs unions and constituents of free-trade areas shall report periodically to the Council for Trade in Goods, as envisaged by the CONTRACTING PARTIES to GATT 1947 in their instruction to the GATT 1947 Council concerning reports on regional agreements (BISD 18S/38), on the operation of the relevant agreement. Any significant changes and/or developments in the agreements should be reported as they occur.

Dispute Settlement

12. The provisions of Articles XXII and XXIII of GATT 1994 as elaborated and applied by the Dispute Settlement Understanding may be invoked with respect to any matters arising from the application of those provisions of Article XXIV relating to customs unions, free-trade areas or interim agreements leading to the formation of a customs union or free-trade area.

Article XXIV: 12

13. Each Member is fully responsible under GATT 1994 for the observance of all provisions of GATT 1994, and shall take such reasonable measures as may be available to it to ensure such observance by regional and local governments and authorities within its territory.

14. The provisions of Articles XXII and XXIII of GATT 1994 as elaborated and applied by the Dispute Settlement Understanding may be invoked in respect of measures affecting its observance taken by regional or local governments or authorities within the territory of a Member. When the Dispute Settlement Body has ruled that a provision of GATT 1994

has not been observed, the responsible Member shall take such reasonable measures as may be available to it to ensure its observance. The provisions relating to compensation and suspension of concessions or other obligations apply in cases where it has not been possible to secure such observance.

15. Each Member undertakes to accord sympathetic consideration to and afford adequate opportunity for consultation regarding any representations made by another Member concerning measures affecting the operation of GATT 1994 taken within the territory of the former.

Appendix 3.3

DIFFERENTIAL AND MORE FAVOURABLE TREATMENT RECIPROCITY AND FULLER PARTICIPATION OF DEVELOPING COUNTRIES

Decision of 28 November 1979
(L/4903)

Following negotiations within the framework of the Multilateral Trade Negotiations, the CONTRACTING PARTIES *decide* as follows:

1. Notwithstanding the provisions of Article I of the General Agreement, contracting parties may accord differential and more favourable treatment to developing countries,[1] without according such treatment to other contracting parties.

2. The provisions of paragraph 1 apply to the following:[2]
   (*a*) Preferential tariff treatment accorded by developed contracting parties to products originating in developing countries in accordance with the Generalized System of Preferences,[3]
   (*b*) Differential and more favourable treatment with respect to the provisions of the General Agreement concerning non-tariff measures governed by the provisions of instruments multilaterally negotiated under the auspices of the GATT;
   (*c*) Regional or global arrangements entered into amongst less-developed contracting parties for the mutual reduction or elimination of tariffs and, in accordance with criteria or conditions which may be prescribed by the CONTRACTING PARTIES, for the mutual reduction or elimination of non-tariff measures, on products imported from one another;

---

[1] The words "developing countries" as used in this text are to be understood to refer also to developing territories.
[2] It would remain open for the CONTRACTING PARTIES to consider on an *ad hoc* basis under the GATT provisions for joint action any proposals for differential and more favourable treatment not falling within the scope of this paragraph.
[3] As described in the Decision of the CONTRACTING PARTIES of 25 June 1971, relating to the establishment of "generalized, non-reciprocal and non discriminatory preferences beneficial to the developing countries" (BISD 18S/24).

(*d*) Special treatment on the least developed among the developing countries in the context of any general or specific measures in favour of developing countries.

3. Any differential and more favourable treatment provided under this clause:

(*a*) shall be designed to facilitate and promote the trade of developing countries and not to raise barriers to or create undue difficulties for the trade of any other contracting parties;

(*b*) shall not constitute an impediment to the reduction or elimination of tariffs and other restrictions to trade on a most-favoured-nation basis;

(*c*) shall in the case of such treatment accorded by developed contracting parties to developing countries be designed and, if necessary, modified, to respond positively to the development, financial and trade needs of developing countries.

4. Any contracting party taking action to introduce an arrangement pursuant to paragraphs 1, 2 and 3 above or subsequently taking action to introduce modification or withdrawal of the differential and more favourable treatment so provided shall:[4]

(*a*) notify the CONTRACTING PARTIES and furnish them with all the information they may deem appropriate relating to such action;

(*b*) afford adequate opportunity for prompt consultations at the request of any interested contracting party with respect to any difficulty or matter that may arise. The CONTRACTING PARTIES shall, if requested to do so by such contracting party, consult with all contracting parties concerned with respect to the matter with a view to reaching solutions satisfactory to all such contracting parties.

5. The developed countries do not expect reciprocity for commitments made by them in trade negotiations to reduce or remove tariffs and other barriers to the trade of developing countries, i.e., the developed countries do not expect the developing countries, in the course of trade negotiations, to make contributions which are inconsistent with their

---

[4]Nothing in these provisions shall affect the rights of contracting parties under the General Agreement.

individual development, financial and trade needs. Developed contracting parties shall therefore not seek, neither shall less-developed contracting parties be required to make, concessions that are inconsistent with the latter's development, financial and trade needs.

6. Having regard to the special economic difficulties and the particular development, financial and trade needs of the least-developed countries, the developed countries shall exercise the utmost restraint in seeking any concessions or contributions for commitments made by them to reduce or remove tariffs and other barriers to the trade of such countries, and the least-developed countries shall not be expected to make concessions or contributions that are inconsistent with the recognition of their particular situation and problems.

7. The concessions and contributions made and the obligations assumed by developed and less-developed contracting parties under the provisions of the General Agreement should promote the basic objectives of the Agreement, including those embodied in the Preamble and in Article XXXVI. Less-developed contracting parties expect that their capacity to make contributions or negotiated concessions or take other mutually agreed action under the provisions and procedures of the General Agreement would improve with the progressive development of their economies and improvement in their trade situation and they would accordingly expect to participate more fully in the framework of rights and obligations under the General Agreement.

8. Particular account shall be taken of the serious difficulty of the least-developed countries in making concessions and contributions in view of their special economic situation and their development, financial and trade needs.

9. The contracting parties will collaborate in arrangements for review of the operation of these provisions, bearing in mind the need for individual and joint efforts by contracting parties to meet the development needs of developing countries and the objectives of the General Agreement.

CHAPTER 4

Regional Approaches to Trade Facilitation

Are Regional Trade Facilitation Measures Discriminatory against Non-members?

4.1 Introduction

Trade facilitation[1] has recently become a hot issue among policy-makers and scholars. While many tariff regimes in Asia-Pacific continue to be liberalized, traders still face difficulties in moving goods across borders. Supporting this view are econometric studies showing that trade facilitation reforms considerably increase international trade and that their impact on trade flows is as equally significant as tariff elimination.[2] Given these propositions, trade facilitation measures aside from tariff elimination are now being seriously discussed as part of the multilateral and regional trade agenda.

Trade facilitation measures conducted at the regional initiative level are important because concrete measures to facilitate trade are often taken or implemented at the regional and bilateral levels, while multilateral institutions such as the World Customs Organization (WCO) and the World Trade Organization (WTO) focus on the establishment of international standards and principles of trade facilitation. Provisions on trade facilitation measures are also usually included in FTAs because of existing substantial non-tariff barriers among FTA members. Despite the elimination or reduction of tariffs, goods may still not always be traded smoothly or timely

---

[1] Because it requires a comprehensive approach, this chapter employs a broad definition of trade facilitation such as transparency, customs procedures and fees, and behind-the-border measures (for the details, see below).

[2] For example, see Anderson and Wincoop (2004); Wilson, Mann, and Otsuki (2005); and Duval and Utoktham (2009).

between FTA members. Trade between FTA partners can be increased through tariff elimination complemented by trade facilitation measures. Bilateral and regional schemes to liberalize trade usually entail cooperation in trade facilitation. FTA policy-makers have begun to realize the significance of trade facilitation and have included trade facilitation provisions in recent FTAs especially those covering the Asia-Pacific region.[3]

The existing literature on trade facilitation has yet to considerably explore one of the most critical questions regarding trade facilitation on a regional context: are regional trade facilitation measures discriminatory? A dominant view is that most trade facilitation measures are non-exclusive and non-discriminatory, unless members adopt specific regional standards (Schiff and Winters, 2003; Maur, 2008; Maur and Shepherd, 2011). For example, it is widely argued that the simplification of customs procedures at the regional level rarely has discriminatory effects (Moise, 2002). However, it cannot be simply assumed that trade facilitation measures at the regional level are always non-discriminatory. Even if the ultimate objective of trade facilitation appears to be multilateral and non-discriminatory, there are some measures that give discriminatory treatment to a limited number of countries. This is especially true for those under FTAs because FTAs are intended to give preferential treatment to their members. There is a possibility that the benefits of trade facilitation reform can be enjoyed only by FTA members, or may be extended to non-FTA members only under certain restrictions. In fact, some observe that concessionary customs fees applicable to FTA members and mutual recognition[4] among members can have discriminatory effects (also see Maur, 2008, p. 14; OECD, 2005).

In the context of "openness" of regionalism, the examination of the exclusive and discriminatory elements of trade facilitation measures at the regional/bilateral level is of particular importance. When the active debates on open regionalism in Asia was conducted in the 1990s, soon after the launch of Asia-Pacific Economic Cooperation (APEC), many theorists as

---

[3]The first FTA in the Asia-Pacific region to include trade facilitation provisions was the South Pacific Regional Trade and Economic Cooperation Agreement, signed in 1980.

[4]Mutual recognition of standards among members may bring exclusive effects to non-members. However, there is also a possibility that non-members can enjoy benefit (Nicolaïdis, 2000). See the Section 4.5 for the details.

well as policy-makers emphasized the importance of trade facilitation in designing open regional trade cooperation scheme. For example, Bergsten (1997) argues that one of the variations of open regionalism in the field of trade is the implementation of trade facilitation measures among regional economies, which tend to be non-discriminatory in nature, rather than the conduct of tariff elimination or reduction among members of regional groupings which inevitably becomes exclusive (also see Garnaut, 1996; Elek, 1995). In fact, in the case of APEC, all APEC members supported trade facilitation activities on the grounds that their benefit can be enjoyed not only by its members but also by non-members, while some proponents of open regionalism among APEC members are skeptical in realizing FTA among the members since preferential tariff treatment inevitably becomes exclusive and there is a risk of jeopardizing the fundamental philosophy of open regionalism.

This chapter provides a detailed analysis of whether trade facilitation provisions of FTAs in Asia-Pacific are discriminatory and, if so, how they can be discriminatory against non-members. In order to show that there are many preferential regional trade facilitation measures, we will examine "likely cases" namely the trade facilitation measures under FTA, since the very purpose of forming FTA is to discriminate partners from others. It also aims to demonstrate that there are various types of differenciated trade facilitation measures under FTAs.[5]

This chapter is structured as follows. The scope of trade facilitation measures in this study is discussed in the remainder of this section. Section 4.2 compares the difference between trade liberalization and trade facilitation in terms of multilateral governance on regionalism. Section 4.3 provides a framework to conduct empirical analysis on discriminatory effects of regional trade facilitation measures and introduces the concept of exclusive as well as differenciated trade facilitation. Section 4.4 briefly reviews the variety of trade facilitation measures covered by FTAs in Asia-Pacific and beyond. Section 4.5 identifies how and to what extent trade facilitation measures can be discriminatory by comparing examples of restrictive and liberal trade facilitation provisions under FTAs in Asia-Pacific. Section 4.6 discusses policy recommendations focusing on how to

---

[5]OECD (2005, p. 154) argues that there is very little evidence of arbitrary discrimination with regard to trade facilitation measures except those under FTAs.

minimize the discriminatory effects of regional trade facilitation measures on non-members. Section 4.7 concludes the discussion of this chapter.

Scope of trade facilitation measures in this chapter. Defining trade facilitation measures is not an easy task.[6] Despite difficulty, it is still useful to specify which trade facilitation measures are discussed in this study. While many FTAs have chapters or sections on trade facilitation, the scope and definition of the term "trade facilitation" various across agreements. Because actual facilitation of trade requires a comprehensive approach, this chapter employs a relatively wide definition of trade facilitation. In the broadest way, the concept of trade facilitation measures is similar to that of non-tariff barriers, which includes all trade barriers other than tariff. However, trade facilitation measures usually do not cover both non-policy-oriented barriers to trade, such as language barriers,[7] and those related to trade policies, such as safeguards. Trade facilitation measures in this chapter hence mainly include measures covered by trade facilitation negotiations at the WTO as well as other critical measures of trade facilitation. Since the Doha Round trade facilitation negotiation group's agenda is limited, it is useful to expand the focus slightly in considering the exclusive and discriminatory elements of trade facilitation. The analysis focuses on five trade facilitation items listed as follows:

First, transparency and publication of trade regulations is of extreme importance in facilitating trade transactions.[8] This issue is covered by GATT Article X and included in one of the critical negotiations issues of the Doha Round. In the context of trade facilitation, transparency includes the availability of trade-related laws and regulations, establishment of enquiry

---

[6]The WTO employs a relatively narrow definition of trade facilitation as "the simplification and harmonization of international trade procedures," and trade procedures as the "activities, practices and formalities involved in collecting, presenting, communicating and processing data required for the movement of goods in international trade" (Dee and Findley, 2006). In contrast, OECD (2002) has a relatively broad definition of trade facilitation: "simplification and standardization of procedures and associated information flows required to move goods internationally from seller to buyer and to pass."

[7]However, unnecessary complicated documentary requirement in the local language can be regarded as non-tariff barriers.

[8]The significance of costs of information barrier should not be underestimated. According to economic literature, information costs barrier is 6% equivalent of tariff (Anderson and van Wincoop, 2004).

points, intervals between publication and implementation of trade laws and regulations, prior consultation on new or amended rules, and effective appeal mechanisms (ADB and ESCAP, 2009). These are important to impartial application of laws and regulations free from discretion.

Second, fees and charges are one of the critical non-tariff barriers and obstacles to trade. GATT Article VIII says "[fees and charges] shall be limited in amount to the approximate cost of services rendered and shall not represent an indirect protection to domestic products or a taxation of imports or exports for fiscal purposes." The effects of fees and charges are similar to those of tariffs, because they directly increase the financial costs of trade. Even if tariffs become low, traders may suffer from fees and charges that actually increase the financial cost of trade. Fees and charges however do not include taxes, which should be applied in a non-discriminatory manner.[9]

Third, formalities or procedures of trade are also important in thinking trade facilitation. GATT Article VIII mentions the need for minimizing the complexity of import and export formalities and for decreasing and simplifying import and export documentation requirements. While customs procedures are its central elements, the requirement of simplification of the formalities trade under GATT Article VIII is extended to cover the following: consular transactions; qualitative restrictions; licensing; exchange control; statistical services; documents, documentation and certification; analysis and inspection; and quarantine, sanitation, and fumigation.

However, these narrowly defined trade facilitation items in the GATT and the WTO negotiations on trade facilitation mentioned are not sufficient to facilitate trade flows. Thus, the fourth item of trade facilitation covered in this research is so-called behind-the-border measures, such as Sanitary and Phytosanitary measures (SPS) and Technical Barriers to Trade (TBT). The assessment of conformity to the standards of each country, not the difference of standards *per se* becomes the obstacles of trade. If the recognition of conformity assessment test conducted in other countries is eased, international trade can be substantially facilitated.

Finally, we consider the origin administration for preferential trade as an important component of trade facilitation under regional initiatives. While all FTAs specify the procedures to get preferential tariff treatment,

---

[9]See GATT Article VIII:1(a) and GATT Article III:1.

both conditions and procedures for preferential access are not the same. This issue of differentiated treatment across FTAs is important. Traders of FTA partners may not use the preferential access if the procedures for availing trade preference are complicated. Under the situation wherein two countries signed an FTA with a common country, it is possible that they receive the same preferential tariff treatment but different treatments in terms of customs procedures and origin administration from their common partner.

Aside from the five items mentioned above, transit trade is another important element of trade facilitation. It is covered by GATT Article V and included in the trade facilitation negotiations of the Doha Round and many FTAs involving Asia-Pacific countries actually have provisions on transit trade.[10] However, transit trade is not covered in the analysis of this chapter primarily because the scope of this chapter is limited to the examination of discriminatory elements of regional trade facilitation measures. GATT Article V requests all WTO Members to guarantee freedom of transit trade and ensure non-discriminatory implementation of transit trade because it prohibits any form of discrimination regarding transit trade.[11]

> GATT Article V Freedom of Transit
>
> 2. There shall be freedom of transit through the territory of each contracting party, via the routes most convenient for international transit, for traffic in transit to or from the territory of other contracting parties. No distinction shall be made which is based on the flag of vessels, the place of origin, departure, entry, exit or destination, or on any circumstances relating to the ownership of goods, of vessels or of other means of transport.
>
> 5. With respect to all charges, regulations and formalities in connection with transit, each contracting party shall accord to traffic in transit to or from the territory of any other contracting party treatment no less favourable than the treatment accorded to traffic in transit to or from any third country. (underline supplied)

---

[10] Asia-Pacific FTAs' tendency of including transit trade issues is high. Among the 21 Asia-Pacific FTAs analyzed, 9 agreements include transit trade and 5 agreements include temporary admission.

[11] Theoretically speaking, however, non-discriminatory treatment applies only to like products being transported on the same route. Thus, discrimination against a third country is possible as far as the type of consignment is different. See Bolhöfer (2007).

4.2 Difference in Multilateral Principle of Regionalism: Trade Liberalization versus Trade Facilitation

It is of primary importance to understand the critical difference between trade liberalization and trade facilitation in terms of the stipulation of the treatment of non-members in FTAs. In the case of tariff (or market access provisions in general), the preferential treatment is all about the tariff treatment for FTA partners, and FTAs usually mention only this aspect, not the tariff treatment of non-members (or third parties). In contrast, stipulations in trade facilitation provisions under FTA can include the treatment of non-members. It is the FTA designers' choice on legal stipulation of preferential treatment rendered to FTA partners and non-members that determines the discriminatory effects of trade facilitation measures. Thus, the FTA could bring about *de jure* non-discriminatory trade facilitation treatment to all countries.

In terms of multilateral governance of regionalism, there is another major difference between trade liberalization and facilitation. In tariff elimination under FTAs, especially GATT Article XXIV-based FTAs, there is at least a fundamental objective: an FTA should eliminate tariffs on "substantially all" the trade among FTA parties as stipulated in GATT Article XXIV:8(a). While there are issues that allow different treatments in the field of tariffs, such as products included in a sensitive list and rules of origin, the underlying objective is to abolish all tariffs among FTA members. As far as tariff policies are concerned, an FTA is an all-or-nothing proposition that leaves minimal discretion to FTA contracting parties. In contrast, trade facilitation measures under FTAs can be tailor-made to suit the actual needs of contracting parties since there is no constraint under the WTO system on these measures that can be adopted by FTAs. GATT Article XXIV:8(a) stipulates in fact that "duties and other restrictive regulations of commerce" shall be eliminated among FTA or customs union members. While there have been debates on the scope of other restrictive regulations of commerce (ORRCs),[12] most trade facilitation measures discussed in this chapter are not ORRCs to be eliminated under FTAs.[13] Thus, FTA

---

[12]On the discussion on the ORRCs, see Trachtman (2003).

[13]For example, there is no obligation to eliminate fees and charges among FTA members (Kim, 2006)

members can maintain these measures for imports from FTA partners and, at the same time, have a large discretion in designing trade facilitation measures under FTAs without considering their external effects and systemic implications. As a result, unlike in trade liberalization, the differentiated treatment in trade facilitation across various FTA partners becomes the issue.

However, at the same time, one should note that the norm of non-discrimination in the field of trade facilitation is very strong. In fact, the grant of special and differential treatment negotiated in the Doha Round is limited to the "implementation" of the obligation regarding trade facilitation such as longer transitional period and capacity building needs and does not include the grant of preferential trade facilitation treatment to products from developing countries (Moise, 2006). This implies that non-discriminatory treatment with regard to trade facilitation is a dominant norm of multilateral negotiations.

Moreover, there are some overarching general guidelines regarding the formulation of various trade facilitation measures designed by WTO members. These include:

- Transparency: WTO Members shall allow reasonable time for other Members to make comments in writing, discuss the comments upon request and take these written comments and the result of these discussions in to account without discrimination (TBT 2.9.4).
- Import and export procedures: The contracting parties of WTO recognize the need for minimizing the incidence and complexity of import and export formalities (GATT Article VIII:1(c)).
- Fees and charges: Fees and charges shall be limited in amount to the approximate cost of services rendered (GATT Article VIII:1(a)).

However, while these stipulations imply that the non-discriminatory application of those measures is desirable, the term "most favored nation" (MFN) treatment is not used. This implies that the norm or guidelines of non-discriminatory trade facilitation measures does not prevent introducing preferential trade facilitation measures. For example, countries are able to offer more favorable treatments to FTA partners than what is required at the multilateral level, such as offering concessional fees and charges to FTA partners that is lower than the approximate cost of services rendered.

The multilateral discipline on regionalism in some issue areas that fall under the category of trade facilitation in this chapter, such as TBT and SPS, is not straightforward. As discussed, the scope of ORRCs in terms of GATT Article XXIV:5 to be eliminated in the course of formation of FTAs is the critical question, and many scholars believe that only unnecessary TBT/SPS measures among FTA members should be eliminated and rea-sonable TBT/SPS measures can be maintained even when the imports are from FTA partners (Trachtman, 2003). Then, the problem lies in whether the violation of the MFN principle is acceptable in designing TBT/SPS mea-sures under FTAs, because both TBT and SPS Agreements clearly stipulate the principle of MFN. The majority of trade lawyers argue that the viola-tion of MFN principle is acceptable so that TBT/SPS Agreements will not become barriers to the formation of FTAs (Trachtman, 2003). Thus, on one hand, FTA members can maintain TBT/SPS for the imports from the part-ners, and on the other hand, they are allowed to freely design preferential TBT/SPS measures applicable only to imports from FTA partners.

In considering the exclusiveness of preferential TBT/SPS measures, the critical question is whether regional initiative for mutual recognition should be open to the third party. Some consider that "open recognition" is necessary.[14] "Open recognition" is achieved when regional condition for recognition is established by the concerned countries in the region but the third parties are permitted to meet those conditions (Nicolaïdis, 2000; Trachtman, 2003).[15] It can be inferred then that regional conditions may be favorable to FTA partners, but the application of condition is conducted in a non-discriminatory manner (as far as regional conditions are met by imports from non-members, those should be treated in the same manner as imports from members).

In summary, the lack of a multilateral guideline on trade facilitation measures under FTA has resulted in discriminatory trade facilitation measures under FTAs. Various tailor-made measures and treatments under different FTAs are possible as along as trade facilitation is concerned. Even FTAs with common members do not guarantee harmonized measures. For example, it is possible that a customs office requires a different number

---

[14]In the case of services, open recognition is strongly encouraged. See GATS Article VII.
[15]If open recognition is stipulated in the agreement, then such is *de jure* extension of preferential treatment. See Figure 4.1.

of documents for goods from different FTA partners (for example, 20 documents from Country A, 10 from B, and 5 from C). The differentiated treatment of trade partners across FTAs is a problem intrinsic to trade facilitation, which is not critical in the case of trade liberalization (especially in tariffs). Thus, with respect to discrimination in the field of trade facilitation, we need to consider not only discrimination by different treatments between FTA members and non-members but also discrimination between various FTA members under different FTAs.

4.3   Analytical Framework for Assessing the Openness of Regional Trade Facilitation

4.3.1   *Typology of discriminatory regional trade facilitation measures*

Non-discrimination is the fundamental philosophy underlying the international trade system. Non-discrimination is also an important principle of trade facilitation efforts at both global and regional levels. For example, the Asia-Pacific Economic Cooperation (APEC) Principles on Trade Facilitation adopted by APEC Ministers responsible for trade in 2001[16] clearly request members to introduce non-discriminatory trade facilitation measures. The APEC Principle discourages two kinds of discrimination. One type is the discriminatory treatment across like products. Discriminatory treatment across like products not only distorts consumption patterns but also has the potential of increasing the risk levels of products. The other type of discrimination, which is the main focus of this chapter, is the differential treatment between domestic and foreign products and across countries. The APEC Principle reaffirms the significance of non-discrimination in the field of trade facilitation in terms of both national treatment and MFN status.

Figure 4.1 gives an overview of the methodology to assess the discriminatory effects of trade facilitation measures in terms of countries. There are in total five questions to evaluate the discriminatory effects of preferential trade facilitation measures stipulated in the agreements. It is

---

[16]APEC Principles on Trade Facilitation states that: "Rules and procedures relating to trade should be applied in a manner that does not discriminate between or among like products or services or economic entities in like circumstances."

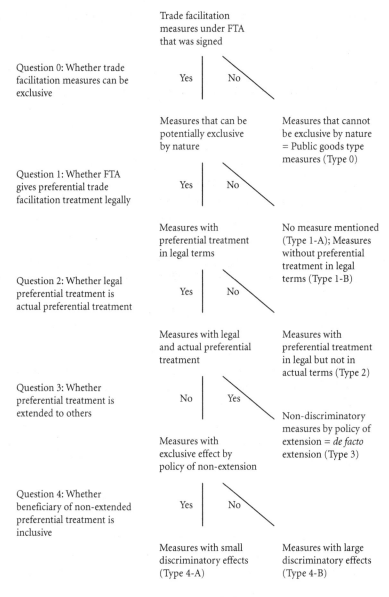

Figure 4.1   Exclusiveness of trade facilitation measures

Source: Author's compilation

important to understand that there are various elements that contribute to the discriminatory effects of trade facilitation measures at regional levels.

In understanding the discriminatory treatment across countries with regard to trade facilitation, first of all, it is useful to consider the exclusiveness of trade facilitation measures. This is because different treatment between members and non-members becomes possible only when the beneficiary of measures can be exclusive. Without the exclusive nature, different treatment across countries is impossible from the beginning. Some measures cannot be exclusive by nature. This type of measures is akin to "public goods" in the economic literature,[17] such as services of a lighthouse. When trade facilitation measures under an FTA are, by nature, non-exclusive, the benefits can be enjoyed even by non-members of the FTA. Such measures like other public goods cannot avoid a free-rider problem because they cannot be made exclusive from the beginning. The same treatment for all countries, irrespective of FTA membership, is guaranteed by this non-exclusive nature of the measures and not by policies. For example, some transparency issues such as publication of trade law and regulation, which is an important component of trade facilitation, cannot be exclusive to FTA members only because information in the public domain is accessible regardless of FTA membership. In fact, an FTA that requires its members to publish customs procedures on the internet makes the information also available to non-members. If certain countries' transparency of trade policy is enhanced by an FTA, the non-members can also enjoy the benefit. Another scenario is when parties agree to adopt or incorporate existing commitments under international conventions (e.g., the Revised Kyoto Convention) or international standards (e.g., Codex Alimentarius Commission), and respect the rights and obligations of the parties in these international conventions.

It is not good to only assume the non-exclusive nature of trade facilitation measures; trade facilitation measures can be discriminatory as emphasized in the earlier sections. If certain trade facilitation measures under an FTA are not public goods-type ("Yes" to Question 0 in Figure 4.1), then we need to assess the technical details of preferential trade

---

[17]A public good in the economic literature has two conditions. The first condition is non-exclusive nature of goods and the second condition is non-rival.

facilitation treatment created by the specific stipulations in the agreements. The exclusivity of measures does not automatically lead to different treatment between members and non-members. It is always a policy decision to include stipulation on exclusive preferential treatment in FTA and to limit the beneficiaries of trade facilitation measures.

It is the FTA negotiators who design FTA in terms of Question 1 ("whether FTA gives preferential trade facilitation treatment legally to partners") in Figure 4.1. The first possibility is that FTA gives preferential trade facilitation treatment to FTA partners ("Yes" to Question 1). In this case, preference is created in legal terms (however, whether this is an actual preference is a different question). The other possibility is that the FTA does not create preferential treatment exclusive to FTA partners ("No" to Question 1). In this case, no preference is created by legal stipulations. This possibility (no preference in legal terms) has three scenarios. The first scenario is the non-inclusion of any stipulation on preferential treatment to partners in FTA.[18] Because FTA does not give preferences to the partner, no discriminatory effect is expected. The second scenario is "explicit *de jure* extension" (Baldwin, Evenett, and Low, 2009, p. 81).[19] In this case, an FTA explicitly mentions that favorable treatment is applicable to both members and non-members and not preferential anymore. The third scenario is implicit extension. In this case, an FTA simply mentions favorable treatment without limiting the scope of country beneficiaries. As an illustration, an FTA states that "the number of required document form import will be five" rather than "the number of required documents from imports originating form partner will be five." In the case of implicit extension, it is not perfectly clear that non-members can enjoy the same level of favorable treatment as FTA members. In brief, FTA designers have four options:

- Stipulation of preferential treatment to members ("Yes" to Question 1)
- No stipulation of preferential treatment given to the partner (Type 1-A treatment)

---

[18]When trade facilitation provisions in an FTA are exactly same as WTO provisions on trade facilitation ("copy and paste" provisions), then such a situation can be regarded as non-inclusion of preferential treatment.
[19]Also see Schiff and Winters (2003) and Maur (2005, 2008).

- Explicit *de jure* extension (Type 1-B-1 treatment)
- Implicit *de jure* extension (Type 1-B-2 treatment)

In analyzing the discriminatory elements entailed by trade facilitation measures under FTA, making a distinction between legal and actual discrimination is important. The fact that there is preferential treatment in legal terms (the agreement stipulates preferential and favorable treatment to members only = "Yes" to Question 1) does not mean that there is actual discrimination. Even if it looks like the FTA gives preferential treatment to partners, there is a possibility that actual treatment applicable to all countries is more liberal than what is written in FTA as a preferential treatment. Question 2 ("whether legal preferential treatment is actual preferential treatment") in Figure 4.1 is vital in this regard because we need to consider if preferential treatment stipulated in FTA is in fact a better treatment than actual policy implemented in a unilateral manner. In a situation where FTA says that the number of required documents for imports from FTA partners should be lower than five, there is a possibility that the number of document actually required to all trading partners is only one.

4.3.2   Analytical focus and caveat on methodology

The purpose of this study is to empirically demonstrate the extent of preferential treatment to FTA partners and to consider how to reduce potential negative effects on non-members caused by discriminatory effects in trade facilitation measures stipulated in FTAs. Thus, we focus the analysis in this chapter on trade facilitation measures that have preferential effects in legal terms by demonstrating these two arguments: one, there are many non-Type 0 trade facilitation measures ("Yes" to Question 0); two, many FTAs in fact include legal stipulations on preferential trade facilitation measure to members only ("Yes" to Question 1). Conversely, existing studies on trade facilitation under regional initiatives that analyze their externality usually emphasize Type 0 trade facilitation measures and tend to conclude that most regional trade facilitation measures also benefit non-members. In other words, the dominant *assumption* is that many trade facilitation measures are Type 0 measures ("No" to Question 0) in Figure 4.1.

Trade facilitation measures with preferential treatment stipulated in agreement would lead to two types of discrimination: (i) exclusive

Only goods from Country A can enjoy the benefit of trade facilitation measures conducted by Country X under the FTA between Country X and Country A. Goods from Country B cannot enjoy the benefits, or may do so only under restrictive conditions.

Figure 4.2   Exclusive preferential trade facilitation measures

Source: Author's compilation

preferential treatment and (ii) differentiated treatment. The first type of discriminatory trade facilitation treatment (exclusive preferential treatment) is the one between FTA members and non-members. We call this as exclusive preferential trade facilitation measures under FTAs. If an FTA gives preferential treatment to partners only, this leads to the situation that the treatment becomes different between FTA members and non-members. As Figure 4.2 illustrates, it is determined whether an FTA creates legal preferential treatment exclusive to goods from a partner country (Country A) and how FTAs between Country X and Country A stipulates the trade facilitation merit for the goods from Country B to Country X.

The second type of discrimination brought about by preferential trade facilitation treatment stipulated in the agreement is the one between members of different FTAs, which can be called differentiated trade facilitation measures. This type of discrimination across countries is between different FTAs. In other words, preferential trade facilitation treatment stipulated in the agreement is not homogenous across agreements. The level of preferential treatment rendered by a country in each FTA where it is engaged in is not the same for all partners. As illustrated in Figure 4.3, Country X, a common partner, may render much better treatment in terms of trade facilitation of goods from Country A than goods from Country B, even if both Country A and Country B have an FTA with Country X. Trade facilitation measures offered by one country under a certain FTA can be different from trade facilitation measures offered by the same country to another partner in another FTA. Even if there are common members, trade facilitation measures covered by different FTAs are not necessarily harmonized. In some cases, trade facilitation measures covered by a specific FTA in which

Country X renders different trade facilitation treatment to goods from Country A versus goods from Country B, even if both have an FTA with Country X.

Figure 4.3   Differentiated trade facilitation measures

Source: Author's compilation

a certain country is a member could be more liberal than those included in another FTA in which the same country is also a member. For example, a country, which requires 10 documents for customs clearance against all trade partners, may request 5 documents from one FTA partner in one FTA, and may accept a single document from another partner in another FTA. This can be possibly explained by the degree of readiness and willingness of different FTA partners to comply with the trade facilitation measures espoused by an FTA member with multiple FTAs. However, there is also a possibility that the country maintains unnecessary burden on trade with some FTA partners.

It is emphasized earlier that it is important to distinguish legal preferential treatment stipulated in FTAs and actual preferential treatment with regard to trade facilitation measures. If unilaterally implemented trade facilitation measures are liberal enough, legally stipulated preferential treatment does not necessarily create effective actual preference. However, this chapter limits its analysis to legal stipulation on the exclusive preferential treatment and differentiated treatment in trade facilitation provisions in each FTA, and it does not cover actual trade facilitation treatment. In other words, we will set out primary analytical focus on Question 0 and 1 in Figure 4.1, and we try to demonstrate that FTAs often include many stipulations on discriminatory/preferential trade facilitation measures whose beneficiaries are limited to the partners in legal terms.

There are mainly two reasons why we focus on Question 0. First, the majority of scholars and policy-makers believe that trade facilitation measures are non-discriminatory even if they are included in FTAs. Thus, it is critically important to examine if such an *assumption* is valid by conducting empirical analysis. Second, if legal stipulations on non-public goods type trade facilitation measures are included in the FTAs, it is likely that such legal preferential trade facilitation measures brings actual discriminatory preferential effects to FTA partners (and the answer to Question 2 is *likely* to be "Yes"). This is because there would be no large incentive for FTA parties to include trade facilitation obligations in FTAs, unless these have actual impacts. In other words, FTA parties try to include specific obligations regarding trade facilitation in FTAs expecting that those actually facilitate trade.

Even if the measures have preferential treatment in both legal and actual terms ("Yes" to Question 2), there is still a possibility that the same treatment between members and non-members is achieved by policies ("Yes" to Question 3). Question 1 is about *de jure* extension of preferential treatment while Question 3 is about *de facto* extension of preferential treatment. With *de jure* extension, legal preferential treatment cannot be created. If an FTA simply gives legal preferential treatment to partners without *de jure* extension, then, the actual preferential treatment can be eliminated by the policy of *de facto* extension. Therefore, policy decisions on the extension of the measures can be made through either legally backed-up extension of measures (*de jure* extension) or actual extension of measures without legal back-up (*de facto* extension). After conducting the empirical analysis of the discriminatory trade facilitation measures, we will return to the issue of *de facto* extension in Section 4.6, where we consider the policy recommendations.

4.4 Overview on Trade Facilitation Measures under FTAs in the World

It is useful to briefly review the frequency of the inclusion of various types of trade facilitation measures in FTAs in Asia-Pacific and elsewhere before delving into the comparison of discriminatory and non-discriminatory cases. It is not easy to conduct comparative analysis of trade facilitation measures across FTAs in a consistent manner in most cases. Each FTA uses the same word/term regarding trade facilitation (such as transparency) in slightly different ways. Moreover, there are instances that a certain trade facilitation item (such as express shipment) constitutes one Chapter or Article, while there is a case where the item is briefly mentioned in a short sentence under different section headings. Furthermore, the same trade facilitation items may appear in very different places in different FTAs. For example, a section on enquiry point may be included in SPS or TBT chapters of a certain FTA, but this may not be included under the chapter on transparency or publication issues. Because many comparative empirical studies also use trade facilitation-related terms differently, comparing the result of those studies is also not easy.

One of the pioneer studies of the comparison of trade facilitation provisions under FTAs was conducted by Bin (2008). Using comparative case analyses of 34 FTAs in Asia and the Pacific, he identified that FTAs are significantly diverse as far as trade facilitation is concerned. Provisions relating to customs procedures and cooperation appear in all of 34 FTAs covered in the study and as high as 94% of these have provisions on technical regulations (e.g., the adoption of international standards). Meanwhile, 61% of these FTAs have transparency provisions and 52% of them mention information technology. He also found that only 17% cover trade finance and 14% cover freedom of transit. Wilee and Redden (2007) conducted detailed case studies on trade facilitation initiatives in major regional trade facilitation frameworks in Asia.[20] Their empirical assessment outlined five elements of trade facilitation in regional agreements: (i) compliance with international agreements, (ii) transparency, (iii) simplification, (iv) harmonization, and (v) technical assistance. Recently, Duval (2011) also studied trade facilitation measures under WTO[21] and six FTAs in Asia[22], by conducting provision-by-provision comparison. He found that the coverage of trade facilitation measures has been significantly expanded in the recent FTAs.

A more comprehensive analysis of trade facilitation provisions across FTAs worldwide is conducted by UNCTAD (2011) recently. It analyzes 54 representative FTAs in the world and compares their coverage with regard to trade facilitation. This study is useful in understanding the diversity as well as convergence of trade facilitation measures of FTAs in the world,

---

[20]The cases covered in this study are limited to ASEAN/AFTA, APEC, SAARC/SAFTA, Pacific Agreement on Closer Economic Relations (PACER), and Australia–Singapore FTA (ASFTA).
[21]Draft consolidated negotiation text on Trade Facilitation.
[22]These include ASEAN Trade in Goods Agreement (ATIGA), ASEAN–Australia–New Zealand FTA, APTA, China–Singapore FTA, Korea–US FTA, and Japan–Vietnam EPA.

Table 4.1   Coverage of trade facilitation under FTAs

		World (54 FTAs)	Asia (21 FTAs)
Transparency	Publication/Enquiry Points	46%	29%
	Advance Rulling	54%	38%
	Review/Appeal	44%	29%
Procedures	Customs Clearance	72%	86%
	Use of ICT/Automarion/Single Window	54%	57%
	Risk Management	50%	38%
	Express Shipment	26%	5%
Fee and Charges		7%	10%

Source: Author's compilation based on UNCTAD (2011)

especially the comparison between trade facilitation covered by GATT Article V, VIII and X and equivalent measures under FTAs. Table 4.1 presents a summary of the comparison of trade facilitation measures under FTAs in Asia and other regions compiled by the author based on the UNCTAD study. Although the comparison of coverage at the heading level has some problems as mentioned, it still gives us a crude representation of the unique feature of trade facilitation measures under FTA in terms of coverage. In general, the coverage of transparency issue is low in the case of Asian FTAs compared with other regions. However, this does not necessarily imply that transparency provisions in Asian FTAs are inadequate because basic issues on transparency are already covered in GATT Article X. As we will see later, some non-Asian FTAs include discriminatory trade facilitation measures relating to transparency (e.g., chance of public comment for the FTA partners on a discriminatory basis). One could argue that the absence of transparency provision in FTA is better than the inclusion of discriminatory transparency provision.

Procedures of importation and exportation are a critical element of trade facilitation and majority of FTAs have some provisions on trade procedures. FTAs in Asia seem to place special emphasis on customs procedures. As high as 86% of FTAs in Asia covers this item, while only 72% of FTA includes this at the global level. Meanwhile risk management is a very popular trade facilitation measure outside Asia but not that much in Asia. Likewise many FTAs outside Asia include express shipment while minority of FTAs in Asia has this provision. Fee and charges are not covered in many FTAs both inside and outside Asia.[23]

4.5 Discriminatory and Non-discriminatory Cases of Regional Trade Facilitation

Below is a review of trade facilitation provisions under FTAs within Asia-Pacific, defined very broadly. The focus of the analysis in this section is to identify the various types of discriminatory regional trade facilitation measures in the region, not to make a general assessment on trade facilitation measures under FTAs within a particular geographical area (e.g., Asia, Asia-Pacific). We compare FTAs in this region to demonstrate that the trade facilitation measures under the said FTAs are quite diverse in terms of their discriminatory and exclusive elements, despite APEC's strong advocacy on the importance of non-discriminatory trade facilitation measures (see footnote 16).

This section presents both discriminatory (either exclusive preferential or differentiated treatment) and non-discriminatory examples of each area of trade facilitation measures, in order to understand how to make trade facilitation measures under regional initiative more open (underlines supplied by the authors to identify and illustrate differences in trade facilitation provisions in FTAs). It attempts to show the variety of trade facilitation measures in terms of discrimination and openness rather than quantify the level of discrimination of each trade facilitation measures, because there is no strict test for determining the level of discriminatory elements entailed by each trade facilitation measure.[24]

4.5.1 *Transparency*

Transparency provisions in FTAs are, in general, multilateral-friendly since pertinent information is readily made available to all interested persons.

---

[23] According to UNCTAD, only four FTAs among 54 FTA analyzed include provision on fees and charges. Those are: APTA; Pakistan–China; EU–Central Africa; and EU–Cote d'Ivoire.
[24] Non-discriminatory principles in trade facilitation can be expressly or implicitly superseded by more specific provisions in the FTA, operational guidelines between the contracting partners, or implementing rules and regulations of customs and other border agencies.

Many FTA provisions on transparency incorporate an important principle of trade facilitation which addresses the differing and sometimes arbitrary interpretation of laws by customs and border officials.

Examples of non-discriminatory treatment in transparency provisions. The effects of many transparency provisions are usually non-discriminatory by nature. In other words, a typical example of Type 0 treatment in Figure 4.1 can be found in the transparency provisions of FTAs. A clear case of a non-discriminatory transparency measure is provided in the Association of Southeast Asian Nations (ASEAN)–Japan Comprehensive Economic Partnership Agreement (CEPA).

> ASEAN–Japan CEPA, Chapter 1 General Provision, Article 4 Transparency
>
> 1. Each Party shall, in accordance with its laws and regulations, <u>make publicly available</u> its laws, regulations, administrative procedures …
> 2. Each Party shall <u>make publicly available</u> the names and addresses of the competent authorities responsible for laws, regulations, administrative procedures …

In other FTAs, obligations related to publication surpass what is required by the WTO. Making relevant trade information available on the internet is one such example. This is also a non-exclusive action because non-members can access the information online. It is technologically not feasible to make information on internet available only to traders in FTA partner country.

> Pakistan–China FTA, Chapter 3 National Treatment and Market Access for Goods, Article 9 Administrative Fees and Formalities
>
> Each Party shall make available <u>through the Internet or a comparable computer-based telecommunications network</u> a list of the fees and charges and changes thereto levied by the central/federal Government, as the case may be, thereof in connection with importation or exportation.

Examples of exclusive preferential treatment in transparency provisions. Transparency requirements are sometimes mentioned in other chapters of an FTA such as under SPS and TBT. In the context of trade facilitation as earlier mentioned, transparency usually includes various issues such as the availability of trade-related laws and regulations, establishment of enquiry points, intervals between publication and implementation of trade laws and regulations, prior consultation on new or amended rules, and effective appeal mechanisms. These provisions usually replicate the obligations set in the SPS and TBT Agreements, and can be considered non-discriminatory, but some WTO-plus requirements could be discriminatory.

The first half of the provision in the China–Singapore FTA mentioned below is essentially non-discriminatory because the clause only obliges the FTA members to notify their partners at the same time that they notify WTO members. However, as to the second half, the 60-day commenting period is guaranteed only to the FTA partner (however, there is also a possibility that 60-day period is granted to all countries on a *de facto* basis). This is because TBT Agreement Article 2.9.4 and SPS Agreement Annex B 5(d) request that WTO members allow reasonable time for other members to make comments, without specifying concrete time span.

China–Singapore FTA, Chapter 7 TBT and SPS, Article 54

Parties shall notify each other through their respective TBT and SPS enquiry points, under the TBT Agreement and the SPS Agreement, of any new technical regulation and SPS measure related to the trade of products in accordance with the TBT Agreement and the SPS Agreement, or any change to them. Each Party shall allow at least sixty (60) days for the other Party to present comments in writing on any notification except where considerations of health, safety, environmental protection, or national security arise or threaten to arise to warrant more urgent action.

Furthermore, some WTO-plus transparency provisions in TBT and SPS, such as participation, may be more clearly restricted to FTA members. Although the development of a country's standards regarding trade facilitation is closely related to national sovereignty, outside parties can assume direct influence so long as they are granted national treatment. The provision of national treatment in the Transparency Chapter in the Australia–United States (US) FTA is a good example.

Australia–US FTA, Chapter 8 TBT, Article 8.7 Transparency

1. Each Party shall allow persons of the other Party to participate in the development of standards, technical regulations, and conformity assessment procedures on terms no less favourable than those accorded to its own persons.

This provision is certainly WTO-plus and contributes to a higher level of transparency because persons outside the country can also participate in the formulation process of standards as long as they are located in the partner countries of the FTA. However, participation is enjoyed only by the parties to the FTA as well as non-governmental bodies in their respective territories. The privilege thus becomes exclusive to contracting parties of the FTA.

4.5.2 *Exemption of fees*

Fees are among the critical factors that affect the cost of importation and exportation. GATT Article VIII stipulates that all fees and charges in connection with importation and exportation shall be limited in amount to the approximate cost of services rendered. This does not constrain FTA members to introduce the concessionary fees or exemption of fees to FTA members. The clause providing for non-application or exemption from duties, fees, and other charges is an example of a trade facilitation provision with the same discriminatory effect as a tariff exemption.

Examples of non-discriminatory treatment in provisions relating to fees. Exemption of fees is seldom applicable across the board. Fees can be waived only when certain goods are traded through a certain method form a certain country. Most FTAs reduce fees on goods originating partner countries. A limited number of FTAs mention fee elimination in a general manner (which means under implicit *de jure* extension). The Turkey–Jordan FTA below is an example of implicit *de jure* extension of fee reduction. Even in these cases, it is not clear if the FTA guarantees that imports from non-member countries can enjoy the exemption of fees because these FTAs simply did not limit the scope of beneficiary rather than state that goods from non-member can enjoy fee exemption (implicit, rather than explicit extension as discussed in Section 4.3).

> Turkey–Jordan FTA, Article 5, Customs Duties on Imports and Charges Having Equivalent Effect
>
> From the date of entry into force of this Agreement <u>no new customs duties on imports</u> or charges having equivalent effect shall be introduced, nor shall those existing be increased, other than as permitted by this Agreement.

Many FTAs stipulate that when these digital products — computer programs, text, video, images, sound recordings, and other products that are digitally encoded — are traded via electronic transmission, fees are exempted.[25] The question is whether the application of this provision is, in practice, liberal or restrictive. The provision is very liberal if the FTA applies fee exemption on the trade of digital products by electronic transmission regardless of their origin. The US–Singapore FTA is a good example of this

---

[25] US–Singapore FTA, Chapter 14, Article 14.4.

case in the sense that digital products produced outside the FTA territory also qualify for fee exemption.[26] This is a typical case of explicit *de jure* extension because this agreement clearly states that the same treatment is rendered to the imports from non-party countries.

US–Singapore FTA, Chapter 14 Electronic Commerce, Article 14.3 Digital Products

1. A Party shall not apply customs duties or other duties, fees, or charges on or in connection with the importation or exportation of <u>digital products</u> by electronic transmission.
3. A Party shall not accord less favorable treatment to some digital products than it accords to other like digital products:

    (a) on the basis that

        (i) the digital products receiving less favorable treatment are created, produced, published, stored, transmitted, contracted for, commissioned, or first made available on commercial terms, <u>outside its territory</u>; or
        (ii) the author, performer, producer, developer, or distributor of such digital products is <u>a person of the other Party or a non-Party</u>, ...

4. (a) A Party shall not accord less favorable treatment to digital products created ... in the territory of the other Party than it accords to like digital products created ... <u>in the territory of a non-Party</u>.
    (b) A Party shall not accord less favorable treatment to digital products whose author ... is a person of the other Party than it accords to like digital products whose author ... is <u>a person of a non-Party</u>.

Examples of exclusive preferential treatment in provisions relating to fees. In general, exemption of fees is very exclusive. Many countries abolish various fees on goods originating from FTA partners only (OECD, 2005, p. 154). For example, the US merchandise processing fee[27] is abolished in recent bilateral trade agreements signed by the US, but these agreements clearly state that the only goods from originating partner countries can be exempted unlike the Turkey–Jordan FTA mentioned earlier. What is interesting is that Turkey–Morocco FTA's provision on fees is more restrictive than Turkey–Jordan FTA because the former is applicable only

---

[26]Singapore–Australia FTA Chapter 14, Article 3 and Korea–Singapore FTA Article 14.4 have similar provisions.
[27]The US charges merchandise processing fees for the processing of merchandise that is formally entering or being released into the US. A fee of an amount equal to 0.21% *ad valorem* is charged unless otherwise adjusted. See Kim (2006).

to trade between the two parties (there is no implicit extension in the case of Turkey–Morocco FTA, unlike Turkey–Jordan FTA).

US-Singapore FTA, Article 2.8: Merchandise Processing Fee

A Party shall not adopt or maintain a merchandise processing fee for originating goods.

Turkey-Morocco FTA, Article 4, Customs Duties On Imports And Charges Having Equivalent Effect

1. No new customs duties on imports or charges having equivalent effect shall be introduced, in trade between the Parties from the date of entry into force of this Agreement.

While the digital product provisions in the US–Singapore FTA mentioned above are very liberal, those contained in the Korea–Singapore FTA limit the application of fee exemptions to digital products that are created, produced, published, stored, transmitted, contracted for, commissioned, or first made available on commercial terms in the FTA partner's territory.

Korea–Singapore FTA, Chapter 14 Electronic Commerce, Article 14.4 Digital Products

1. Each Party shall not apply customs duties or other duties, fees, or charges on or in connection with the importation or exportation of a digital product of the other Party by electronic transmission.
3. A Party shall not accord less favourable treatment to a digital product than it accords to other like digital products:

    (a) on the basis that:

        (i) the digital product receiving less favourable treatment is created, produced, published, stored, transmitted, contracted for, commissioned, or first made available on commercial terms in the territory of the other Party; or
        (ii) the author, performer, producer, developer, or distributor of such digital product is a person of the other Party, …

4.5.3 Customs procedures

Since it is the customs office that assesses the origin of imported products, it seems possible to apply discriminatory customs procedures depending on the origin of imports. Similar to the application of preferential tariff, preferential customs procedure may be applied to imports from partner country only. However, in this case, there is a paradox: It is only *after* the examination at the customs when the origin of the products can be identified. It is not possible to precisely know the origin of imports *before* the customs examination. Thus, the application of preferential customs procedures exclusive to FTA partners does not seem to be a practical option. It is more reasonable to give the same favorable treatment with regard to customs procedures to all trading partners.

However, in reality, most provisions on simplification of customs procedures in FTAs in place are applicable to FTA partners only. There are many FTAs that give preferential customs procedures exclusive to FTA partners although the origin of the product can be determined only after customs examination. It is critical for policy-makers to acknowledge that the fundamental goal of customs reform is to expedite customs procedures for all goods, not only for goods traded between FTA members.

Examples of non-discriminatory treatment in customs procedures provisions. One of the few examples that do not limit the application of prompt customs procedures is probably the ASEAN–Australia–New Zealand FTA cited below. This FTA does not limit the application scope of prompt customs procedures (*cf.* ASEAN-Japan CEPA below). Thus this falls under implicit *de jure* extension (Type 1-B-2 treatment) rather than explicit *de jure* extension (Type 1-B-1 treatment), as discussed in Section 4.3. This is because this agreement simply says "expeditious clearance of goods" not "expeditious clearance of goods originating partners *and* other countries."

> ASEAN–Australia–New Zealand FTA, Chapter 4 Customs Procedures, Article 1 Objectives
> The objectives of this Chapter are to:
>
> a. ensure predictability, consistency and transparency in the application of customs laws and regulations of the Parties;
> b. promote efficient, economical administration of customs procedures, and the expeditious clearance of goods;
> c. simplify customs procedures; and
> d. promote cooperation among the customs administrations of the Parties.

Express shipment refers to expediting the clearance of goods through pre-arrival information processing, acceptance of a single manifest or document, and submission thereof through electronic means, if possible. Express shipment is critical to trade facilitation because it can significantly reduce the amount of time spent crossing a border. While only goods traded between parties can use express shipment, most express shipment provisions mention the importance of the efficient clearance of all shipments (which is not applicable in the case of US–Korea FTA discussed later). The US–Singapore FTA cited below is a good example because it recognizes that express shipment is a second-best option. It can be said that the US–Singapore FTA has a better approach to express shipment from the perspective of non-members.

> US–Singapore FTA, Chapter 4 Customs Administration, Article 4.10 Express Shipments
>
> Each Party shall ensure efficient clearance of all shipments, while maintaining appropriate control and customs selection. In the event that a Party's existing system does not ensure efficient clearance, it should adopt procedures to expedite express shipments. Such procedures shall…

An example of exclusive preferential treatment in customs procedures provisions. Most provisions on customs procedure in FTAs state that customs procedures should be simplified for goods traded between contracting parties, rather than encompassing "all goods or shipments." In these cases, the focus is narrower and it seems reasonable to consider that preferential treatment given to FTA partners tends to be exclusive. ASEAN–Japan CEPA is a good example of this.

> ASEAN–Japan CEPA, Chapter 2 Trade in Goods, Article 22 Customs Procedures
>
> 3. For prompt customs clearance of goods traded among the Parties, each Party, recognizing the significant role of customs authorities and the importance of customs procedures in promoting trade facilitation, shall endeavor to:
>
> a. simplify its customs procedures; and …

Examples of differentiated treatment in customs procedures provisions. When express shipment is covered by FTAs, the prescribed level of speed is applicable to goods traded between members only and is thus discriminatory. Further, differentiated treatment in terms of the speed of customs clearance across FTAs can become an issue due to different stipulated time limitations prescribed for the different FTA partners of a country. Given the resources of US customs, for example, different time requirements across FTAs in terms of express shipment does not seem to be a large problem (six hours for imports from Singapore and four hours for imports from Korea). However, for less developed countries, it is more efficient to adhere to a single expedited amount of time to avoid maintaining several lanes — regular lanes, express lanes, super-express lanes — which would entail additional administrative costs.

US–Singapore FTA, Chapter 4 Customs Administration, Article 4.10 Express Shipments
… Such procedures shall:

(e) allow, in normal circumstances, for an express shipment to be released within six hours of the submission of necessary customs documentation.

US–Korea FTA, Chapter 7 Customs Administration and Trade Facilitation, Article 7.7 Express Shipments
Each Party shall adopt or maintain expedited customs procedures for express shipments while maintaining appropriate customs control and selection. These procedures shall:

(e) under normal circumstances, provide for clearance of express shipments within four hours after submission of the necessary customs documents, provided the shipment has arrived.

4.5.4   *Mutual recognition: Conformity assessment of standards*

Product standards (SPS and TBT) are at the core of behind-the-border issues in a broader definition of trade facilitation. In view of this, some FTAs try to achieve the harmonization of product standards to facilitate trade. However, harmonizing standards is challenging because each country has a distinctive approach to consumer protection as well as safety of health. Although difficult, mutual recognition of each other's standards seems to be a more doable approach to the issue. Mutual recognition is the arrangement between two or more parties to mutually recognize or accept some or all aspects of one another's standards.[28] The mutual recognition of standards among limited member countries seems to entail some discriminatory elements and bring some negative effect on non-members (Nicolaïdis, 2000).[29] However, while mutual recognition plays an important role in the regional integration process in Europe, most FTAs in Asia,

---

[28] Under the Singapore–Australia FTA, "a Party shall accept a food standard of the other Party as equivalent even if the standard differs from its own…[if such] achieves the purposes of the importing Party's food standard" (Food Sectoral Annex 3.1.1).

[29] However, there is a possibility that a third country can be benefited by mutual recognition (of standards) signed by others. Suppose that Country A and B signed mutual recognition agreement on product standards. If Country C's standards are recognized in Country A, but not in Country B, and there is mutual recognition between Country A and Country B, then products of Country C may be regarded as products that meet Country B's standards for Country A. For the details on this topic, see Bartels (2005).

with a notable exception of ASEAN, do not have strong mutual recognition system.[30]

It is important to distinguish mutual recognition of conformity assessment results (e.g., test reports and certificates of compliance) as opposed to mutual recognition of standards. Some FTAs provide for mutual recognition of conformity assessment of results, which is relatively easier than mutual recognition of standards but still have great potential for trade facilitation. Moreover, the problem of mutual recognition of conformity assessment continues to exist even if countries harmonize standards (Nicolaïdis, 2000, p. 270). The fact that FTAs include only mutual recognition of conformity assessment result as opposed to mutual recognition of standards is not necessarily insignificant in facilitating trade flows. Because the mutual recognition of standards is rare in Asia, this section focuses on mutual recognition of conformity assessment.

The scope of the analysis for this item in this section is the preferential treatment to the conformity assessment test conducted in the territory of FTA partners. Based on the methodology earlier, the argument focuses on the question of whether FTA gives preferential treatment to partners with regard to conformity assessment in terms of legal stipulations in FTA (Question 1 in Figure 4.1), and not on whether exporters in non-FTA partner can enjoy the conformity assessment services conduced in FTA partners (Question 4, which focuses on rules of origin). As an illustration, given a situation where Country A and Country B signed an FTA with conformity assessment issues, the analysis here will focus on the question of whether the Country A/B gives preferential treatment to the conformity assessment bodies in Country B/A (provided that there is mutual recognition of conformity assessment between Country A and B). It will not address whether firms in Country C can use the services of conformity assessment bodies in Country A when they wish to export to the Country B markets, which is related to the rules of origin (ROO) concepts (Question 4 in Figure 4.1).[31]

---

[30]Whether the exclusive mutual recognition agreement is WTO-consistent is a difficult question. For the extensive argument on this topic, see Trachtman (2003).

[31]The restrictiveness of rules of origin with regard to the conformity assessment is a very important technical detail that determines the openness of conformity assessment measures under regional initiatives. Many discuss that rules of origin is leaky in the case of conformity assessment (Baldwin, Evenett, and Low, 2009, p. 116). In contrast, Hoekman and Winters

Examples of non-discriminatory treatment in conformity assessment provisions. ASEAN member countries signed a framework on mutual recognition arrangements (MRAs) in 1998. A few years later, sectoral MRAs were agreed upon for electrical and electronic equipment (EEE),[32] telecommunications,[33] and cosmetics.[34] ASEAN MRAs require parties to accept the test reports and certifications issued by the testing laboratories and certification bodies of the other parties.[35] This reduces, if not eliminates, duplicate testing and certification requirements in all ASEAN territories.[36] Furthermore, the MRA on EEE provides an extremely liberal approach to conformity assessment. ASEAN is also open to the possibility that the conformity assessment might be conducted outside ASEAN (unlike other FTAs such as Australia–US FTA). This is another good example of explicit *de jure* extension of preferences.

> ASEAN Harmonized Conformity Assessment Procedures for EEE, Appendix C
>
> 1.2. Test Reports and/or Certificates of Conformity issued by Conformity Assessment Bodies located outside ASEAN in compliance with the requirements of this Agreement may be accepted provided that ASEAN enters into a Mutual Recognition Agreement with the country or countries where the said Conformity Assessment Bodies are situated.

An example of exclusive preferential treatment in conformity assessment provisions. Specific conformity assessment provisions can also be territorial in nature and hence exclusive to FTA members. This includes the national treatment in conformity assessment bodies as in the case of the Australia–US FTA, and unlike the case of ASEAN Harmonized Conformity Assessment Procedures mentioned above.

(2009) argue that some mutual recognition arrangements (MRAs) do impose restrictive rules of origin contrary to what is widely believed.

[32] ASEAN sectoral MRAs for Electrical and Electronic Equipment (EEE) and ASEAN Harmonized Electronic Equipment Regulatory Scheme were signed in April 2002 and December 2005, respectively.

[33] To date, MRAs have been signed between Singapore and Indonesia, Singapore and Brunei, and Singapore and Malaysia.

[34] ASEAN Harmonized Cosmetic Regulatory Scheme was signed in September 2003.

[35] ASEAN EEE MRA Article 3, paragraph 1.

[36] The implementation of the MRAs, however, has yet to be extended to ASEAN's external partners in ASEAN-plus FTAs. In the case of Europe, the extension of mutual recognition to EU's partner countries such as Turkey becomes an issue. See Bartels (2005).

Australia–US FTA, Chapter 8 TBT, Article 8.6 Conformity Assessment Procedures

3. Each Party shall accredit, approve, license, or otherwise recognise conformity assessment bodies in the territory of the other Party on terms no less favourable than those it accords to conformity assessment bodies in its territory...

Examples of differentiated treatment in conformity assessment provisions. Japan's Economic Partnership Agreements (EPA) with Singapore, the Philippines, and Thailand feature a case of differentiated treatment of conformity assessment bodies across different FTA partners. It can be argued that the first EPA (with Singapore) is more liberal than the other two. The Japan–Singapore EPA allows the designation of conformity assessment bodies (CABs) by the host country and registration with the other party. This means that both Singapore and Japan only need to register under this agreement with the CABs, and each of their designating authorities is assigned to issue certificates of conformity. In contrast, the Japan–Philippines EPA and Japan–Thailand EPA require that CABs issuing certificates of conformity assessments in the Philippines and Thailand must be accredited by the Japanese government.

Japan–Singapore EPA, Chapter 6 Mutual Recognition, Article 46 General Obligations[37]

Each party shall accept, in accordance with the provisions of this Chapter, the results of conformity assessment procedures required by the applicable laws, regulations and administrative provisions of that Party specified in the relevant Sectoral Annex, including certificates and marks of conformity, that are conducted by the registered conformity assessment bodies of the other Party.

Japan–Philippines EPA, Chapter 6 Mutual Recognition, Article 60 General Obligations[38]

Each Party shall, in accordance with the provisions of this Chapter, permit participation of conformity assessment bodies of the other Party, in the system of the former Party providing for conformity assessment procedures and shall accept the results of conformity assessment procedures required by its applicable laws, regulations and administrative provisions specified in the relevant Sectoral Annex, including certificates of conformity, that are conducted by the conformity assessment bodies of the other Party registered by the Registering Authority of the former Party.

---

[37] Singapore–Korea FTA has the same provision (Article 8.5.3). Article 53 (Registration of Conformity Assessment Bodies) of Japan–Singapore FTA stipulates the actual procedures of registration.

[38] Japan–Thailand EPA has a similar provision (Chapter 6, Article 62).

The Japan–Singapore EPA's MRA has wider coverage than the Japan–Philippines EPA. Under the EPA with Singapore, the mutual recognition of conformity assessments includes electrical products, telecommunications terminal equipment, and radio equipment (Annex III, Sectoral Annex), while under the other two Epas, the mutual recognition covers only electrical products (Annex 4 of each EPA).

4.5.5   *Origin administration for preferential tariff treatment*

Origin administration provisions in FTAs are meant to ease the procedure for establishing the origin of goods. Some studies (for example, Roy and Bagai, 2005) find that the goods from FTA partners take a longer time for import procedures than goods from non-partners due to additional procedures required. Thus, streamlining the origin administration for preferential treatment is critically important. Establishing the origin of the goods in question is necessary for claims of preferential tariff treatment. However, the degree of ease in obtaining a certificate of origin for claims of preferential tariff varies across FTAs. Therefore, this gives rise to the issue of differentiated treatment across FTAs presented in different provisions below.

In some FTAs, a certificate of origin shall be issued by government authorities (e.g., under the ASEAN–China FTA). A more liberal approach to the issuance of a certificate of origin would be to allow relevant parties designated by the government, such as associations, to issue the certificate (e.g., under the ASEAN–Japan CEPA).

Framework Agreement on ASEAN–China FTA, Annex 3 Rules of Origin for the ASEAN–China FTA, Attachment A

Rule 1: The Certificate of Origin shall be issued by the Government authorities of the exporting Party.

ASEAN–Japan CEPA, Annex 4 Operational Certification Procedures

Rule 2: Issuance of Certificate of Origin

1. The competent governmental authority of the exporting Party shall, upon request made in writing by the exporter or its authorized agent, issue a CO or, under the authorization given in accordance with the applicable laws and regulations of the exporting Party, may designate other entities or bodies (hereinafter referred to as "designees") to issue a CO.

A "self certificate" is the most liberal approach to establishing origin. Self-certification, or certification that emanates from the traders as a means of application for preferential treatment, is certainly less burdensome than an application for a certificate of origin emanating from government authorities. A certificate can usually be issued by importers, but under some FTAs, it can be issued by exporters.[39]

> ASEAN Free Trade Area (AFTA), Annex 8 Operational Certification Procedure for the Rules of Origin under Chapter 3, Rule 5 Application for Certificate of Origin
>
> At the time of carrying out the formalities for exporting the products under preferential treatment, the exporter or his authorized representative shall submit a written application for the Certificate of Origin (Form D) together with appropriate supporting documents proving that the products to be exported qualify for the issuance of a Certificate of Origin (Form D).

> Malaysia–New Zealand FTA, Annex 3 Procedures and Verifications, Article 1 Declaration of Origin
>
> 1. A claim that goods are eligible for preferential tariff treatment shall be supported by a declaration as to the origin of a good from the exporter or producer.

> US–Singapore FTA, Chapter 3 Rules of Origin, Article 3.13: Claims for Preferential Treatment
>
> 1. Each Party shall provide that an importer may make a claim for preferential treatment under this Agreement based on the importer's knowledge or on information in the importer's possession that the good qualifies as an originating good.

Furthermore, other FTAs waive the application for the certificate of origin for any consignment of goods below the defined customs value, ranging from a ceiling of US$200 to over US$2,000 free on board (FOB). The varying thresholds for a certificate of origin exemption in FTAs can also be discriminatory between partners of a country with multiple FTAs.[40] Under AFTA, for example, if the export value (FOB) does not exceed US$200, Form D (certificate of origin for claims of preferential treatment) is waived.

---

[39]The divergence regarding the certification of origin is significantly wide across FTAs. EU ROO regime requires certificate issued by exporting country, while NAFTA relies on certification by interested parties. See Estevadeordal, Harris, and Suominen (2009).

[40]Under US$200 FOB for AFTA, ASEAN–China FTA, ASEAN–Japan CEPA; under US$600 FOB for China–Singapore FTA and China–Chile FTA; and under US$1,000 FOB for Japan–Mexico FTA, Japan–Malaysia EPA, and Korea–Singapore FTA.

Instead of Form D, a simplified declaration by the exporter that the goods have originated in the exporting member state will be accepted.

> **AFTA Common Effective Preferential Tariff (CEPT), Annex 8 Operational Certification Procedure for the Rules of Origin under Chapter 3, Rule 15 Waiver of Certificate of Origin**
>
> In the case of consignments of goods originating in the exporting Member State and not exceeding <u>US$200</u> FOB, the production of Certificate of Origin (Form D) shall be waived and the use of simplified declaration by the exporter that the goods in question have originated in the exporting Member State will be accepted. Goods sent through the post not exceeding <u>US$200</u> FOB shall also be similarly treated.

> **Japan–Singapore EPA, Article 29 Claim for Preferential Tariff Treatment**
>
> 1. … the importing Party shall not require a certificate of origin form importers for:
>
> (a) an importation of a consignment of a good whose aggregate customs value does not exceed <u>JPY200,000</u> or its equivalent amount.[41]

4.6   Policy Suggestions: Minimizing Negative Externality of Regional Trade Facilitation

An FTA aims principally to promote international trade by eliminating tariffs between or among its members. By nature, an FTA offers preferential tariff treatment to FTA members only. Therefore, whether an FTA is a building block or stumbling block to a multilateral trading system is a critical question for trade economists (Bhagwati, 1995).[42]

However, the very idea of trade facilitation would be fundamentally very liberal because it seeks to eliminate unnecessary barriers to trade even if measures are included in FTAs. Some argue that several FTAs stipulate *de jure* non-discriminatory treatment on trade facilitation; FTAs do not have preferential trade facilitation effects in legal terms (Schiff and Winters, 2003; Maur, 2005). In fact, we confirmed earlier that some trade facilitation measures written in FTAs in fact cover the treatment of imports from non-members, such as the case of exemption of fees on digital products

---

[41] JPY200,000 is equivalent to US$2350 (US$1 is roughly JPY85 as of June 2010).

[42] Proponents, while recognizing FTAs as being second-best to multilateralism, argue that FTAs generate large trade creation effects. Critics of regionalism through FTAs focus on the significant trade diversion effects and caution that FTAs could lead to a decline in global welfare. The building block versus stumbling block debate on trade liberalization remains.

and the conformity assessment bodies located outside the counteracting parties.

If preferential treatment is created by FTAs, then the FTA parties have two choices in terms of the application of such measures: (i) extend the application of measures to non-members or (ii) not to extend the application of measures to non-members. The latter implies exclusive treatment beneficial only to partners that causes negative effects to non-members similar to the effect of preferential tariff elimination (e.g., trade diversion). As we have seen, in most cases, trade facilitation measures can be enjoyed by FTA members only.

Thus, it is critical for policy-makers to understand the impact of trade facilitation measures under FTAs to non-members, particularly those that may have discriminatory elements against non-members. The best scenario is to multilateralize or extend the application of trade facilitation measures under the FTA to all non-members on either *de jure* or *de facto* basis. If there is a need to implement trade facilitation measures that can be enjoyed only by FTA partners, then the second-best policy is to minimize the negative effects against non-FTA members. At the same time, differentiated treatment — in terms of trade facilitation measures across FTAs with common partners — should also be considered. Therefore, it is important that negotiators and policy-makers consider the four questions or issues below in designing trade facilitation measures in FTAs.

Recommendation 1: Trade facilitation reform triggered by FTA negotiations

The most essential issue is the impetus of reforms including trade facilitation policy reforms established in FTAs (Maur, 2008). From the policy-making perspective, it is important to maximize the reform incentives of any trade facilitation measures that is brought about by the negotiations on FTA. There are many areas of trade facilitation in FTAs rather than the multilateral approach to trade facilitation that can lead to improvement and reforms (World Bank, 2005, p. 81[43]). Moreover, trade facilitation reforms

---

[43]Those include: alignment of customs codes with international standards; simplification and harmonization of procedures; enhancement of transparency; implementation of customs valuation agreements; establishment of joint border posts; and establishment of joint training centers. See Chapter 1 for more details.

under FTA can have a much wider scope than relatively narrow approach to trade facilitation taken by WTO (Wilson *et al.*, 2002, p. 74).

It is ideal if unilateral trade facilitation reform is conducted when an FTA is signed. Many argue that even if the impetus for reform comes from regional rather than multilateral sources, the reductions in trade costs are largely non-discriminatory (Maur and Shepherd, 2011). In this case, even if an FTA includes some stipulations of preferential trade facilitation measures legally applicable only to FTA partners, actual preferential effects will not be created. Actual policy applicable to any country in this case is at least as liberal as what is written in the FTA due to the unilateral reform achieved ("No" to Question 2 in Figure 4.1 = Type 2 Treatment). Both members and non-members can enjoy the benefit of trade facilitation reform if this is conducted in a unilateral manner.

However, given the resource constraint that developing countries are facing, it is understandable if the scope of the beneficiary of initial reform in trade facilitation is limited to FTA partners. In this respect, the reforms at the regional level can be identified as a "pilot project." At the outset, trade facilitation measures under FTAs that have both legal and actual preferential treatment exclusive to FTA partners ("Yes" to Question 2 in the said Figure), which is not extended to non-members ("No" to Question 3, thus either Type 4-A or 4-B treatment) are acceptable. Once they find that the pilot project described earlier is useful, however, it is advisable to expand the beneficiaries of trade facilitation reform ("Yes" to Question 3 = Type 3 Treatment).

Recommendation 2: Extension of exclusive preferential regional trade facilitation measures to non-members

FTA countries should make every effort to multilateralize or implement the trade facilitation measures across all countries when they initially intro-duce measures that can be enjoyed only by partners.[44] For example, as we have seen, when an FTA allows parties of member countries to participate in the formulation process of new standards with a national treatment status, it should be understood why such a treatment cannot be granted to par-ties of non-member countries. Likewise, when an FTA allows conformity

---

[44]Lucenti (2003) is against the idea of plurilateral trade facilitation agreement on the ground that it creates *de facto* and *de jure* discrimination against non-members.

assessment bodies in an FTA partner's territory to conduct a conformity assessment test, it is important to consider why a test conducted by CABs outside the FTA territory would not be acceptable.

The extension of the same measures to non-members as members may be easily achieved on a *de facto* basis rather than *de jure* basis. Thus, Question 3 in Figure 4.1 is critical to address the problem associated with the exclusivity of regional trade facilitation measures, once FTAs are already signed. For example, given a scenario where an FTA says that paperless trade is allowed between members and the paperless trade is introduced after the FTA implementation, paperless trade may be also enjoyed by all trading partners. The weakness of *de facto* extension is that some traders may regard that the newly introduced measures are not perpetual.

Even if extension is on *de facto* basis without *de jure* extension, there is still a way to enhance the credibility of the extension of the trade facilitation reforms. If there is no international mechanism that guarantees the application of such newly introduced favorable treatment to non-FTA parties (which means that there is no *de jure* extension of preferential treatment), *de facto* extension can be embedded in the domestic system such as paperless trade law introduced by the country. This can be called domestic legislation back-up *de facto* extension of measures.

Listed below are examples of multilateralizing trade facilitation measures originally targeted at FTA partners.

(i) When FTA members allow parties of FTA member countries to participate in the standards formulation process, the members must consider why parties in non-member countries cannot get involved in the process.

(ii) When FTA members reduce the number of required documents for FTA partners, the members must consider why it may be impossible to apply the same measures to non-FTA partners.

(iii) When FTA members introduce concessional fees to FTA partners, the members must consider why the same fees cannot be made applicable to non-FTA partners.

(iv) When FTA members agree with the mutual recognition of conformity assessment, the members should consider why the testing laboratory should be located in the territory of FTA members.

The extension of preferential trade facilitation treatment to non-members can be achieved with some time lag. There is no need to extend the same treatment immediately. This is especially true in the case of developing countries that started the trade facilitation reforms brought about by FTA negotiation with a limited initial scope as a pilot project. Such a situation is understandable because it is widely recognized that the implementation of trade facilitation reform is not straightforward even if the benefit of trade facilitation reform is limited to FTA partners.

Recommendation 3: Reduced burden on non-members after the introduction of preferential exclusive measures

There is a risk that regional trade facilitation measures bring negative external effects on non-members if these are not extended to them. When an FTA introduces trade facilitation measures that can be enjoyed only by FTA partners, the treatment of non-FTA members must be better when compared with the treatment they received before the introduction of the regional trade facilitation measures. One of the three conditions for FTAs stipulated under GATT Article XXIV for goods integration — trade barriers to non-members should not become more restrictive when FTAs are introduced (GATT XXIV-5) — can be a helpful guideline in minimizing the negative effects of trade facilitation measures under FTAs. The following are examples of extending trade facilitation measures under FTAs to reduce the burden of non-members.

(i) When FTA members decide to make trade rules and regulations available via a website, the members should ensure that the paper-based information is not made less efficient as a result. Paper-based information is critical for traders without internet access especially in the least developed countries.

(ii) When FTA members introduce the express shipment system for FTA partners, this should not lead to longer customs clearance times at the lane used by non-FTA partners.

(iii) When FTA members introduce automated customs clearance systems, the existing paper clearance system for other countries (particularly least developed countries) that are unable to introduce an electronic system should, as much as possible, remain efficient or be made as efficient as the electronic system. If the paper-based system becomes less efficient because resources are reallocated to the electronic system, then this effectively creates higher barriers to trade for non-members.

(iv) When a concessional fee system for FTA partners is introduced, fees for non-members should not be increased.

Although this problem is easily understood conceptually, observing this principle in the actual design of trade facilitation measures under regional initiatives is not simple. For example, in the case of fees, GATT Article VIII:1(a) says that fees and charges shall be limited in amount to the approximate cost of services rendered. If fees and charges are actually identical to services costs, the introduction of concessional fee for FTA partners may lead to increase of fees to non-members, unless additional financial resources will be in place to cover the costs associated with the services rendered to the trade with partners. The cost of reducing or exempting fees for FTA partners should not be incurred by non-FTA partners. In order to achieve this, it is critical to separate the services costs rendered to the trade with partners and those with non-partners.

Recommendation 4: Inclusion of non-party MFN clause in trade facilitation provisions under FTAs

When a country has FTAs with various countries, it is important to consider the consistency of trade facilitation measures included in each FTA. Differentiated trade facilitation treatment of a country across various FTA partners may sometimes cause confusion. The distinction of goods from FTA partner and non-partners seems to be more straightforward than the situation in which a country has different rules for each FTA partner. This can be achieved by the following instances:

(i) When a country with multiple FTAs introduces express shipment, it may be advisable to have one express shipment lane for all FTA partners. For example, having a regular lane (for non-FTA partners), express lane (for certain FTA partners), and a super-express lane (for other FTA partners) makes the overall process complicated and inefficient.

(ii) When FTA members accept self-certificate under a certain FTA, but require a certificate issued by government authorities under another FTA, origin administration may become complicated from a business as well as customs perspective. Different threshold values for the exemption of submitting certificates across FTAs may also be confusing for traders.

The problem resulting from differentiated trade facilitation treatment measures across FTAs with common partners can be addressed by a considerable degree through the introduction of automatic MFN status in terms of trade facilitation (non-party MFN clause). At the WTO level, while the unconditional grant of MFN treatment is an obligation of the members, unconditional grant of MFN treatment particularly in the field of trade facilitation is not required.[45]

There are some FTAs that provide for automatic MFN, wherein a party is obliged to extend the same favorable trade liberalization/facilitation treatment as those agreed in its existing and future FTAs to its partner. For example, in the case of tariff, if the preferential rate under a newly agreed FTA is lower than its old FTAs with other partners, the former will be applied to the import from the partner of an old FTA, provided that it has automatic MFN clause. The automatic MFN clause can be also adopted in trade facilitation where the FTA states that parties agree to use certain more favorable trade facilitation measures with any non-party or future FTA partner, then such measures should be automatically incorporated in the FTA.

India–Singapore CECA[46] Annex I

The Parties confirm...that in the event that India adopts and implements the usage and concepts of De Minimis and Outward Processing in any bilateral, regional, or global trade agreement with any third party or parties, India shall adopt and implement the same usage and concepts...for the Agreement.

4.7 Summary

Are trade facilitation measures under FTAs discriminatory? This chapter tackles the question by providing detailed empirical analysis on whether trade facilitation provisions in FTAs are exclusive to contracting FTA partners, and how the measures can be discriminatory against non-members. Although the relationship between regionalism and

---

[45] For example, SPS Agreement contains "conditional" recognition of other WTO members' SPS measures. See Schroder (2011, p. 143).

[46] Comprehensive Economic Cooperation Agreement.

multilateralism in the field of trade facilitation merits equal attention to that in tariff elimination, the systemic problem regarding trade facilitation seems to have been overlooked by both policy-makers and international trade experts. This chapter also analyzed the implications of differentiated trade facilitation treatment across various FTAs. The analysis found that despite the multilateral scope and non-discriminatory objectives of trade facilitation measures, some trade facilitation measures under FTAs may actually be discriminatory similar to the impact of preferential tariff elimination.

Trade facilitation measures are significantly diverse in terms of their openness. This is partly because these are not strictly regulated by WTO agreements and countries have relatively large space of discretion in drawing up the regional trade facilitation measures unlike regional trade liberalization where the GATT treaty provides the guiding principles of regionalism (GATT Article XXIV). While GATT Article XXIV sets three conditions[47] for tariff elimination among FTA members, there is no equivalent guideline in the field of trade facilitation. For example, some FTAs allow the nationals of FTA partners to participate in the formulation process of standards on the national treatment. In this case, the rationale behind the exclusion of nationals of other countries in the formulation of standards should be considered. Likewise, the stipulation on the location of the conformity assessment bodies varies across agreements. Some FTAs stipulate that the conformity assessment bodies should be located in the contracting parties of FTA, while other FTAs does not set any geographical condition on the location of the conformity assessment bodies.

It is important to stress that it is policy decisions that make trade facilitating measures exclusive and discriminatory. Extending the same trade facilitation treatment to non-members is always possible. Such an extension can be easily achieved on a *de facto* basis. Designers of trade facilitation provisions in FTAs need to consider (i) how to maximize the impetus of trade facilitation reforms that is brought about by FTA

---

[47]Three conditions stipulated in GATT Article XXIV are: (i) substantially all the trade should be covered by the FTA (GATT Article XXIV-8), (ii) the FTA should be formed within a reasonable time frame (GATT Article XXIV-5c), and (iii) trade barriers against non-FTA members should not be higher or more restrictive than those prior to the formation of the FTA (GATT Article XXIV-5a).

negotiations; (ii) whether exclusive preferential trade facilitation treatment that discriminate non-members *vis-à-vis* FTA members is necessary, and (iii) how to avoid or minimize any negative impacts on non-members of introducing trade facilitation measures under FTAs. Furthermore, applying the same trade facilitation treatment across various FTA partners, rather than differentiated treatment for different FTA partners, significantly contributes to easing the administration of the flow of goods across borders.

While the primary analytical focus of this chapter is on trade facilitation measures under FTAs, the argument on the exclusive and discriminatory elements of trade facilitation measures is also applicable to any regional project that entails trade facilitation. This is the reason why the title of this chapter uses "regional approaches to trade facilitation" or "regional trade facilitation measures," rather than trade facilitation measures under FTAs. In fact, there are many cross-border transport agreements (CBTAs) at the bilateral and regional level that entail trade facilitation measures (Maur, 2011). These CBTAs are not usually treated as trade agreements since they are transport agreements and are not governed by the WTO or GATT Article XXIV. However, as far as those CBTAs entail trade facilitation-related measures such as streamlining the customs procedures, it is critical to consider if those have exclusive and discriminatory elements *vis-à-vis* non-members.

CHAPTER 5

Regional Services Agreements

What Is the Value of GATS-plus Regional Services Commitments?

5.1 Introduction

There is a general consensus on the growing economic significance of services that recognizes that they are as important as goods. In many countries, more than half of the national wealth is created by service industries. One can easily list the essential services used by households and businesses, such as financial and telecommunications services, while services in more minor sectors, such as the environment, are also flourishing. Services account for a considerable share of international trade too. Even the process of importing and exporting goods involves services, such as transportation and storage. Recent technological developments allow the international transaction of many services through the internet (Mode 1). Moreover, establishing a commercial presence to supply services locally, such as opening a branch of a commercial bank, is within the scope of trade in services (Mode 3). In addition, the significance of services provided by individual foreign professionals, such as lawyers and engineers who move across borders (Mode 4), and consumption abroad by domestic nationals (Mode 2), should not be overlooked despite the accurate measurement of these transactions being extremely difficult.[1]

Nevertheless, as far as economic and trade research is concerned, services have not won serious attention relative to their economic significance. In other words, empirical analysis of trade in services is very

---

[1]For the measurement of international services trade, see WTO (2010). On the measurement of Mode 3 and Mode 4 of services trade, see Drake-Brockman (2011) and Maurer and Magdeleine (2011).

limited, unlike trade in goods. This is primarily because of the lack of comprehensive data on services. It is difficult to accurately measure the amount of cross-border services traded through the internet or provided by the movement of foreign nationals. Various notional difficulties, such as the difficulty in distinguishing domestic and international services transactions, are another reason for the stagnant research output. For example, if a foreign bank opens an overseas branch with a minority share participation, should services provided by the branch to local consumers constitute international trade in services? Despite these notional and measurement difficulties, however, we can still conduct some analysis on services trade and agreements in a qualitative manner and draw some policy implications.

Trade economists usually have trade in goods in mind in examining trade theories and the studies on trade regionalism are no exception. In particular, a fundamental question of trade regionalism theory — whether or not regionalism contributes to the multilateral trading system — is usually examined from the perspective of goods trade, especially concerning tariffs. Theoretical debates relating to regional trade agreements have been dictated by goods specialists and they hardly cover the nature of trade in services sufficiently. But in reality, the progress of services liberalization at the regional level has been remarkable even when compared to multilateral efforts to liberalize services trade under the General Agreements on Trade in Services (GATS) as we will see in detail later. If we properly take services into consideration, commonplace views on the trade regionalism debate will be altered significantly.

This chapter considers the value and effects of regional services agreements, in particular, the discriminatory effects that regional services agreements have *vis-à-vis* non-members, with emphasis placed on the evolutionary nature of services liberalization at the regional level.[2]

---

[2]Regional services agreements may have several types of discrimination other than those against non-members. First, in a plurilateral services agreement (where there are more than three members), there is a possibility that treatment offered by one member to fellow members may not be identical (no most favored nation (MFN) status among parties). Second, treatment of members under different agreement may not be the same. This problem can be solved by the inclusion of a "non-party" MFN provision in agreements. For details on various types of discrimination in the field of services, see Chapter 2 of this book. See also Miroudot, Sauvage, and Sudreau (2010).

While there are several interesting studies on the value and effects of regional services agreements, the majority of them seem to assume that regional services agreements and commitments are static in nature. Many studies compare regional and multilateral commitments at a particular time and attempt to examine if the former has substantial multilateralism-plus elements. For example, Roy, Marchetti, and Lim (2008) tackle the question of how much further regional services agreements go beyond GATS by comparing the commitments of GATS and regional agreements, concluding that Southeast Asian countries' regional commitments do not have substantial GATS-plus commitments based on the available data in 2006.[3] However, a usually overlooked fact is that the subject of analysis, namely services commitment at the regional level, evolves continuously, and regional services trade liberalization is not a one-off event, unlike trade in goods integration. Accordingly, this chapter examines the dynamic development of regional services commitments and considers the implications of such regional services commitments.

In this chapter, the term regional services agreements, rather than services liberalization under FTAs or services chapters in FTAs, will be used. This is due to the fact that a regional scheme to liberalize services trade should be notified to the World Trade Organization (WTO) under GATS Article V, unlike other goods-related issues such as technical barriers to trade (TBT), which can be regarded as a subcomponent of FTAs to be notified under the General Agreement on Tariffs and Trade (GATT) Article XXIV. In other words, the frameworks to liberalize trade in goods and trade in services are different creatures under the WTO legal system. In fact, many agreements covering various issues such as services are notified to the WTO under both GATT Article XXIV and GATS Article V.[4]

This chapter analyzes regional services liberalization schemes in the Association of Southeast Asian Nations (ASEAN). Although the regional services agreement in ASEAN — the ASEAN Framework Agreement on Services (AFAS) — has achieved significant liberalization, it is seldom mentioned in the academic literature. This is in sharp contrast to ASEAN's

---

[3]Their study compares Southeast Asian countries' GATS commitments against AFAS 5 commitments in 2006. As Section 5.3 discusses in detail, AFAS concluded its ninth package in 2012.

[4]The term Economic Integration Agreement (EIA) is used in GATS Article V.

trade liberalization scheme in goods — the ASEAN Free Trade Area (AFTA) — which has been examined in detail. Moreover, the majority of studies on AFAS, albeit limited, tend to focus on a static comparison with GATS and conclude that its achievements are insignificant (see Section 5.4 for more detail). Instead, this chapter conducts a dynamic analysis of the evolution of AFAS to understand its real contribution to the world trading system. One important caveat is that AFAS has not been notified to the WTO as we will see later.

The remainder of this chapter is structured as follows. Section 5.2 considers the differences between trade in goods and services, especially from the perspective of the multilateral governance of regionalism. Section 5.3 presents the analytical framework for assessing the openness of regional services agreements and commitments, and explains the typology of regional services agreements in terms of discriminatory effects. Section 5.4 gives an overview of regional services agreements around the world. Section 5.5 empirically assesses regional services agreements using the case of a services trade regionalist project in ASEAN. Based on these empirical data, Section 5.6 considers the value of GATS-plus commitments in regional services agreements and proposes the best institutional framework for integrating regional efforts at services liberalization into the multilateral system. It is critical to properly design the appropriate institutional framework that defines the relationship between the two so that regional services agreements will be able to contribute to global trade in services. Section 5.7 summarizes the main discussions of this chapter.

5.2　Differences in Multilateral Principles of Regionalism: Goods versus Services

5.2.1　*Comparison of GATT Article XXIV and GATS Article V*

It is important to recognize the fundamental difference between trade liberalization in goods and services in terms of the multilateral governance of regionalism. In the case of goods, the complete elimination of tariffs after a transitional period is implicitly assumed when countries form an FTA based on GATT Article XXIV. In other words, the event of trade liberalization in goods is one-off. In fact, any interim agreement regarding an FTA should be terminated within a reasonable length of time

(GATT Article XXIV-5(c)). This period is usually considered to be 10 years as stipulated in the Understanding of GATT Article XXIV. A timely completion of interim agreements and the formation of the FTA is a critical requirement; otherwise agreements covering only selected sectors will continue to exist on the ground that they are "interim" agreements.

Because the elimination of tariffs entails large economic impacts on outside parties, some requirements for forming an FTA are stipulated in GATT Article XXIV. Satisfying these conditions is essential to maximizing the trade creation effect and minimizing the trade diversion effect. First, duties and other restrictive regulations of commerce with respect to "substantially all the trade" among FTA members should be eliminated (GATT Article XXIV-8). The elimination of tariffs with regard to all the intra-FTA trade mainly contributes to trade creation (Sampson, 1996). It should also be noted that meeting this condition is important to avoid the risk of trade diversion because countries may have an incentive to reduce intra-FTA tariffs only on the products that would lead to trade diversion, not on the highly protected products that would lead to trade creation from political economy considerations (Lamy, 2002, p. 1411). Second, duties and other regulations applicable to WTO members other than FTA members should not on the whole be higher or more restrictive than those prior to the formation of the FTA (GATT Article XXIV-5a). This condition is important to minimize trade diversion (Sampson, 1996).[5]

In the case of services, however, progressive liberalization through successive rounds of negotiations is common practice, though the modality of future services negotiations is still unpredictable. The GATS has a dedicated article on regional integration in the field of services trade (GATS Article V), which is equivalent to GATT Article XXIV in the case of goods trade. GATS Article V lists similar, but not the same, conditions that need to be satisfied by regional services agreements *vis-à-vis* FTAs. In comparison to GATT Article XXIV, GATS Article V has two distinct conditions that are related to the nature of services trade.

First, services agreements should have substantial sectoral coverage (GATS Article V-1a). According to the footnote in GATS Article V-1, this

.

---

[5]However, theoretically speaking, what is important is to maintain trade effects neutral so that an FTA does not lead to a reduction of trade with non-partners (Macmillan, 1993).

condition of substantial coverage should be understood in terms of the number of sectors, volume of trade affected, and modes of supply. It should be emphasized that GATS does not simply say either "substantially all the trade in services" or "substantially all restriction on trade in services," unlike the case of goods. The way the "substantial sectoral coverage" is examined is not simple. This is mainly because the concept of services trade and services *per se* is elusive, and measuring the amount of services trade and the level of restrictions on services trade is extremely difficult.

Second, substantially all discrimination regarding national treatment in the sector covered should be eliminated "on the basis of a reasonable time-frame" (GATS Article V-1(b)).[6] What should be eliminated are national treatment restrictions, not market access restrictions. More importantly, the time-frame of integration is not a strict requirement in the case of services, unlike the case of goods wherein an FTA should be completed within 10 years. It only says "on the basis of a reasonable time-frame," not "within a reasonable time-frame." As long as a reasonable time-frame is presented, such a services integration scheme satisfies this condition (this is exactly the reason why progressive liberalization is possible for regional services agreements). As a result, it is extremely difficult for GATS to prevent the formation of insubstantial regional services agreements only on the basis of their inconsistency to GATS Article V. This in turn means that services agreements have not been effectively governed by the current formulation of GATS.

One of the reasons why GATS Article V renders much greater flex-ibility with regard to the formation of regional agreements than GATT Article XXIV is that regional services agreements should be based on GATS Article V, not the Enabling Clause. This is unlike the case of goods agreements where the Enabling Clause, which sets much less demanding conditions than GATT Article XXIV, can be used as long as all contract-ing parties are developing countries. Because regional services agreement should be based on GATS Article V, even if all members are developing countries, GATS Article V cannot be as demanding as GATT Article XXIV. In fact, GATS Article V-3 specifically mentions flexibility for developing countries, unlike in GATT where non-reciprocal trade liberalization is

---

[6]New or more discriminatory measures are also prohibited by GATS Article V-1(b).

not allowed and the room of special and differentiated treatment among members is very limited.[7] GATS Article V allows greater flexibility than GATT Article XXIV partly because the flexibility to cope with developmental concerns is more directly addressed by GATS.

However, even though that flexibility allowed for (developing) countries under regional services agreement based on GATS Article V is partly because of the loophole of the WTO Agreemen — regional services agreements cannot be based on the Enabling Clause — the multilateral governance of regionalism between trade in goods and services are different mainly because of the difference in the nature of trade in goods and services. The fundamental philosophies of liberalization in goods trade and services trade are different even at the multilateral level as we will see in the next section.

5.2.2 *Modality of services liberalization: Progressive liberalization*

Because the multilateral principles of the governance of regionalism in trade in goods and services are different, it is useful to identify the modalities (or principles) of liberalization that are distinct to services. Services were negotiated for the first time in the Uruguay Round and GATS was finally agreed to in 1994. The overarching negotiations principles for services liberalization applicable to any WTO round of negotiations regarding services liberalization are laid out in the GATS Preface.

> GATS Preface
> *Desiring* the early achievement of progressively higher levels of liberalization of trade in services through successive rounds of multilateral negotiations aimed at promoting the interests of all participants on a mutually advantageous basis and at securing an overall balance of rights and obligations, while giving due respect to national policy objectives (underline added).

Progressive liberalization is the fundamental philosophy of services negotiations. No country is expected to liberalize services at once, and

---

[7]This is partly because in the world of goods trade, it is implicitly assumed that regional trade agreements are among developed countries (GATT Article XXIV-based) or developing countries (Enabling Clause-based) and therefore "mixed" agreements between developed and developing countries are not assumed. For a detailed discussion on mixed regional trade agreements, see Chapter 2.

the gradualism of achieving a higher level of services liberalization is encouraged. Part IV of GATS is titled "Progressive Liberalization" and the way in which services liberalization negotiations are conducted as well as how to make and modify or withdraw commitments is elaborated in three Articles: XIX, XX, and XXI.

However, the grand ideas of services negotiations modality as laid out in the GATS Preface have not been implemented so far. The Doha Round was suspended twice — in July 2006 and July 2008 — and there is no clear prospect of concluding the negotiations in the near future. As a result, no improved overall services commitments have been approved since the Uruguay Round, and the progressive liberalization of services has faced a serious problem at the WTO-level, although several WTO Members submitted initial and revised offer of services commitments in 2003 and 2005.

It is safe to consider that the fundamental principle of regional services liberalization is consistent with multilateral services liberalization. Just as progressive liberalization is expected at multilateral services negotiations, the same should be expected at services negotiation at the regional level. Progressive liberalization is the principle of not only multilateral services negotiations and commitments but also regional services negotiations and commitments. It is widely argued that regional services agreements are not expected to deliver immediate free trade in all services sectors (Fink and Molinuevo, 2008, p. 266). Gradualism is the norm at both the multilateral and regional level as far as services are concerned. In contrast, as we have already seen, the formulation of FTAs in goods is basically a one-off event. In short, while gradual trade liberalization is required under regional services agreements, the elimination of tariff in a relatively short time is required under FTAs in goods.

5.3   Analytical Framework for Assessing the Openness of Regional Services Agreements

5.3.1   *Typology of regional services commitments in terms of discriminatory effects*

When we discuss services liberalization, it is important to distinguish two types of services liberalization: services liberalization commitments and actual status of services (de)regulations. Services liberalization commitment usually takes the form of services schedules, wherein a certain level of liberalization is "bound" internationally (e.g., a schedule of specific commitments). The commitment in the services schedule specifies the minimum level of market access that will be maintained in future. Introducing a more restrictive policy than commitment is possible but subject to compensation, because this entails the withdrawal of the commitments. Thus, it can be said that services commitment (at the multilateral level) is equivalent to the most favored nation (MFN) bound rate in the case of goods. Progressive liberalization, mentioned earlier, is the principle of services liberalization in terms of services commitment.

In the case of the actual level of services (de)regulation, the question concerns the restrictiveness of the ongoing regulatory framework in place, which is equivalent to the MFN applied tariff rate in goods trade. However, similar to the case of goods trade where the actual tariff (MFN applied tariff rate) could be lower than the multilaterally committed tariff "cap" (MFN bound tariff rate), the actual services regulatory status may be more liberal than what is committed internationally.[8] Thus, a poor international commitment in terms of the services schedule does not imply that the actual services transaction is highly restricted (Miroudot, Sauvage, and Sudreau, 2010). In fact, countries usually conduct deregulation at home, which is implemented unilaterally irrespective of the progress of multilateral negotiations (Alam, Yusuf, and Coghill, 2010). The gap between actual regulation and international commitments is regarded as a policy space because there is room for governments to introduce regulations that are tighter than the current regulations.

WTO Members are expected to liberalize actual regulations as well, though the right to regulate services industries is granted to all countries and not limited to developing countries.[9] The GATS encourages countries to liberalize services trade and industries at home. The principle of services liberalization in terms of actual (de)regulation is called "autonomous liberalization" (GATS Article XIX-3). Thus, autonomous liberalization is the principle for the deregulation of actual regulatory status, which is not necessarily committed to internationally. Countries are expected to

---

[8] In the case of services, not only multilateral services commitment but also regional services commitment can be more restrictive than actual regulations.

[9] The GATS Preamble recognizes that this is especially important to developing countries.

liberalize services in an autonomous manner even if they are not committed to do so internationally. In such cases, they have the freedom to tighten the regulations without being subject to providing compensation. At the same time, countries are expected to bind some of the liberalization achieved at home by making commitments at the international level through round negotiations. Thus, during the negotiations of commitments, whether or not to request the binding of past autonomous liberalization becomes an issue. GATS does not seek to eliminate policy spaces, saying "negotiating guidelines [for each round negotiations] shall establish modalities for the treatment of liberalization undertaken autonomously by Members since previous negotiations ..." (GATS Article XIX-3).

Thus, in order to understand the value and discriminatory effects of regional services commitments under various scenarios, we need to conduct two types of comparative analysis. There are various types of regional commitments based on the two types of comparison:

- First, we need to compare regional commitments and GATS commitments because, unlike the case of goods where preferential treatment is likely, regional services commitment can be exactly the same as GATS services commitments.
- Second, we need to compare regional commitments against actual regulatory status because identifying the difference between services commitments and services deregulation is necessary to understand the significance of regional commitments.

However, before going into the technical details of discriminatory effects of regional commitments, it is important to make clear that this study assumes that services policy can be preferential or discriminatory.[10] Some argue that preferential regulations are not meaningful and *de jure* preferential regulations tend to be *de facto* MFN regulations (Anirudh and Sauvé, 2011). This, however, does not mean that services regulation cannot be preferential or discriminatory like public goods in economics literature. It is reasonable rather to consider that countries tend to extend *de jure*

---

[10] See Figure 2.4 in Chapter 2 for the measures that cannot be preferential in nature. In this case (public goods type measures), preferential or discriminatory treatment is impossible from the beginning.

preferential regulation to all countries on a *de facto* basis (Fink, 2008, p. 124). While it is possible to actually implement preferential regulations, countries decide to implement such policies in a discriminatory manner. (This is Type 3 scenario, which we will discuss next).

Figure 5.1 provides the classification of regional services commitments mainly based on the two types of comparison mentioned above (regional versus multilateral services commitments and commitment versus actual

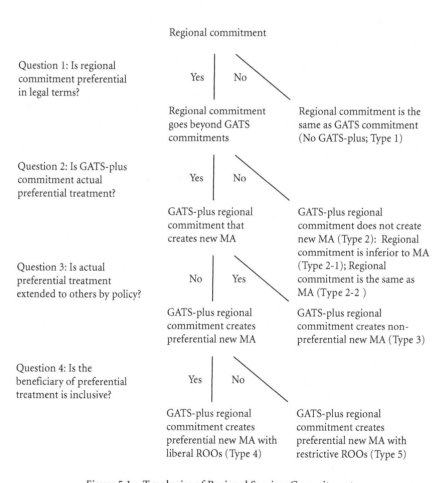

Figure 5.1   Typologies of Regional Services Commitments

Note: MA = market access

Source: Author's compilation based on Fink (2008)

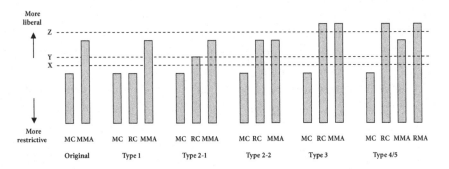

Figure 5.2   Level of commitments and market access

Source: Author's illustration

regulations), which is originally based on Fink (2008).[11] It has four tree-type questions to identify the discriminatory effects of regional services commitments.[12] Thus, there are in total five major types of regional commitment in terms of discriminatory effects.

Figure 5.2 illustrates the level of commitments at the regional level (RC) and the level of commitments at the multilateral level (MC) as well as MFN-basis market access or multilateral market access (MMA) and preferential market access to regional members (RMA), if applicable under each scenario described in Figure 5.1. A GATS-plus commitment in a certain country's regional commitment is described as the difference between its RC and MC. The policy space allowed for a particular country is described as either the difference between the level of MMA in that country's service industry and its MC (identified as multilateral policy space), or the difference between MMA (or RMC when this is more liberal than MMA[13]) and RC (identified as regional policy space). Multilateral and regional policy spaces can be easily understood with a concrete example of a foreign equity

---

[11] He argues that most commitments under regional services agreements in Asia are Type 2, 3, or 4 and their discriminatory effects are small.

[12] In Chapter 1, we identified five technical questions to determine the level of discriminatory effects of regional agreement (Figure 2.4 in Chapter 1). Question 0 in Figure 2.4, which is about the nature of measures in terms of exclusives, is not assessed in this chapter because it is obvious that services market access can be exclusive.

[13] RMA becomes an issue only under the scenario 4/5, wherein GATS-plus regional commitments "push up" the level of market access at the regional level (RMA), but not that at the multilateral level (MMA).

cap for a certain services industry. For example, under the Type 2 scenario (Type 2-1), the foreign equity cap commitment at the regional level (RC) is 50% and the foreign equity cap commitment at the multilateral level (MC) is 40%, while actual regulation (MMA) allows up to 70% foreign participation. In this case, the RC is MC-plus (since 50%>40%) and the country has the regional policy space to reduce the foreign equity cap by 20% *vis-à-vis* regional members (the difference between 70% and 50%) and have the multilateral policy space to reduce the foreign equity cap by 30% *vis-à-vis* non-regional members (the difference between 70% and 40%).

In assessing the value of regional commitments, we first need to examine if they create preferences for partners in legal terms (Question 1). This is a question of whether the regional commitment has any GATS-plus commitments. When the regional commitment simply reproduces the multilateral commitment ("No" to Question 1), there is no preference given to services agreement partners in legal terms (Type 1). This happens when the regional commitment simply "copies and pastes" the GATS commitment. This type of commitment does not have discriminatory effects (Miroudot, Sauvage, and Sudreau, 2010). However, some may question the value-added of regional commitments if they are neither economically nor legally meaningful when they are exactly the same as GATS commitments. Many studies on regional services agreements in Asia conclude that regional services agreements in Asia generally do not have GATS-plus commitments.[14]

When the regional commitment has GATS-plus elements ("Yes" to Question 1), we can say that such a regional commitment is "preferential binding." Then, the question regarding the implications of GATS-plus commitments to non-members arises. We need to consider if this entails actual deregulation or new market access (Question 2). The fact that preferences are given to partners in legal terms (GATS-plus regional commitments) does not automatically mean that actual preferences are created. If the regional commitment is superior to the multilateral commitment but not superior to actual regulations ("No" to Question 2), such a commitment does not lead to new market access (Type 2). From

---

[14]Some regional services commitments are GATS-minus, which means that the coverage and/or depth of a certain country's regional services commitments are inferior to its GATS commitments.

a market access-centric perspective, this type of regional commitment is not meaningful because it does not enhance business opportunities. There are two types of GATS-plus regional commitments without new market access, which has different implications in terms of lock-in effect, which will be discussed later:

- GATS-plus regional commitment without new market access that allows regional policy space (Type 2-1)
- GATS-plus regional commitment without new market access that does not allow regional policy space (Type 2-2)[15]

But if the GATS-plus regional commitment actually entails new market access or deregulation ("Yes" to Question 2), then the next critical question in terms of the discriminatory effects is whether new market access is enhanced in a discriminatory manner (Question 3). As Fink (2008) observes,[16] enhanced market access brought about by a regional commitment is usually implemented in a non-discriminatory manner ("Yes" to Question 3, Type 3). This is certainly beneficial in terms of the business of non-members. However, even if new market access is granted in a non-discriminatory manner, there is a possibility that tighter regulations will be introduced in future that may be applied in a discriminatory manner (discriminatory regulations). This scenario means that a country introduces new regulations applicable only to non-members in order to avoid offering compensation to members. There is no option of introducing new regulations within existing policy space because the country does not have the policy space *vis-à-vis* regional members under the Type 3 scenario in Figure 5.2. A regional commitment without policy space may induce the introduction of discriminatory regulations in future even if this does not bring immediate discriminatory market access. Thus, the Type 3 regional commitment is a double-edged sword; on one hand it enhances market access even for non-members, but on the other hand it may induce discriminatory regulations in future.

---

[15] Standstill commitments do not allow countries to have policy space when commitments are made. Thus, standstill commitments also do not entail new market access.

[16] Also see Hoekman, Mattoo, and Sapir (2007). However, they argue that Mode 4 services commitments in regional agreements tend to give actual preferential treatment to members.

Moreover, one should not forget that new market access or actual deregulation could be implemented in a discriminatory manner ("No" to Question 3), contrary to the observations made by Fink (2008). There is the possibility that GATS-plus commitments bring preferential new market access exclusive to members that entail serious discriminatory effects (Type 4/5). In this case, the magnitude of the discriminatory effects depends on the restrictiveness of the rules of origin (ROOs). The discriminatory effects are small when ROOs are liberal (Type 4), but they are large when ROOs are restrictive (Type 5). However, it is important to note that liberal ROOs can reduce, not eliminate, discriminatory effects of preferential treatment.

Various scenarios regarding the level of commitment and actual regulations have different lock-in effects. In this regard, it is important to examine policy space under each scenario. Type 2-1 commitments seem to be beneficial to non-members in terms of the lock-in effects (see Figure 5.2), because, under this scenario, it is reasonable to consider that a country tends to introduce tighter regulations in future within a regional policy space in a non-discriminatory manner (Regulation Y for all countries) rather than introducing either discriminatory regulations that are tighter than the regional commitment and applicable only to non-members (Regulation X for non-members; Regulation Y for members[17]), or non-discriminatory regulations that are tighter than the regional commitment and subject to compensation being offered to regional members (Regulation X for all countries).[18] In short, the regional policy space seems to function as a buffer by creating an incentive for countries to avoid discriminatory measures. Thus, the benefit of lock-in effects of regulations brought about by the regional commitment can also be enjoyed by non-members

---

[17] In this case, non-regional members will be worse-off in actual terms.

[18] Despite some lock-in effects mentioned above, we cannot rule out that a country under the scenario of Type 2 in Figure 5.2 will still introduce regulations tighter than the regional commitment (e.g., Regulation X). If regulations tighter than the regional commitment are introduced in a non-discriminatory manner, the discriminatory effect is small (discrimination in terms of compensation where only members can be compensated). If regulations tighter than the regional commitment are applicable only to non-members and the same preferential treatment continues to be applied to partner countries, the discriminatory effect is large. However, this scenario is unlikely because discriminatory policy is harmful in the long-run. The more likely scenario is to avoid any discriminatory measure.

(non-regional members can free ride on GATS-plus commitments in others' services agreements). In short, a GATS-plus regional commitment without new market access has two interrelated positive effects: (i) incentives for countries to introduce regulations within regional policy space in a non-discriminatory manner, and (ii) confidence-building for non-members due to the lock-in effects of regional commitments.

This effect (the creation of an incentive to introduce tighter non-discriminatory regulations within regional policy space), however, cannot be expected when regional commitment is the same as actual regulations (Type 2-2), because there is no regional policy space in this case. Likewise, a "GATS-plus regional commitment with new market access" ("Yes" to Question 2 = Type 3/4/5) is not necessarily a good thing because (immediate) new market access (for all countries) implies that there is no regional policy space, just like the Type 2-2 scenario mentioned above. On one hand, new market access is certainly beneficial for services-exporting countries, but several issues should be carefully considered from the perspective of the services-importing country. On the other hand, from a developing country perspective at least, enhancing market access and immediately binding enhanced market access to the international commitments, which implies no policy space between a regional commitment and actual policy, is too risky because any policy drawback in future would be subject to compensation to regional members. Given that the autonomous liberalization of domestic services industry is the fundamental philosophy of regulatory reform (GATS Article XIX), the immediate binding of new market access seems to be too demanding. (Moreover, the absence of policy space would lead to the future introduction of discriminatory regulations under a certain circumstance as we will see below.)

The various scenarios of regional services commitments that would lead to discriminatory or preferential regulations can be summarized as follows. First, preferential market access is directly created if a regional services commitment satisfies a set of conditions that leads to the Type 4/5 scenario: (i) regional commitment has GATS-plus elements ("Yes" to Question 1), (ii) GATS-plus regional commitment is more liberal than the actual regulation ("Yes" to Question 2), and (iii) countries do not want to provide the same treatment to all other countries on a *de facto* basis ("No" to Question 3). An alternative scenario of discriminatory or preferential regulations introduced is that a GATS-plus regional services commitment brings non-discriminatory new market access to all countries (Type 3), but the government later decides to introduce a tighter regulation that is applicable only to non-members to avoid having to offer compensation to regional members.

5.3.2 *Analytical focus and caveat on methodology*

The focus of this chapter is regionalism in terms of services agreements as opposed to unilateral services liberalization or reform at home. This chapter attempts to demonstrate that regional services agreements have GATS-plus commitments ("Yes" to Question 1). Whether there are GATS-plus commitments in regional services agreements is an important issue because this is the first question in considering the multilateral implications of regional services agreements. In fact, many existing studies attempt to tackle this empirical question because regional services agreements (or commitments) have direct implications on multilateral trading systems (Roy, Vivas, and Vea, 2007; Fink, 2008; Miroudot, Sauvage, and Sudreau, 2010).

Though useful, one of the weaknesses of the classification of services commitments discussed above is that the analysis summarized in Figure 5.1 does not have a dynamic perspective, which is necessary in analyzing services liberalization from two angles: regional commitments and regulatory reforms. First, a regional commitment is likely to be dynamic. If this is so, it is not fruitful to continue endless debates on whether regional commitments at a particular point in time have GATS-plus elements (especially when the commitment is made). The discussion on the size of GATS-plus elements also tends to be fruitless because the reference point is unclear.[19] An important perspective is that the GATS-plus element of regional commitments is getting more substantial across time. Even if regional and multilateral commitments are identical at a particular point in time, it is likely that a regional commitment becomes deeper than the multilateral commitment as the regional commitment evolves. In short, we should examine

---

[19]Accordingly, existing studies tend to analyze GATS-plus elements across regional services agreements and compare the relative size of GATS-plus elements under each agreement despite the fact that each country has different ideas and norms on making commitments.

how quickly GATS-plus elements in regional commitments are evolving, rather than the question of whether a regional commitment is GATS-plus and/or whether such GATS-plus elements are substantial based on static analysis, which is common in existing studies. This implies that Question 1 is highly relevant in considering the multilateral implications of regional commitments.

Second, it is also important to note that the actual regulatory status also changes as reforms of services policy are conducted. If we admit the evolutionary nature of services industry reform, then Question 2 (whether immediate new market access is created by a regional commitment) is too narrow to assess the real development of new market access enhancement in the long-run because long-term reform, which is indirectly brought about by regional services negotiations and commitments, also enhances long-term market access. Therefore, in assessing the quality of services liberalization at the regional level, it is important to have a dynamic perspective of regulatory reform rather than a static comparison between commitments and actual regulatory status. This implies that "Yes" to Question 2 (Type 3 and Type 4/5) is not necessarily superior to "No" to Question 2 (Type 2) in enhancing long-term market access. We will return to this point in Section 6.

In summary, this chapter analyzes regional services commitments mainly in terms of Question 1, namely from the perspective of GATS-plus commitments. But the argument is not limited to the question of whether a regional commitment has GATS-plus elements and/or whether these are substantial. Rather, it attempts to demonstrate that the level of regional commitment steadily improves (thus GATS-plus elements of regional commitment also rapidly increase). Thus, regional commitments generate impetus for reviewing the existing regulations, which leads to future reform of the services sector. Regional commitments also have some positive effects on non-members if the country avoids introducing regulations that are tighter than regional commitments and applicable only to non-members.

5.4   Overview on Regional Services Agreements

As of December 2011, there were 92 regional services agreements in force and notified to the WTO, excluding notifications of the accession into existing regional services agreements.[20] Because the Enabling Clause cannot be used for an agreement on services, unlike the case of an agreement on goods, those 92 regional services agreements are all GATS Article V-based. However, it should be noted that there are several regional services agreement that have not been notified to the WTO; AFAS is one of the notable examples.[21]

The exhaustive list of the 92 regional services agreements in force and notified to the WTO is included in Table 5.1. Agreements covering various issues such as trade in goods, trade in services, investment, and others

Table 5.1   92 regional services agreements

Regional trade agreement	Date entry into force
European Community (EC) Treaty	01-Jan-1958
Australia–New Zealand (ANZCERTA)	01-Jan-1989
European Economic Area (EEA)	01-Jan-1994
North American Free Trade Agreement (NAFTA)	01-Jan-1994
Costa Rica–Mexico	01-Jan-1995
Colombia–Mexico	01-Jan-1995
Canada–Chile	05-Jul-1997
Mexico–Nicaragua	01-Jul-1998
Chile–Mexico	01-Aug-1999
EU–Mexico	01-Oct-2000
New Zealand–Singapore	01-Jan-2001
Mexico–Guatemala (Mexico–Northern Triangle)	15-Mar-2001
Mexico–El Salvador (Mexico–Northern Triangle)	15-Mar-2001
Mexico–Honduras (Mexico–Northern Triangle)	01-Jun-2001
EFTA–Mexico	01-Jul-2001
Dominican Republic–Central America	04-Oct-2001
US–Jordan	17-Dec-2001

(*Continued*)

---

[20]There are three notifications regarding accession into an existing regional services agreement: European Community (EC) (15) Enlargement in 1995, EC (25) Enlargement in 2004, and EC (27) Enlargement in 2007.

[21]Unlike agreements on goods, it is not easy to grasp the number of regional services agreement not notified to WTO. The ESCAP Database, which covers not only notified but also agreements not notified to WTO, only includes non-notified agreement on goods. Other than AFAS, there seem to be a large number of services agreement not notified to the WTO, such as the US–Lao PDR trade agreement covering services (Fink and Molinuevo, 2008).

Table 5.1   (*Continued*)

Regional trade agreement	Date entry into force
Chile–Costa Rica (Chile–Central America)	15-Feb-2002
Chile–El Salvador (Chile–Central America)	01-Jun-2002
European Free Trade Association (EFTA)	01-Jun-2002
Caribbean Community and Common Market (CARICOM)	04-Jul-2002
Japan–Singapore	30-Nov-2002
EFTA–Singapore	01-Jan-2003
Panama–El Salvador (Panama–Central America)	11-Apr-2003
Singapore–Australia	28-Jul-2003
China–Macau	01-Jan-2004
China–Hong Kong	01-Jan-2004
US–Singapore	01-Jan-2004
US–Chile	01-Jan-2004
Panama–Chinese Taipei	01-Jan-2004
Korea–Chile	01-Apr-2004
EU–Former Yugoslav Republic of Macedonia	01-Apr-2004
EFTA–Chile	01-Dec-2004
Thailand–Australia	01-Jan-2005
US–Australia	01-Jan-2005
EU–Croatia	01-Feb-2005
EU–Chile	01-Mar-2005
Japan–Mexico	01-Apr-2005
Thailand–New Zealand	01-Jul-2005
India–Singapore	01-Aug-2005
Jordan–Singapore	22-Aug-2005
Southern Common Market (MERCOSUR)	07-Dec-2005
US–Morocco	01-Jan-2006
CAFTA–DR	01-Mar-2006
Korea–Singapore	02-Mar-2006
Trans-Pacific Strategic Economic Partnership	28-May-2006
Guatemala–Chinese Taipei	01-Jul-2006
Japan–Malaysia	13-Jul-2006
Panama–Singapore	24-Jul-2006
US–Bahrain	01-Aug-2006
EFTA–Korea	01-Sep-2006
Iceland–Faroe Islands	01-Nov-2006
ASEAN–China	01-Jul-2007
Chile–Japan	03-Sep-2007
Japan–Thailand	01-Nov-2007
Pakistan–Malaysia	01-Jan-2008
Nicaragua–Chinese Taipei	01-Jan-2008

(*Continued*)

Table 5.1 (*Continued*)

Regional trade agreement	Date entry into force
Honduras–El Salvador–Chinese Taipei	01-Mar-2008
Panama–Chile	07-Mar-2008
Japan–Indonesia	01-Jul-2008
Chile–Honduras (Chile–Central America)	19-Jul-2008
Brunei Darussalam–Japan	31-Jul-2008
China–New Zealand	01-Oct-2008
EU–CARIFORUM States EPA	01-Nov-2008
Panama–Costa Rica (Panama–Central America)	23-Nov-2008
Japan–Philippines	11-Dec-2008
US–Oman	01-Jan-2009
China–Singapore	01-Jan-2009
Panama–Honduras (Panama–Central America)	09-Jan-2009
US–Peru	01-Feb-2009
Peru–Chile	01-Mar-2009
Australia–Chile	06-Mar-2009
EU–Albania	01-Apr-2009
ASEAN–Korea	01-May-2009
Chile–Colombia	08-May-2009
Peru–Singapore	01-Aug-2009
Canada–Peru	01-Aug-2009
Japan–Switzerland	01-Sep-2009
Japan–Vietnam	01-Oct-2009
Pakistan–China	10-Oct-2009
ASEAN–Australia–New Zealand	01-Jan-2010
Korea–India	01-Jan-2010
Peru–China	01-Mar-2010
EU–Montenegro	01-May-2010
Chile–China	01-Aug-2010
Hong Kong–New Zealand	01-Jan-2011
EU–Korea	01-Jul-2011
EFTA–Colombia	01-Jul-2011
India–Malaysia	01-Jul-2011
India–Japan	01-Aug-2011
Peru–Korea	01-Aug-2011
Canada–Colombia	15-Aug-2011

Note: CAFTA-DR = Dominican Republic–Central America–United States Free Trade Agreement
Source: Author's compilation based on WTO website

are often notified under both GATS Article V and GATT Article XXV (the Enabling Clause).[22] However, the number of the regional services agreements is much fewer than goods agreements. This seems to imply that a large number of regional cooperation schemes include only cooperation in goods trade and not services trade. Goods agreements based on the Enabling Clause, such as the Asia-Pacific Trade Agreement (APTA), usually do not entail regional services agreements. MERCOSUR is the only agreement whose goods section is notified under the Enabling Clause, but entails a services agreement notified under GATS Article V.

Several interesting observations can be made from this list. First, two regional services agreement existed even before the launch of GATS: the European Community (EC) (1958) and the Australia–New Zealand Closer Economic Relations Trade Agreement (ANZCERTA) (1989). Second, there were only seven regional services agreements that came into force in the 1990s. The majority of regional services agreements were signed in the 2000s. Third, the number of regional services agreements in Asia is limited. In particular, the services trade agreement among Asian countries (intra-Asian regional services agreement) is very limited as far as agreements notified to the WTO are concerned. Fourth, most regional services agreements are bilateral.[23] This is partly because plurilateral regional cooperation schemes usually include only goods agreements under the Enabling Clause, which does not have a services cooperation scheme.

5.5　Case Study: Achievements of the ASEAN Framework Agreement on Services

This section reviews the services liberalization scheme within ASEAN, the ASEAN Framework Agreement on Services (AFAS), which is a typical Asian services agreement based on a positive list approach. While services commitments can take the form of either positive or negative list approaches,[24] it is said that the philosophy of progressive liberalization is

---

[22]While GATT Article XXIV-based goods agreements usually entail GATS Article V–based regional services agreements, the only minority among Enabling Clause–based goods agreements entail services agreements.

[23]On the bilateralism of regional services agreements, see Adlung and Molinuevo (2008).

[24]A negative list approach is very rare in regional services agreement within Asia. While several agreements involving Asian countries and countries from the Americas, such as

better reflected in the positive list approach, which is popular among Asian countries (Arup, 2008). In fact, AFAS members make commitments in line with a GATS-style positive list approach through consecutive round negotiations unlike the negative list approach of the North American Free Trade Agreements (NAFTA). AFAS also follows GATS classification of services that has 12 categories, using the W/120 classification.[25]

AFAS began in December 1995 at the meeting of the ASEAN Economic Ministers (AEM) in Bangkok, Thailand. Leaders recognized the growing importance of trade in services at the regional level and established AFAS in adherence to GATS principles:

> Reiterating their commitments to the rules and principles of the General Agreement on Trade in Services (GATS). . . and noting that Article V of GATS permits the liberalizing of trade in services between or among the parties to an economic integration agreement. . .

One important caveat relating to the relationship between AFAS and GATS is that AFAS has not been notified to WTO under GATS Article V. While the question of whether the original AFAS in 1997 was consistent with GATS Article V may be controversial,[26] recent AFAS packages, which included broad sectoral coverage, seem to be consistent with GATS. ASEAN's efforts to notify AFAS to WTO should be encouraged so that its achievements regarding services liberalization will be widely recognized as WTO compliant.

This section empirically examines AFAS achievements relevant to the principles of services liberalization that were discussed in Section 5.2. It analyzes the evolution of AFAS round negotiations in terms of progressive liberalization. The analysis below first focuses on whether or not at least one sub-sector under a certain sector is covered. Although it may be true that the question of whether whole sub-sectors under one sector are covered

---

the Japan–Mexico EPA, employ a negative list approach (Fink and Molinuevo, 2008), the Singapore–Korea FTA is the only regional services agreement between Asian countries that uses a negative list approach.

[25] The W/120 classification on which GATS commitments are based has 12 sectors. However, the 12th sector ("others") will not be analyzed in this chapter.

[26] In particular, it is uncertain whether AFAS 1997 satisfied GATS V-1a because its coverage was limited to the tourism sector. For GATS V-1a, see Section 5.6.

is critical from a business perspective, the distinction between the perfect exclusion of one whole sector and the situation where at least one sub-sector is included is important from the political and legal perspectives. As previously discussed, the *a priori* exclusion of one whole sector in regional services negotiations is not allowed. We will also examine the GATS-plus elements of past AFAS packages in a more quantitative manner. We will use the Hoekman index to see whether AFAS packages actually bring GATS-plus commitments.

Some argue critically that regional services agreement in ASEAN do not have "GATS-plus" commitments by comparing GATS offers to AFAS commitments, such as is the case when new GATS offers are submitted (Rajan, 2002; Roy *et al.*, 2007; Stephenson and Nikomborirak, 2001; Sally, 2007; Ochiai, Dee, and Findley, 2009). In other words, they consider AFAS as a Type 1 preferential treatment in Figure 5.1. However, it is important to note that they conduct a static comparison between GATS and AFAS at a particular point in time and tend to use old data.[27] Thus, it is a useful exercise to examine the GATS-plus commitments of AFAS in a dynamic manner.

5.5.1 *The evolution of AFAS commitments in terms of coverage*

So far, eight packages of services commitments were achieved as a result of round negotiations of AFAS. However, it should be noted that one round of negotiations sometimes resulted in two packages and thus the number of the negotiations and packages concluded are not identical.[28]

AFAS 1 (The 1997 Package). Soon after the Bangkok meeting, the first AFAS round of negotiations was launched, and the first overall package was agreed to in December 1997. All nine ASEAN members, including the two newest members — Myanmar and the Lao Peoples' Democratic Republic (Lao PDR) — submitted services schedules, a remarkable achievement given that the two had only become members in July 1997.

---

[27] Fink (2008, p. 119) argues that AFAS's recent achievement can be said to be remarkable.
[28] The first round of negotiations resulted in two packages (AFAS 1 and 2). While the second and third round of negotiations resulted in only one package per round (AFAS 3 and 4), the fourth round of negotiations again resulted in two packages (AFAS 5 and 6). Beginning again with the fifth round of negotiations, each subsequent round resulted in only one package. See the ASEAN Secretariat (2011).

While the 1997 AFAS package was not very ambitious, basically covering only tourism and transport, the former was included in the schedules of all nine AFAS members. Five out of nine members covered transport. The Philippines also covered business services (audit) and Vietnam covered some telecommunications services. It is quite remarkable for ASEAN members to have started liberalization in services in the same year that the Asian financial crisis struck.

AFAS 2 (The 1998 Package). There was a marked improvement in the commitments in new and existing sectors. Four new sectors (business, communications, construction, and financial services) appeared in most countries' commitments for the first time. All AFAS members made commitments in business services and, except for two relatively new ASEAN members — Myanmar and Vietnam — all countries expanded commitments in telecommunications sector.[29] Nearly all improved their commitments in construction and finance (except Indonesia in finance), a marvelous achievement in 1998 given that finance and telecommunications were the most difficult sectors in GATS negotiations.

The scope of commitments in tourism and transport, meanwhile, was significantly broadened. All countries, except Brunei Darussalam,[30] enhanced the coverage of commitments in the transport sector, and most countries advanced their commitments in tourism. Interestingly, even countries that had already made transport commitments in 1997 did so again in 1998. This showed that ASEAN members were attempting to adjust their commitments proportionately and balance "marginal" efforts among members in each round of AFAS negotiations.

Cambodia, which was supposed to have joined ASEAN in 1997 but its entry was postponed due to internal political struggle, immediately submitted its AFAS commitment after accession to ASEAN in 1999. The coverage of its 1999 commitments was limited to four sectors (business, finance, tourism, and transport), but the country gave its best effort given its level of economic development and the prevailing international environment. (For example, Cambodia was not even a WTO member at that time).

---

[29]Vietnam's 1997 Package had already made goods commitments in telecommunications.
[30]Brunei's 1997 Package had already made goods commitments in transportation, ranging from air to maritime.

AFAS 3 (The 2001 Package). The third package in 2001 covered almost the same sectors as in 1998, but two important features of this package should be highlighted. First, members significantly deepened commitments in five sectors (business, communications, construction, tourism, and transport). ASEAN paid significant attention to the balance in terms of "marginal" efforts. In fact, all members, including those who had already made commitments in 1998, improved in all five sectors. Cambodia's communications and construction sectors, and Myanmar's communications sector were first covered in the 2001 package. Second, members made no commitment in sectors other than the five listed above.[31] This implies that ASEAN was practical by carefully avoiding liberalization in sectors where political sensitivity was an issue. Another practical reason for the limited coverage of the 2001 package may have been the launching of the WTO Doha Round. It is understandable that countries would have strong reservations about improving their regional commitments when international negotiations are about to start. (The Doha Ministerial meeting was held in November 2001.)

AFAS 4 (The 2004 Package). The Bali Concord II was adopted at the ASEAN Summit in Bali in October 2003; it agreed on two major points: (i) the free flow of services should be achieved by 2020, and (ii) the application of the "ASEAN minus X" formula in the implementation of member countries' services commitments. Under this formula, a subset of ASEAN members (more than two) that are ready to liberalize a certain services sector on a reciprocal basis may do so without extending concessions to non-participating countries.

Nevertheless, no new sectors were covered in 2004, with improvements limited to those four that were already covered by the 2001 package. It is difficult to provide a definitive answer, but the principal reason for this stagnant outcome was probably the then-ongoing Doha Round negotiations. It was also not specified in the protocol how to implement the ASEAN minus X formula, and members did not actually use the formula in making commitments in the 2004 Package.[32]

---

[31] Except Malaysia's distribution sector, as Malaysia's 2001 schedule included wholesale and retail services.

[32] Moreover, this rule has not yet been used because realizing "ASEAN minus X" entails operational difficulty, although it is philosophy attractive. Accordingly, all commitments made so far by members were on a non-discriminatory basis in terms of the ASEAN minus

AFAS 5 (The 2006 Package). By 2006, AFAS commitments grew significantly more complicated. To understand the whole picture of a member's commitment, one should refer to the first, second, third, and fourth packages because only changes in commitments from the previous package were inscribed in their respective overall packages. In addition to past overall packages, one should also refer to independent financial packages and air transport packages. Because the decision on liberalization of some service sectors was highly technical, ministers in charge of specific fields started the negotiations in their respective sectors instead of the economic ministers. The liberalization of services in the field of finance and air transport fell under this category. In 2002, finance ministers agreed to a services package exclusively for financial services.[33] Likewise in 2005, the first independent air transport package was concluded.[34] As a consequence of the above developments, it resulted in too many documents for each country's commitments and monitoring the commitments became very tedious.[35]

The fifth package overcame these problems to a certain degree by consolidating the four previous schedules. By simply looking at this package, it is easy to understand the status of commitments as of 2006, except for sectors covered by specialized ministers' meetings such as finance and air transport. The only drawback of this methodological change was the difficulty in identifying any improvement from previous commitments; generally, one should carefully compare old and new commitments to find improvements (and possibly setbacks as well). The consolidation of past commitments under the fifth package is an excellent example of ASEAN's full support of the GATS approach even at a very technical level.

X approach. The ASEAN minus X method, however, can be said to be politically important, because liberalization among a "coalition of the willing" was supported at the minister level.

[33] This agreement is called the second package because the 1998 overall package covered some financial services and is regarded as the first financial package.

[34] This is usually called the fourth air transportation package because, as with financial services, the overall package in 1997, 1998, and 2001 included air transportation.

[35] In particular, the relation between the ASEAN minus X approach and the MFN Exemption List is unclear. From the GATS perspective, discriminatory treatment among members is prohibited unless the member had registered sectors where such treatment could be introduced beforehand.

The fifth package made significant improvements in actual commitments as well. All difficult sectors that had not been covered in previous packages were included in the 2006 package, including distribution, education, environment, and recreation services. For example, liberalization in the distribution sector is politically sensitive in many ASEAN countries because family-run stores often face difficulty from competition with foreign shopping centers. The environment (e.g., sewerage) and education are also very difficult to liberalize because they are closely linked to government regulations and governmental services. But by 2006, AFAS achieved comprehensive sectoral coverage.

At the same time, the fifth package continued to observe ASEAN's flexibility principle, though not the ASEAN minus X principle. Half of ASEAN's members did not make commitments in environmental services in 2006, but they eventually did in later years, as will be discussed in the next section. Flexibility was also extended by other ASEAN members to Vietnam, which allowed Vietnam to avoid making commitments in some sectors (distribution, education, and environment) because it was about to complete its accession negotiations with incumbent WTO Members. Had Vietnam's 2006 AFAS commitments been too good, they would have undermined its bargaining position with regard to WTO accession.

AFAS 6 (The 2007 Package). Vietnam joined the WTO in December 2006 and its AFAS commitments made significant improvement in 2007. Other ASEAN members were freeriding on Vietnam's new commitments and also improved on their own commitments. While Indonesia, Malaysia, and Lao PDR reserved making commitments in environmental services in their 2006 schedules, these countries covered some environment sub-sectors in 2007.

The sixth package has substantial GATS-plus elements in many ASEAN countries' AFAS commitments. But because the GATS offers submitted by ASEAN countries in 2006 were basically confidential, it is difficult to compare thoroughly ASEAN's 2007 AFAS commitments with their GATS commitments. Malaysia is the only ASEAN country that made its latest GATS offer, submitted in 2006, public.[36] As far as Malaysia is concerned,

---

[36] Alongside developed countries that are proponents of services liberalization, Malaysia agreed to make its GATS offer available on the website of Coalition of Service Industries. See http://www.uscsi.org/wto/.

AFAS 2007 (and 2006) commitments included sectors that were not covered by its latest GATS offer. For example, distribution services, educational services (other than higher education), and health services (other than private hospitals) were included in Malaysia's AFAS 2006, while they were not covered in its GATS 2006 offer. Similarly, Malaysia decided to make AFAS commitments in environmental sectors in 2007, which it has not offered under GATS.

As a result, the AFAS 6 coverage was significantly more comprehensive. Aside from some limited exceptions, all countries made some commitments in all sectors. The country-sector matrix of making commitments under the AFAS scheme was almost completed by 2007 and, thus, the future agenda of AFAS entail upgrading or improving existing commitments in various sectors.

AFAS 7 (The 2009 Package). The package in 2009 was the result of the fifth round of negotiations. What was interesting in this round of negotiations was the kind of numerical approach that was adopted. It was agreed that all members should take on an additional 10 new sub-sectors (ASEAN, 2009). This implies that ASEAN members recognize the importance of improving the quality of their AFAS commitments.

As a result, sectoral coverage of each member's commitments also improved in this package. Members made an effort to make some commitments even in their sensitive sectors. Therefore, the sectors that still did not have any commitments were limited to the following: Brunei Darussalam's distribution and environmental sectors, Lao PDR's recreation sector, Myanmar's education sector, and the Philippines' education sector. Except for these five sectors, some commitments had now been made in all services sectors.

AFAS 8 (The 2010 Package). While the eighth package was concluded in 2010, the commitments schedules were not available on the ASEAN Secretariat website as of May 2012. It was agreed that all members should make commitments in an additional 15 new sub-sectors in AFAS 8. Thus, some improvements from AFAS 7 were made, though the interval between the two packages was not long.

ASEAN's plans for further liberalizing services are ambitious. During the ASEAN Summit in December 2005, the members agreed to accelerate services liberalization in non-priority sectors by 2015 "with flexibility."

The target year was moved earlier by 5 years from the date set at the Bali Concord II in 2003. The ASEAN Economic Community Blueprint adopted at the ASEAN Summit in November 2007 seeks to "remove substantially all restrictions on trade in services for all services sectors [other than priority sectors] by 2015" and includes detailed parameters of the services liberalization process.

Three more AFAS packages are planned to achieve the goals of the ASEAN Economic Community with respect to services liberalization. The plan is to conclude AFAS 9 in 2012, AFAS 10 in 2014, and AFAS 11 in 2015. It was agreed that all members should make commitments in an additional 20 sub-sectors in both AFAS 9 and AFAS 10, and seven additional sub-sectors in AFAS 11 (MITI, 2011).

5.5.2 *The Hoekman index quantitative analysis of AFAS*

The Hoekman index is one of the most widely used indexes to quantitatively measure the comprehensiveness of services commitments in the positive list schedules, based on which both GATS and AFAS commitments are made. The methodology was originally proposed by Hoekman in 1995. In this method, a score is given to the inscription of each of eight cells in each sector: a Market Access column and National Treatment column for four modes of supply. The score given is 1.0 for full commitment ("none"), 0.5 for partial commitment ("some limitations"), and zero for no commitment ("unbound"). Thus, the closer to 1.0 the index is, the more liberal the commitment. While there are some methodological problems with the Hoekman index, such as weighting and the arbitrary manner of coding, this is so far the most widely used quantitative method to assess the quality of services commitments.[37]

The average of the Hoekman index for all ASEAN countries' commitment under AFAS and GATS is provided in Table 5.2. The overall assessment is consistent with the analysis in terms of coverage in the previous section. In terms of the Hoekman index, while AFAS 5 is only slightly better than

---

[37] Some consider that the score allocated to a partial commitment (0.5) should be more than half that of a full commitment (1.0). For example, Roy (2012) gives a score of 0.75 for partial commitments. Another problem of the Hoekman index is that this method assumes that all partial commitments are similar in terms of effects. Finally, the equal weight distributed to each sector is also major problem of this index.

Table 5.2   Hoekman index of GATS and AFAS commitments

	Business	Communication	Construction	Distribution	Education	Environment	Finance	Health	Tourism	Recreation	Transport	Overall
Brunei												
GATS	0.12	0.05	0.00	0.00	0.00	0.00	0.13	0.00	0.00	0.00	0.01	0.03
AFAS 5	0.36	0.08	0.31	0.00	0.00	0.00	0.33	0.31	0.27	0.11	0.17	0.18
AFAS 7	0.38	0.10	0.33	0.00	0.45	0.00	0.33	0.31	0.28	0.11	0.21	0.23
Cambodia												
GATS	0.30	0.28	0.50	0.70	0.45	0.75	0.35	0.19	0.46	0.15	0.17	0.39
AFAS 5	0.30	0.28	0.50	0.75	0.45	0.75	0.44	0.19	0.52	0.30	0.20	0.43
AFAS 7	0.30	0.30	0.51	0.75	0.45	0.75	0.44	0.19	0.53	0.30	0.20	0.43
Indonesia												
GATS	0.05	0.10	0.22	0.00	0.00	0.00	0.21	0.00	0.17	0.00	0.03	0.07
AFAS 5	0.22	0.13	0.50	0.00	0.36	0.00	0.25	0.00	0.48	0.08	0.07	0.19
AFAS 7	0.27	0.16	0.53	0.21	0.48	0.42	0.25	0.66	0.61	0.24	0.30	0.38
Lao PDR												
AFAS 5	0.11	0.03	0.55	0.00	0.00	0.00	0.24	0.00	0.14	0.00	0.01	0.10
AFAS 7	0.35	0.28	0.75	0.34	0.56	0.56	0.24	0.27	0.42	0.00	0.14	0.36
Malaysia												
GATS	0.30	0.04	0.09	0.00	0.00	0.00	0.21	0.16	0.22	0.18	0.03	0.11
AFAS 5	0.32	0.09	0.50	0.15	0.24	0.00	0.28	0.16	0.53	0.18	0.09	0.23
AFAS 7	0.50	0.19	0.50	0.43	0.39	0.34	0.28	0.33	0.56	0.23	0.14	0.35
Myanmar												
GATS	0.00	0.00	0.00	0.00	0.00	0.00	0.00	0.00	0.34	0.00	0.01	0.03
AFAS 5	0.09	0.09	0.63	0.30	0.10	0.16	0.09	0.25	0.36	0.18	0.10	0.21
AFAS 7	0.25	0.35	0.63	0.38	0.48	0.47	0.09	0.50	0.52	0.30	0.13	0.37

(Continued)

Table 5.2   (*Continued*)

	Business	Communi-cation	Constru-ction	Distri-bution	Education	Environ-ment	Finance	Health	Tourism	Recreation	Trans-port	Over-all
Philippines												
GATS	0.03	0.22	0.00	0.00	0.00	0.00	0.34	0.00	0.36	0.00	0.16	0.10
AFAS 5	0.16	0.33	0.31	0.16	0.00	0.00	0.45	0.14	0.45	0.00	0.37	0.22
AFAS 7	0.42	0.52	0.35	0.28	0.00	0.27	0.45	0.14	0.47	0.30	0.38	0.33
Singapore												
GATS	0.21	0.14	0.15	0.00	0.00	0.00	0.32	0.00	0.28	0.15	0.03	0.12
AFAS 5	0.27	0.16	0.75	0.30	0.15	0.25	0.34	0.23	0.66	0.15	0.08	0.30
AFAS 7	0.52	0.38	0.75	0.60	0.15	0.25	0.34	0.38	0.66	0.30	0.14	0.41
Thailand												
GATS	0.22	0.10	0.41	0.10	0.30	0.69	0.20	0.00	0.52	0.14	0.11	0.25
AFAS 5	0.35	0.15	0.64	0.10	0.34	0.69	0.39	0.13	0.52	0.14	0.14	0.33
AFAS 7	0.66	0.20	0.64	0.60	0.58	0.75	0.39	0.31	0.64	0.64	0.24	0.51
Vietnam												
GATS	0.34	0.27	0.50	0.25	0.20	0.44	0.41	0.25	0.36	0.09	0.12	0.29
AFAS 5	0.36	0.32	0.56	0.25	0.28	0.50	0.49	0.30	0.38	0.10	0.14	0.33
AFAS 7	0.39	0.33	0.56	0.25	0.43	0.50	0.49	0.63	0.52	0.18	0.19	0.41
ASEAN Ave.												
GATS	0.15	0.12	0.22	0.09	0.08	0.18	0.23	0.05	0.27	0.06	0.06	0.14
AFAS 5	0.25	0.17	0.53	0.20	0.19	0.23	0.33	0.17	0.43	0.12	0.14	0.25
AFAS 7	0.41	0.28	0.55	0.38	0.40	0.43	0.33	0.37	0.52	0.26	0.21	0.38

Source: Author's compilation based on Ishido and Fukunaga (2012).

GATS commitments, AFAS 7 is much better than GATS. All sectors, with the notable exception of finance, made significant improvement between AFAS 5 and AFAS 7. Sectors where commitments were made at an early stage (AFAS 1 or 2), such as construction and tourism, are also sectors where the Hoekman index is high in the AFAS 7 package. For example, both the construction and tourism sectors' Hoekman index exceed 0.5 in AFAS 7. The transport sector is an exception since it was initially covered by AFAS 1 but has not seen substantial progress across AFAS round negotiations. The transport sector's Hoekman index as of AFAS 7 remained low at 0.2.

In terms of countries, Thailand (0.51) had the highest score at the time of AFAS 7, followed by Cambodia (0.43). Brunei Darussalam (0.23) had the lowest score, with the Philippines (0.33) as the next lowest. Except for the highest and lowest scores of Thailand and Brunei Darussalam, respectively, the Hoekman index scores are more or less similar among ASEAN members. It is interesting to note that the less developed member countries of ASEAN who joined the organization as late comers are not necessarily poor performers in terms of their services liberalization commitments as assessed by this index.

In summary, AFAS countries tend to upgrade their commitments every 1 or 2 years. AFAS achieved significant liberalization of the services sectors through consecutive rounds of negotiation, with almost all sectors covered by 2007. The enhanced level of market access commitments was also confirmed by analysis based on the Hoekman index. It is possible to argue that AFAS has better achieved what GATS attempted to do, namely progressive liberalization through round negotiations. AFAS will take two decades to complete its liberalization project on services that started in 1995, with the final package to the submitted in 2015. Given the difficulty in liberalizing services sectors and the principle of progressive liberalization, we can conclude that AFAS has developed relatively fast.

Finally, it is worth noting that GATS-plus commitments of AFAS sometimes lead to actual discriminatory market access. This implies that some ASEAN members introduce actual preferential or discriminatory regulations favorable to members. In the financial services, Thailand relaxed restrictions on hiring foreign personnel on a preferential basis (Dee and Ncnaughton, 2011, p. 17). Malaysia and Lao PDR allowed cross-border lending and deposit taking on a preferential basis, which was not permitted in the past (Dee, 2012, p. 32). In health services, Indonesia relaxed the minimum number of beds for foreign-invested hospitals on a preferential basis (Dee and Ncnaughton, 2011, p. 17). In the case of the maritime sector, both Malaysia and Indonesia made preferential concessions on foreign equity limits (Dee, 2012, p. 21).

5.6   Policy Issues: Regional Services Agreements as a Trigger for Services Reforms

5.6.1   *Policy question: Immediate discriminatory new market access or long-term unilateral reform*

As we have seen, the development of regional services commitments is progressive. ASEAN's effort to improve AFAS commitments, even during the Doha Round, should not be overlooked. It is misleading to overemphasize the relatively minor outcome of AFAS 3 in 2001, the year the Doha Round started. AFAS concluded five services packages during the Doha Round (2004, 2006, 2007, 2008, and 2009) and as a result ASEAN members' services commitments have been deepened significantly. This means that ASEAN has steadily liberalized services sectors in the region regardless of the progress (or the lack of) in multilateral GATS negotiations. It should not be assumed that making commitments at the regional level is a one-off event.

Thus, the static comparison between multilateral commitments against regional commitments at a particular point of time is misleading because regional commitments improve gradually though successive rounds of negotiations, which are usually much more frequent than multilateral services negotiations. As illustrated in Figure 5.3, although the level of commitment is insubstantial at an early stage of implementing regional liberalization, it is enhanced through progressive liberalization. The level of liberalization contained in multilateral and regional commitments may be identical at a particular point in time ("t1" in Figure 5.3), but GATS-plus elements contained in regional commitments can outpace those of multilateral commitments over time ("t3" and "t4"). The important point of the analysis is that the GATS-plus elements of regional commitments are dynamic. Most existing studies of AFAS underevaluate the achievements of AFAS, mainly because they cover only the

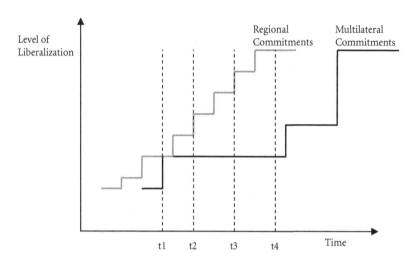

Figure 5.3   Dynamics of GATS-plus regional commitments
Source: Author's illustration

inauguration stage of AFAS when the commitments being made were insubstantial.

If a regional commitment is GATS-plus ("Yes" to Question 1 in Figure 5.1), then we tend to focus on the next question in assessing the value of regional services commitments: whether a regional services commitment leads to new market access (Question 2). However, immediate market access brought about by a regional commitment implicitly assumes that the regional commitment is a one-off event. Existing literature emphasizes new market access on the grounds that one-off commitments exercised at the regional level should be large enough to produce new market access. In other words, new market access is created only if a "large" commitment increases the level of liberalization in terms of actual regulations (Figure 5.4(a)). In short, existing studies' preoccupation with new market access at the time of commitments is partly because they assume that making a commitment is a one-off event.

However, if a regional commitment is evolving, the question of whether a commitment is large enough to create new market access (or whether an actual commitment to deregulation is achieved during negotiations) seems to be secondary. Moreover, the narrow focus on new market access at the time of making commitments is misleading. The more important

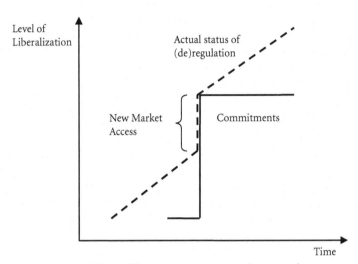

(a) One-off large commitments and new market access

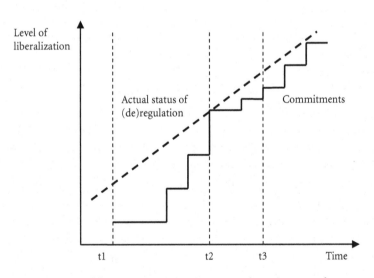

(b) Progressive commitments and continuous reform

Figure 5.4   One-off vs. progressive commitments

Source: Author's illustration

question is: whether commitments are long-term reform inducing or not. This is because even if a new commitment is not large enough to create immediate new market access, this does not mean that market access is not enhanced indirectly in the long-run. Negotiations over international services commitments induce long-term reforms that can lead to enhanced market access in the future. It is important to understand that the issue is not limited to the regulatory reform that is directly induced by negotiations leading to immediate market access.[38] As long as negotiations and commitments bring some impetus for policy-makers to consider the necessity of future policy reform, we can say that negotiations and commitment are reform-inducing. This type of effect brought about by regional commitments can be referred to as "reform-inducing effects." Although whether or not autonomous and continuous regulatory reforms are induced by regional round negotiations is a difficult empirical question, it is undeniable that regional negotiations can be a good opportunity to examine the relevancy of regulations from a policy perspective. As long as regional negotiations and commitments give impetus to further autonomous deregulation and liberalization, we should consider that market openings are induced by making commitments. (See Section 6.2 for the further discussion on the reform-inducing effects of regional commitments).

Another important aspect of regional commitments is their lock-in effects of reforms. By making commitments, a certain level of reform achieved in the past is locked-in and the risk of policy drawback is reduced because it would be possible only with compensation. Thus, when regional commitments have GATS-plus elements, they bring additional lock-in effects. What should be locked-in via a regional commitment can be past reforms, not the latest reforms. The lock-in of past reform contributes to the predictability of policy. The lock-in effects of regional commitments can even be enjoyed by non-members if countries attempt to introduce tighter regulations within policy space in a non-discriminatory manner, as we have already discussed in Section 5.3.1.

---

[38] In discussing reform brought about by commitments, some literature over-emphasizes regulatory reform that leads to immediate market access (Francois and Hoekman, 2010). Though identifying the causality is difficult, the impetus for future reform is more important in assessing long-term effects.

Thus, the overall dynamic relationship between progressive liberalization and continuous unilateral reform can be explained in this order: a country can initially conduct autonomous deregulation that liberalizes market access (without international commitments), then makes a commitment, especially at a regional level, once it feels comfortable, which may be followed by further autonomous deregulation when the country becomes confident enough (Figure 5.4(b)).[39] Empirical literature suggests that unilateral liberalization is a kind of precondition for making a services commitment (Alam, Yusuf, and Coghill, 2010). While the commitment can sometimes be deeper than the actual regulation, this is because policymakers attempt to use international commitments as a device of reform rather than the outcomes of negotiations over new market access.[40] While a country sometimes loses policy space ("t2" in Figure 5.4(b)), the country regains some policy space after conducting autonomous liberalization with regard to actual regulations ("t3"). The usual outcome is that both the level of liberalization, in terms of international commitments, and the actual regulation improve gradually with some policy space being maintained.

An important perspective in examining the pros and cons of immediate new market access and long-term reform includes indentifying their respective discriminatory effects. Services sector reform usually takes the form of unilateralism. The autonomous liberalization or reform of regulations is usually unilateral. In contrast, new market access achieved by regional commitments may be preferential, which means that the discriminatory treatment between members and non-members is introduced in actual terms (Bosworth and Trewin, 2008, p. 647). As we have seen, AFAS led to actual preferential or discriminatory regulations favorable to partner countries in some services sectors. This implies that preferential market access tends to be created when countries are required to provide commitments during regional services negotiations. It is important to

[39] In a similar line, Cornish and Findlay (2010) argue that the creation of the environment in which services regulation reform happens is more important than negotiating a services agreement that seeks new market access.
[40] In the case of GATS commitment, Alam, Yusuf, and Coghill (2010) find that the commitments of Vietnam and China are deeper than actual regulations. However, note that those are newly acceding members of the WTO.

understand that preferential or discriminatory market access is a result of a poor regulatory framework (Bosworth and Trewin, 2008; Dee, 2010). Thus, members of a regional services agreement need to carefully think what would contribute most to the long-term development of services industries in their respective countries as well as the region as a whole: long-term reform, which leads to unilateral market access enhancement, or immediate new market access, which can be discriminatory. Even though rules of origin (ROOs) in services agreements tend to be liberal or "leaky" (Fink, 2008; Anirudh and Sauvé, 2011; Fink and Nikomboriak, 2007; Hamanaka, 2011b) and thus the discriminatory effects of preferential treatment are not huge, one should recognize that leaky ROOs do not eliminate the discriminatory effects. (Scholars who emphasize the leaky nature of ROOs for services tend to consider preferential services treatment as Type 4 in Figure 5.1, which is not true).

5.6.2   *Policy proposal: The amendment of GATS Article V*

Regional commitments (especially GATS-plus regional commitments) have two effects: reform-inducing and reform-binding. However, different magnitude of reform-inducing effects and reform-binding effects are brought about by multilateral and regional commitments.

It is reasonable to consider that services commitments at the multilateral and regional levels contribute to services industry reform in the long-run. While economic literature has not fully captured the long-term reform-inducing effects of commitments because of methodological difficulties (Francois and Hoekman, 2010),[41] this is a policy-oriented question rather than a theoretical debate. Many authors have emphasized that multilateral negotiations on services can be used as an effective driver of services sector reform in WTO member countries (Hoekman and Mattoo, 2011). Regional commitments sometimes include the future liberalization of services (Hoeknam, Mattoo, and Sapir, 2007, p. 382) and this implies the significance of the long-term reform or future reform-inducing effects of

---

[41]This is partly because it is not easy to identify the real impetus for long-term reform effects. Thus, the research tends to focus on reform that leads to immediate market access in analyzing the reform effects of commitments.

regional commitments.[42] Moreover, regional cooperation that envisages the long-term goal of comprehensive economic integration similar to the case of the ASEAN Economic Community undoubtedly contributes to the member countries' attitude toward long-term reform. In fact, many ASEAN countries conducted ambitious services reform recently and it is difficult to argue that such reforms are not related to regional services liberalization cooperation.[43] Several country-level and industry-level studies suggest that AFAS contributed to regulatory cooperation and reform in member countries in many important services sectors.[44] In this context, it is also important to note that priority sector liberalization, such as logistics, significantly contributed to ASEAN countries' regulatory reform in the sector (Trewin *et al.*, 2008, p. 52). Thus, both multilateral and regional negotiations on liberalizing services can be a trigger of services reform efforts (Dee, 2011, p. 17).

A careful examination is necessary to assess the consequences of making commitments in terms of lock-in effects. The question is whether a country is willing to bind its ongoing regulatory status through international services commitments. There is a gap between commitments and actual regulations; this is especially true in the case of multilateral commitments (Hoekman and Mattoo, 2011). Countries are reluctant to bind the *status quo* of actual regulations at the multilateral level because the consequences of policy drawback are too large. Regional commitments could be a good tool to bind the past efforts of reform. It is true that a GATS commitment is more desirable than a regional commitment in terms of the lock-in effects alone (Hoekman and Mattoo, 2011; Mattoo and Sauvé, 2008, p. 251), but we should not overlook the negative side of making commitments at the multilateral level compared with the regional level. If a government needs to introduce regulations that are tighter than its current commitments to cope with something unexpected, the country needs to compensate the entire WTO Membership if these commitments have been made at

---

[42] This can also happen to multilateral commitments. But in most cases, future commitments of future deregulation are included in newly acceding members' schedules.

[43] On the intensive discussion over reform effects brought about by AFAS, see Trewin *et al.* (2008).

[44] On issues regarding regulatory cooperation and reform in the health services sector under the AFAS scheme, see Arunanondchai and Fink (2007).

the multilateral level. Thus, it is reasonable for countries to first conduct deregulations and then make commitments at the regional level, which may be followed by multilateral commitments. Even before multilateralizing regional commitment to GATS, however, we can expect some degree of lock-in effects that is equally beneficial to regional and non-regional members.

What is the appropriate and practical mechanism for the WTO to govern regional services agreements? The key is found in the fundamental nature of services liberalization — progressive liberalization. As we have seen, both GATS and AFAS attempt to achieve progressive liberalization, but the latter has been more successful. In the case of goods, the principal multilateral concern is to minimize the negative effects of a one-off elimination of tariffs in the region by setting requirements for regionalism. But because of the fundamental nature of services liberalization, which entails autonomous and progressive liberalization, the direct control of regional services agreements by setting requirements is not practically feasible. Without discretion in deciding the scope, mode, and speed of liberalization, a regional services agreement does not become fruitful for its members. Thus, rather than tightening the conditions to be met with the formation of a regional services agreement, reflecting regional-level progressive liberalization in multilateral progressive liberalization, with some time-lag present, is a better way to cope with services trade regionalism.

The basic premise is that a particular level of liberalization achieved through regional commitments is expected to be multilateralized within GATS after a reasonable period. GATS services commitments should at least cover what has been achieved at the regional level in the past. What has been achieved at the regional level should be replicated in multilateral commitments after a reasonable period of time. The essence of this proposal is explained in Figure 5.5. The level of liberalization of services commitments at the multilateral level is illustrated as a large stair-shaped line (black line), while regional services commitments are described as a small stair-shaped line (gray line).

Accordingly, GATS Article V *ter* is proposed as a new paragraph in the current GATS.

GATS V *ter* Regional Integration and GATS (Proposal)
Specific commitments regarding regional integration shall be, to the extent possible, reflected in specific commitments of GATS after a reasonable period of time.

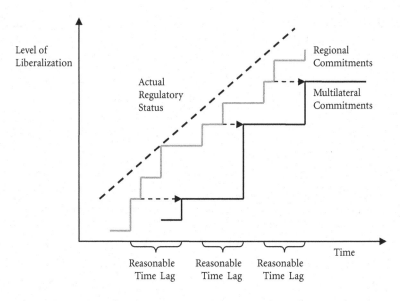

Figure 5.5   Regional and multilateral commitments

Source: Author's illustration

If this is achieved, there will be no need for WTO services negotiators to engage in *ad hoc* bargaining in each round of negotiations in order to request that other WTO Members realize GATS commitments that are comparable to their regional commitments. While a similar idea has been introduced by Mattoo and Sauvé (2010, p. 16), who argue that WTO Members should pre-commit to future multilateral liberalization in GATS commitments and signal a timeframe in which regional preferences may be progressively eroded and/or eliminated, there is no guarantee that this will actually happen. If GATS Article V *ter* is added, such a move is institutionally secured without the need for *ad hoc* negotiations on whether the future multilateralization of regional preferences should be included in a GATS commitment.

5.7   Summary

In this chapter, we analyzed the relationship between multilateralism and regionalism in the field of services using the case study of AFAS. Members of regional trade agreements covering goods are expected to eliminate trade barriers, especially tariffs among members, within 10 years. However, in the case of services, autonomous liberalization (unilateral reforms) and progressive liberalization (making commitments) are the fundamental philosophies of both multilateral and regional services negotiations. Members of regional services agreements are not expected to eliminate all services barriers in a short period of time; the gradual expansion of sector coverage under a regional agreement is allowed.

Despite the fact that AFAS is not notified to WTO, its services round negotiations replicate GATS round negotiations. And while services negotiations at the WTO level have not made substantial progress, AFAS services negotiations have brought fruitful results. This is mainly because holding round negotiations more frequently is possible at the regional level.

Finally, we should consider the possibility of generalization. One may argue that AFAS, which employs frequent round negotiations, is very unique and ASEAN's experience cannot be the model of regional services cooperation. In this regard, three issues should be pointed out that are favorable toward the possibility of generalization. First, several regional services agreements in Asia, especially South–South services agreements, employ the GATS-style or AFAS-style consecutive round negotiations format. For example, the first package of the ASEAN–China services agreement was concluded in 2007 and the second package was signed in 2011. Second, built-in review mechanisms in regional services agreement (or FTAs that have a services chapter) can substitute for round negotiations. The frequent review of past commitments seems to be useful to improve commitments, given the rapid progress of services technologies. For example, the Japan–Singapore Economic Partnership Agreement (JSEPA) signed in 2002 has a provision on periodical reviews. JSEPA Article X (General Review) says that the review should be conducted in 2007 and every 5 years thereafter; improved services commitments were submitted in 2007 by both parties. Third, a series of different regional service agreements with different partners can serve as a vehicle for the continuous reform of services sectors. Making the level of commitment in newer agreements progressively higher, even if the partners are different, is possible.

Appendix 5.1

GATS Article V Economic Integration

1. This Agreement shall not prevent any of its Members from being a party to or entering into an agreement liberalizing trade in services between or among the parties to such an agreement, provided that such an agreement:

   (a) has substantial sectoral coverage[1] and
   (b) provides for the absence or elimination of substantially all discrimination, in the sense of Article XVII, between or among the parties, in the sectors covered under subparagraph (a), through:

   (i) elimination of existing discriminatory measures, and/or
   (ii) prohibition of new or more discriminatory measures,

   either at the entry into force of that agreement or on the basis of a reasonable time-frame, except for measures permitted under Articles XI, XII, XIV and XIV bis.

2. In evaluating whether the conditions under paragraph 1(b) are met, consideration may be given to the relationship of the agreement to a wider process of economic integration or trade liberalization among the countries concerned.

3. (a) Where developing countries are parties to an agreement of the type referred to in paragraph 1, flexibility shall be provided for regarding the conditions set out in paragraph 1, particularly with reference to subparagraph (b) thereof, in accordance with the level of development of the countries concerned, both overall and in individual sectors and subsectors.

   (b) Notwithstanding paragraph 6, in the case of an agreement of the type referred to in paragraph 1 involving only developing countries, more favourable treatment may be granted to juridical persons owned or controlled by natural persons of the parties to such an agreement.

---

[1]This condition is understood in terms of number of sectors, volume of trade affected and modes of supply. In order to meet this condition, agreements should not provide for the *a priori* exclusion of any mode of supply.

4. Any agreement referred to in paragraph 1 shall be designed to facilitate trade between the parties to the agreement and shall not in respect of any Member outside the agreement raise the overall level of barriers to trade in services within the respective sectors or subsectors compared to the level applicable prior to such an agreement.

5. If, in the conclusion, enlargement or any significant modification of any agreement under paragraph 1, a Member intends to withdraw or modify a specific commitment inconsistently with the terms and conditions set out in its Schedule, it shall provide at least 90 days advance notice of such modification or withdrawal and the procedure set forth in paragraphs 2, 3 and 4 of Article XXI shall apply.

6. A service supplier of any other Member that is a juridical person constituted under the laws of a party to an agreement referred to in paragraph 1 shall be entitled to treatment granted under such agreement, provided that it engages in substantive business operations in the territory of the parties to such agreement.

7. (a) Members which are parties to any agreement referred to in paragraph 1 shall promptly notify any such agreement and any enlargement or any significant modification of that agreement to the Council for Trade in Services. They shall also make available to the Council such relevant information as may be requested by it. The Council may establish a working party to examine such an agreement or enlargement or modification of that agreement and to report to the Council on its consistency with this Article.

   (b) Members which are parties to any agreement referred to in paragraph 1 which is implemented on the basis of a time-frame shall report periodically to the Council for Trade in Services on its implementation. The Council may establish a working party to examine such reports if it deems such a working party necessary.

   (c) Based on the reports of the working parties referred to in subparagraphs (a) and (b), the Council may make recommendations to the parties as it deems appropriate.

8. A Member which is a party to any agreement referred to in paragraph 1 may not seek compensation for trade benefits that may accrue to any other Member from such agreement.

CHAPTER 6

Economic Cooperation under Ftas

Do Ftas Impose WTO-plus Technical Assistance Obligations on Members?

6.1 Introduction

What kind of technical assistance and capacity building[1] benefits do developing countries enjoy if they sign a free trade agreement (FTA) with developed countries? This is a frequently asked question among developing country officials involved in FTA policy-making as they seek to understand the direct and immediate benefits of FTAs aside from the long-term and often ambiguous impacts such as productivity increases and industrial specialization based on comparative advantages. While policy-makers should understand these long-term effects of FTAs, identifying the direct short-term benefits can be even more important in order to sell FTAs to a domestic audience.

We tend to normatively insist that an FTA should lead to a win–win situation for all contracting parties, irrespective of developmental level. We may then propose that the developed members of an FTA should provide technical assistance to developing country partners so that the latter can maximize the benefits and minimize the costs of the FTA. However, empirical assessments of technical assistance mechanisms under FTAs have

---

[1] By (trade-related) "technical assistance," this chapter refers to assistance in trade promotion and trade policy. Recently, the term "technical cooperation" has been gaining popularity because it emphasizes that development programs will work if there is collaboration between technical assistance providers and recipients. For the same reasons, the term "capacity building" is usually added to highlight the importance of local ownership and absorption of technical assistance (Kostecki, 2001; Shaffer, 2006). However, this chapter mainly uses the term technical assistance because the focus of the analysis is on the provision of technical assistance to developing members by developed FTA members.

not yet been thoroughly conducted.[2] An analysis of technical assistance mechanisms under FTAs, in terms of obligations (required actions) and the roles of concerned parties (technical assistance providers and recipients), is necessary to assess the overall effects of FTAs.

By conducting a detailed textual analysis of World Trade Organization (WTO) agreements and various FTAs, this chapter identifies whether, what type of, and how much more technical assistance can be enjoyed by developing countries if they sign an FTA, particularly with developed countries. Given that there are many WTO agreements that include stipulations on technical assistance, it is important to compare technical assistance obligations under FTAs against those under WTO agreements. More specifically, we tackle the question of whether technical assistance obligations in a certain issue area under FTAs are more robust than those under the WTO and whether a particular FTA has technical assistance obligations in a unique area that is not covered by WTO agreements. In doing so, we will indentify WTO-plus elements in technical assistance obligations under FTAs.

This chapter is structured as follows. Section 6.2 points out that the multilateral governance on developmental issues is very weak and developmental issues are scattered across many agreements under the WTO system. Section 6.3 explains the concept of WTO-plus technical assistance and introduces two types of WTO-plus technical assistance under FTAs: (i) additional technical assistance and (ii) unique technical assistance. Section 6.4 analyzes technical assistance mechanisms under WTO agreements and identifies the level of technical assistance obligations under the WTO system. We will analyze nine agreements under the WTO framework that have provisions for technical assistance. Section 6.5 analyzes technical assistance under FTAs. We first see whether FTAs have additional technical assistance obligations compared with those stipulated in each WTO Agreement. We also examine if there is a unique area of technical assistance peculiar to each FTA. We will analyze various Japan–Association of Southeast Asian Nations (ASEAN) Agreements as representative of North–South agreements with ample room for technical assistance given

---

[2]There is some literature that focuses on technical assistance in a certain issue under FTAs such as intellectual property. As an example, see Roffe *et al.* (2007).

the differences in developmental levels among participating countries. Section 6.6 attempts to draw some implication on the regionalism–multilateralism problem from the perspective of developmental issues. Section 6.7 summarizes the empirical findings and concludes the argument by considering the policy implications of WTO-plus technical assistance on the debate over multilateralism versus regionalism.

6.2 Multilateral Governance on Developmental Issues

Under the WTO framework, there are no specific agreements on either development or technical assistance. While some scholars argue that the WTO system should introduce a set of rules focusing on the facilitation of development under one agreement, which could be referred to as an Agreement on Development Facilitation (ADF), this has remained at the conceptual stage and failed to win widespread support in negotiations in Geneva (Lee, 2006).

One of the few WTO documents that directly addresses developmental issues is the Decision on Measures in Favor of Least Developed Countries, which was agreed upon by ministers participating on the Trade Negotiation Committee on December 15, 1993. While this document emphasizes the importance of technical assistance to least developed countries, it lacks operational specificity. It says:

> WTO Trade Negotiation Committee Decision on Measures in Favor of Least Developed Countries. 15 December 1993
>
> [Ministers] agreed that ... Least developed countries shall be accorded substantially increased technical assistance in the development, strengthening, and diversification of their production and export bases including those of services, as well as in trade promotion, to enable them to maximize the benefits from liberalized access to markets.

Nevertheless, the WTO system has many agreements that do include articles, provisions, or paragraphs on technical assistance. As a result, developmental issues such as technical assistance are decentralized and scattered across many agreements under the WTO framework. Therefore, we need to examine each WTO agreement that contains developmental issues to understand the whole picture of multilateral governance on development.

Not surprisingly, provisions on technical assistance under those agreements are very diverse. Required actions are very different across agreements, and the parties that are expected to be a provider or recipient of technical assistance also differ across agreements. The level of ambition set in each agreement significantly varies. While some agreements set binding obligations, others include softening language, such as "mutually agreed terms and conditions," and provisions for technical assistance that are not automatic.

6.3   Analytical Framework for WTO-plus Elements of Technical Assistance under FTAs

6.3.1   *Comparison between WTO Agreements and FTAs*

The fundamental research question of this chapter is: whether FTAs include WTO-plus elements of technical assistance (technical-level Question 1 discussed in Chapter 2, Section 2.4). In conducting assessments of technical assistance under FTAs in comparison with those under the WTO, we first need to identify the WTO-plus elements of such agreements.[3] We should compare specific obligations to provide technical assistance in a certain issue area (e.g., sanitary and phytosanitary [SPS] standards) under FTAs and WTO agreements. If technical assistance provisions under an FTA simply repeat the same language as stipulated in WTO agreements, we cannot say that an FTA's technical assistance mechanism is substantial, at least from a legal perspective.

There are two important caveats on the methodology of comparative analysis. Theoretically speaking, the degree of technical assistance, which is generally provided by developed members to developing partners, depends on the level of obligation included in the agreement binding all contracting parties, including developing countries. This is because technical assistance is often required by developing countries to implement general obligations. For example, it is reasonable for the level of technical assistance obligations in the field of intellectual property to be high when the level of general obligations in intellectual property protection is demanding.[4] Thus, in theory, we have to compare the difference in general

---

[3] For an example of comparative analysis of technical assistance between FTAs and WTO agreements, see Roffe *et al.* (2007).
[4] Shadlen (2008) suggests the possibility that the high level of WTO-plus commitments made by developing countries in the field of intellectual property under FTAs (i.e., the low

obligations in a certain issue area between the WTO and an FTA against the difference in technical assistance obligations in that issue area between the WTO and the FTA. In other words, WTO-plus general obligations should be compared against WTO-plus technical assistance obligations. A simple comparison of technical assistance obligations alone is not sufficient.

However, even a simple comparison focusing only on WTO-plus technical assistance obligations is useful in considering the relation between multilateralism and regionalism in the field of development issues. First, it is an interesting exercise to examine if there are any WTO-plus technical assistance obligations included in FTAs, especially North–South FTAs. While some literature suggests that a North–South FTA can be an avenue for technical assistance,[5] empirical evidence, particularly evidence based on analysis of binding technical assistance obligations under Asian FTAs, is quite limited.[6] Second, even if the receipt of technical assistance under an FTA occurs in exchange for a high level of general obligations, technical assistance provided by developed FTA partners actually contributes to capacity building in a developing country in a general manner. For example, if a certain developing country signs an FTA in which it commits to a higher level of protection for the intellectual property of its FTA partners, institutions established with technical assistance under the FTA will contribute to the developing country's intellectual property policy in general. In short, a narrowed focus on the reciprocity of obligations (WTO-plus technical assistance obligations on developed members of an FTA versus WTO-plus general obligations on developing members of the FTA) would

level of "flexibility utilization") may be due to the form of technical assistance provided to them. However, Shadlen discusses technical assistance from global institutions such as the World Intellectual Property Organization (WIPO) and not technical assistance under FTAs.

[5] For example, see Hoekman and Schiff (2002). See Stolen (2009) for FTA technical assistance obligations in the field of SPS and TBT.

[6] If there are WTO-plus technical assistance provisions under an FTA, the succeeding research question should be whether or not such WTO-plus technical assistance is due to the higher level of general obligations under the FTA *vis-à-vis* the WTO. While it has been determined that WTO-plus general obligations (e.g., intellectual property protection) are included in some FTAs (Sell, 2009), there is little discussion on WTO-plus technical assistance obligations.

be misleading in the case of technical assistance. We will re-visit this issue in the conclusion (Section 6.7).

The second caveat is related to the study's narrow focus on legal text analysis, which can be classified into two sub-categories. Critics may argue that even the stipulation of binding and specific obligations on technical assistance in an agreement does not guarantee the actual provision of technical assistance. It is true that what is written in the legal text may differ from what will actually be implemented.[7] Nonetheless, a detailed analysis of commitments under FTAs is still critical, especially in the field of technical assistance. From a policy-making perspective, the inclusion of binding and specific technical assistance obligations under FTAs is a good mechanism for developing countries to request and actually receive technical assistance from FTA partner countries, despite the possibility that such an obligation may not be fulfilled.

Another problem of the narrow focus on legal text analysis is opposite to the case above — the fact that obligations on technical assistance are not written in a legal text does not mean that technical assistance is not provided at all. Again, *de jure* technical assistance differs from *de facto* technical assistance, but in a positive manner, in this case. Even if some WTO agreements do not mention the technical assistance obligations of the Secretariat, it may still provide technical assistance to members, for instance, by organizing training courses.[8] Likewise, FTA members may provide technical assistance to partners even if it is not required under an FTA. In fact, even without the signing of FTAs (or any type of treaties), many developing countries provide technical assistance to developing countries. However, *de facto* technical assistance, especially bilateral versus multilateral assistance (e.g., WTO Secretariat), may not be continued in the long-run. Technical assistance backed by legal instruments is more resilient to changes in the external environment.

---

[7] Related to this, some may argue that technical assistance is supply-side driven and does not actually contribute to the recipient's enhanced capacity to draw up necessary policies. See Deere (2005) and Jones, Deere-Birkbeck, and Woods (2010).

[8] See Kostecki (2001) for a discussion on technical assistance programs of the WTO Secretariat. Especially since the WTO Seattle Meeting in 1999, the technical assistance programs for capacity building of the Secretariat has enormously expanded, primarily with the help of voluntary contributions from developed countries as well as some developing countries such as China.

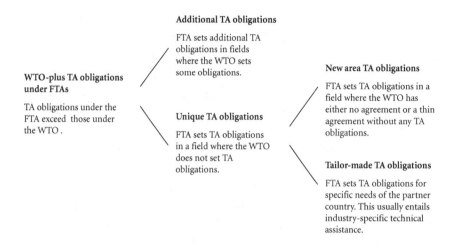

Figure 6.1   WTO-plus technical assistance obligations under FTAs
Note: TA = technical assistance
Source: Author's illustration

6.3.2   Classification of WTO-plus technical assistance and typology of obligations

In conducting a comparative analysis of technical assistance under FTAs and the WTO, we should note that there are two types of WTO-plus technical assistance under FTAs (Figure 6.1). The first type of WTO-plus technical assistance is "additional" technical assistance. When WTO Agreements covering a certain issue area already have some provisions on technical assistance, the additionality that an FTA has in terms of a technical assistance obligation in the same issue area becomes a problem. We should consider whether FTAs bring additional technical assistance obligations to members, akin to the case of tariff liberalization where a preferential tariff is compared with the most favored nation (MFN) tariff (preferential margin).

The second type of WTO-plus technical assistance that FTAs may have is "unique" technical assistance. In this case, FTA sets technical assistance obligations in a field where the WTO does not. Unique technical assistance has two sub-categories. First, when an FTA sets technical assistance obligations in a field where the WTO has either no agreement (e.g., competition) or a thin agreement without any technical assistance obligations (e.g., investment), the FTA has new area technical assistance obligations. As will be discussed later in more detail, this type of technical assistance is evident in the so-called Singapore issues,[9] which have not yet been included in the WTO's purview. Second, when an FTA sets technical assistance obligations based on the specific needs of a partner country, the FTA has tailor-made technical assistance obligations, for example, if a certain FTA includes a binding obligation to provide capacity building programs for the automobile industry. Technical assistance obligations included in each FTA's chapter on cooperation usually fall under the tailor-made category.

How can we assess the significance of additional and unique obligations under each agreement? Abbott *et al.* (2000) identify three critical elements in analyzing the legalization of international relations: (i) the level of binding obligations, (ii) the precision of rules, and (iii) the delegation of power. The first two elements are highly relevant in analyzing obligations regarding technical assistance under FTAs and the WTO.[10] We need to look at whether obligations are binding or not. If the required actions are not compulsory, they may not be implemented. We should also consider whether or not the agreements set out specific obligations. If required actions are not specific and operational, obligations may not be fulfilled as expected. Thus, in total, there are four types of technical assistance: (i) binding and specific, (ii) binding and non-specific, (iii) non-binding and specific, and (iv) non-binding and non-specific (Table 6.1). Note that various combinations of these four types of obligations are also possible. For example, a binding and non-specific obligation, such as "member shall provide technical assistance," can be accompanied by a non-binding and specific obligation, such as "technical assistance may include the organization of seminars and exchange of staff."

---

[9]Investment, competition, trade facilitation, and transparency in government procurement are the four Singapore Issues. Chapters included in FTAs covering the first three issues sometimes include technical assistance.

[10]The third element of legalization is delegation of power, which is also theoretically important. Whether or not a particular dispute settlement mechanism is entitled to make a decision on the implementation of technical assistance obligations is a critical question. However, given that it is unlikely that an FTA member would use a dispute settlement mechanism to provide proof of another party's non-fulfillment of technical assistance obligations under FTAs, the delegation of power will not be discussed in this chapter.

Table 6.1   Examples of binding and specific obligations

	Binding	Non-binding
Specific	"Member shall provide technical assistance through the organization of seminars and exchange of staff."	"Technical assistance may include the organization of seminars and exchange of staff."
Non-Specific	"Member shall provide technical assistance."	"Members shall consider technical assistance "Members shall provide technical assistance, on mutually agreed terms and conditions."

Source: Author's compilation

6.4   Overview on Technical Assistance Provisions under WTO Agreements

As discussed, many agreements under the WTO framework have stipulations on technical assistance. Nine WTO agreements below include some provisions on technical assistance.

(i)   Technical Barriers to Trade (TBT) Agreement
(ii)   Sanitary and Phytosanitary (SPS) Agreement
(iii) Customs Valuation Agreement (CVA)
(iv)   Agreement on Preshipment Inspection (PSI)
(v)   General Agreement on Trade in Services (GATS)
(vi)   Agreement on Trade-related Aspects of Intellectual Property Rights (TRIPS)
(vii) Understanding on Rules and Procedures Governing the Settlement of Disputes (DSU)
(viii) Trade Policy Review Mechanism (TPR)
(ix)   Agreement on Government Procurement (GPA)

Below is the textual analysis of technical assistance provisions for each of the aforementioned WTO agreements.[11] Each agreement's obligations regarding technical assistance are discussed from two different angles. The

---

[11] The WTO Secretariat's website is used as reference in summarizing the background of each WTO agreement.

first angle relates to the comprehensiveness of obligations. The textual analysis will identify what kind of specific actions are required and whether or not they are compulsory. The second angle relates to the scope of concerned parties. Who are the concerned parties with regard to the implementation of the obligations? More specifically, who are the expected providers of technical assistance and who are the expected recipients of technical assistance?

TBT Article 11 "Technical Assistance to Other Members" sets the obligations regarding technical assistance, which fall upon all WTO Members, which means that even developing country Members are expected to provide technical assistance when required. In addition, while special consideration is given to developing country Members as recipients of technical assistance, even developed country Members can be recipients of technical assistance regarding TBT. First, the TBT requests Members to advise other Members on policies regarding various TBT-related issues if requested (the term "on mutually agreed terms and conditions" is not used).[12] The scope of advisory technical assistance includes (i) the preparation of technical regulations; (ii) the establishment of national standardizing bodies, regulatory bodies, conformity assessment bodies, various institutions, and legal frameworks; and (iii) participation in international standardizing bodies. Second, the article also requests that Members grant actual technical assistance on mutually agreed terms and conditions with regard to (i) the establishment of national standardizing bodies, regulatory bodies, conformity assessment bodies, various institutions and legal frameworks; and (ii) participation in international standardizing bodies.[13] Strong language such as "shall … grant [other Members, especially developing country Members] technical assistance" is always accompanied with softening language such as "based on mutually agreed terms and conditions." Thus, if an envisaged technical assistance provider does not agree upon the terms and conditions of technical assistance, such assistance will not

---

[12] Basically, Members shall advise other Members, but in some cases, Members shall take reasonable measures so that advisory assistance is provided by regulatory bodies within their territory (see Article 11.3). Article 11.4 also does not state that Members shall provide advisory assistance. Instead, it requests Members to take reasonable measures.

[13] There is no obligation to grant technical assistance regarding the preparation of technical regulations (Article 11.1).

be granted. In a sense, technical assistance providers can refuse to provide assistance. While such a situation is reasonable because the autonomy and ownership of both technical assistance providers and recipients are important, there is a risk that no technical assistance will be provided under such a weak arrangement (a much stronger and more operational term is used in CVA, for example).

SPS Article 9 "Technical Assistance" sets an obligation to facilitate the provision of technical assistance, not to grant technical assistance, on all WTO Members (Article 9.1). Just like in the case of TBT, the concerned parties involved are all WTO Members, both providers and recipients of technical assistance, though emphasis is placed on developing country Members as recipients. Technical assistance granted under Article 9.1 may take the form of advice, credits, donations, or grants. Financial assistance may also be considered technical assistance under the SPS (other than the SPS, only the TRIPS mentions financial assistance). It also specifically mentions that technical assistance in SPS includes the provision of technical expertise, training, and equipment to allow such countries to adjust to and comply with SPS measures. Article 9.2 stipulates that importing Members shall consider providing technical assistance when substantial investment is required by exporting developing country Members. Article 9.2 also distinguishes exporting from importing countries in order to determine the provider and recipient of technical assistance, not by the distinction between developed and developing country Members. Again, what is required is the consideration, not the actual provision of, technical assistance. Thus, we can maintain our argument that this article's level of ambition is not that high. Partly because the requirement is limited to the facilitation or consideration of technical assistance, the term "on mutually agreed terms and conditions" is not included in the SPS agreement, unlike in the case of the TBT. Given that the level of ambition is low, softening language is not required.

Paragraph 3 in Article 20 of Part III on special and differential treatment of the CVA stipulates the technical assistance obligations of developed country Members, not all WTO Members, in the field of customs valuation. The recipient of technical assistance is limited to developing country Members insofar as this agreement is concerned. The CVA is one of the few agreements under the WTO framework that imposes technical assistance obligations only on developed country Members and limits the recipients to developing country Members (other than the CVA, the TRIPS Agreement has similar provisions). The CVA attempts to address developmental concerns in a direct manner. The obligations imposed on developed country Members are also very clear in this agreement. While the first half of Paragraph 3 mentions the provision of technical assistance on mutually agreed terms and conditions, the second half of the article stipulates specific operational requests. It states that developed country Members shall draw up programs of technical assistance that may include the training of personnel, assistance in preparing implementation measures, access to sources of information regarding customs valuation methodology, and advice on the application of the provisions of the agreement.

Many developing countries conduct preshipment inspections on prospective imports before they are shipped from the exporting country,[14] mainly because the capacity of some developing country's customs services is often not enough to perform the full range of customs functions. The private companies that carry out the inspections verify that the price, exchange rate, financial terms, quantity, quality, and customs classification of the transaction are consistent with what was ordered. PSI provides that such processes should not give rise to unnecessary delays or unequal treatment. It establishes an agreed upon set of transparent procedures, including deadlines for inspections, and creates an independent and impartial review body to resolve disputes between importers and preshipment inspection companies. "Article 3: Obligation of Exporter Members" of PSI includes a provision on technical assistance (Paragraph 3). What is unique about the PSI is that it uses the concept of exporter Members and user Members of preshipment inspection to define the rights and obligations of Members, including technical assistance ($c.f.$ Article 9.2. of the SPS). A user Member is defined as "a Member of which the government or any government body contracts for or mandates the use of preshipment inspection activities" (Article 1.1). With regard to the required actions, upon request exporter Members shall offer to provide (not "shall provide") on mutually agreed terms to user Members of preshipment inspection, which are usually developing country Members, technical assistance directed toward the achievement of the

---

[14]The Preamble of the Agreement on Preshipment Inspection states that "noting that a number of developing country Members have recourse to preshipment inspection ... ."

objectives of the agreement. A footnote in the agreement indicates that technical assistance may be given on a bilateral, plurilateral, or multilateral basis.

GATS Article XXV is on technical cooperation, which includes two paragraphs, each paragraph comprising only one sentence. Article XXV:1 stipulates the use of a contact point with a special reference to Article IV:2. GATS Article IV:2 (Increasing Participation of Developing Countries) states that developed country Members, and other Members to the extent possible,[15] shall establish contact points to facilitate access for developing country Members' services suppliers to information that relates to their respective markets.[16] Meanwhile, Article XXV:1 states that the services suppliers of Members, which is not limited to suppliers in developing country Members,[17] that are in need of technical assistance shall have access to the contact points. Article XXV:2 calls for the provision of technical assistance to developing country Members by the WTO Secretariat on a multilateral basis, with decisions made by the Council of Trade in Services. First, the parties that receives technical assistance are developing country Members and not developing country Members' services suppliers as is the case under Article XXV:1. It is important to note that the scope is limited to developing country Members and not all Members. Second, the party providing technical assistance is the Secretariat and not (developed country) Members. Thus, there are no mandatory rules or methods of cooperation imposed on developed country Members under this provision.[18] The obligation of the Secretariat to provide technical assistance is multilateral and not automatic since it is subject to the decision of the Council for Trade in Services.

The TRIPS contains provisions that allow a degree of flexibility and sufficient room for countries to accommodate their own patent and intellectual property systems, and developmental needs. Article 67: Technical

---

[15] It is possible to argue that the obligation is imposed only on developed country Members. For more details, see Footer and George (2005).

[16] These include (i) commercial and technical aspects of the supply of services; (ii) registration, recognition, and obtaining of professional qualifications; and (iii) availability of services technology.

[17] Nartova (2008).

[18] Nartova (2008).

cooperation requires developed country Members, if requested, to provide technical and financial cooperation to developing country Members on mutually agreed terms and conditions. The developmental dimension is clear in this agreement because the technical assistance providers are limited to developed country Members and the recipients are developing country Members. What is unique in the TRIPS agreement is that financial assistance is mentioned in parallel with technical assistance. Except for the TRIPS agreement, the SPS agreement is the only other agreement that mentions financial assistance. Article 67 also specifies the measures by which technical assistance is to be provided in terms of intellectual property issues. Cooperation in this field shall include assistance in the preparation of laws and regulations on the protection and enforcement of intellectual property rights and the prevention of their abuse, and support regarding the establishment or reinforcement of domestic offices and agencies relevant to these matters, including the training of personnel.

The DSU (Annex 2 of the Marrakesh Agreement) introduced greater discipline in the length of time needed to settle a case (with flexible deadlines set at various stages of the procedure) than old GATT by setting out the details for the procedures and the timetable to be followed in resolving disputes. Article 27: Responsibilities of the Secretariat of the DSU is the only article under this agreement that mentions technical assistance. This seems only natural since, irrespective of their level of development, Members may have a dispute with one another and imposing technical assistance obligations on only one Member (even a developed country Member) would be counterintuitive. The Secretariat, which maintains a neutral position, has the technical assistance obligation. The scope of technical assistance stipulated under this article includes the provision of legal advice (Article 27.2). Experts are the ones actually providing legal services to developing country Members and the responsibility of the Secretariat is to make available a qualified legal expert from the WTO and to monitor the experts' technical assistance in order to ensure the impartiality of the services rendered by these experts. The recipients of legal advisory services are limited to developing country Members (*c.f.* Article 27.3). The Secretariat is also expected to conduct special training courses on dispute settlement procedures and practices for interested Members (Article 27.3). In this case, the beneficiaries of the training courses were all interested Members of the WTO, including developed country Members. Strong language such as "the

Secretariat shall conduct special training courses" appears in Article 27.3 absent any softening language such as "mutually agreed terms and conditions."

Annex 3 (Trade Policy Review Mechanism) of the Marrakesh Agreement is a three-page document without a dedicated article to technical assistance or developmental issues. However, Paragraph D includes language on technical assistance, although the stipulation is very general. It states that the Secretariat has the responsibility for providing TPR technical assistance. In order to ensure the neutrality of the policy debate, technical assistance relating to TPR should be provided by the Secretariat and not by Members. This is similar to the DSU since Members may have disputes with one another even at the TPR sessions. Although the stipulation is not as clear as that of the DSU, the responsibility of the Secretariat is to make available technical assistance to developing country Members.[19]

GPA is a plurilateral agreement under the WTO framework that is applicable only to the signatories to this particular agreement.[20] While current signatories are limited to developed country Members or middle-income developing country Members, it has an article on "Special and Differential Treatment for Developing Countries," and its subsection, "Technical Assistance for Developing Country Parties," includes three paragraphs on technical assistance (Paragraph 8, 9, and 10). The obligation lies on developed country Parties (not developed country Members of the WTO), while the recipients of technical assistance are limited to developing country Parties (not developing country Members of the WTO). The most distinctive feature of GPA in terms of technical assistance is that the provision of assistance is not based on "mutually agreed terms and conditions." No such term, which is common in other WTO agreements, can be found in this agreement. Thus, when technical assistance on government procurement is required by developing country Parties, developed

---

[19]This is because unlike in the case of the DSU, the TPR makes no mention of experts. The agreement states that the Secretariat shall make available technical assistance in response to requests from developing country Members, particularly least-developed country Members.

[20]While the number of signatories was limited to 23 when this agreement was launched after the Uruguay Round, as of January 2013 there were 42 countries (or economies) who are signatories to the agreement. Most signatories are developed country Members or developing country Members that have already achieved middle income status.

country Parties shall provide all technical assistance deemed appropriate. The level of automaticity is higher in this agreement than in other WTO agreements. The scope of technical assistance is also very specific. Technical assistance that aims to solve technical problems relating to the awarding of a specific contract is of particular importance. It also includes translation of qualification documentation and tenders made by suppliers of developing country parties into an official language of the WTO (English, French, Spanish) as designated by the entity. If developed country Parties deem such translation to be burdensome, this obligation can be exempted if an explanation is provided to developing country Parties and/or their entities (Paragraph 10).

Finally, some agreements under the WTO system do not touch upon technical assistance including the (i) Agreement on Trade-related Investment Measures (TRIMs),[21] (ii) Agreement on Subsidies and Countervailing Measures, and (iii) Agreement on Safeguards.[22] Thus, when the chapters of an FTA covering these issues include technical assistance obligations, they become unique technical assistance (new area technical assistance) obligations as defined in Section 6.3. Also, the WTO system does not include agreements in several fields that have a major impact on international trade. Customs procedures and competition,[23] which are two of the four Singapore issues, are illustrative examples.

The empirical findings of the analysis above are summarized in Table 6.2. The providers and recipients of technical assistance vary from one Agreement to another. There are three main types of agreement. First, in the case of TBT and SPS, all WTO Members are expected to provide technical assistance. In this case, all Members can be a recipient as well, but

---

[21] TRIMs is a thin agreement covering only trade related aspects of investment. Investment was supposed to be included in the negotiation agenda of the WTO Doha Round, but was excluded after the Cancun Ministerial Meeting in 2003.

[22] However, the absence of stipulations on obligations regarding technical assistance does not mean that there is no actual technical assistance given. For example, there are many capacity building training courses organized by the WTO Secretariat focusing on anti-dumping and subsidies, which target developing country officials, particularly in least developed countries.

[23] The existing agreements relating to customs cover only limited areas of customs administration. The CVA covers only customs valuation issues while the Agreement on Preshipment Inspection covers only preshipment inspection issues.

Table 6.2 Technical assistance obligations under WTO agreements

	Technical Assistance Obligations			Concerned Parties	
	Required Actions	"On mutually agreed terms"	Specific Form of Technical Assistance	Provider	Recipient
TBT	Shall advise	Not used	No further explanation on advise	All members	All members, especially developing member
	Shall grant technical assistance	Used	Not mentioned	All members	All members, especially developing members
SPS	Agree to facilitate the provision of technical assistance	Not used	May take the form of advice, credits, donations, and grants for the purpose of training personnel	All members	All members, especially developing members
	Shall consider providing technical assistance	Not used	Not mentioned	Importing members	Exporting developing members
CVA	Shall furnish and draw up programs of technical assistance	Used	May include training personnel	Developed members	Developing members
PSI	Shall offer to provide technical assistance	Used	Not mentioned	Exporter members	User members

(*Continued*)

Table 6.2   (*Continued*)

	Technical Assistance Obligations			Concerned Parties	
	Required Actions	"On mutually agreed terms"	Specific Form of Technical Assistance	Provider	Recipient
GATS	Shall provide technical assistance	Not used	Not mentioned	Secretariat	Developing members
TRIPS	Shall provide technical and financial assistance	Used	Shall include training personnel	Developed members	Developing members
DSU	Shall make available a qualified legal expert	Not used	The obligations in the left column are already specific	Secretariat	Developing members
	Shall conduct special training courses	Not used	The obligations in the left column are already specific	Secretariat	All members
TPR	Shall make available technical assistance	Not used	Not mentioned	Secretariat	Developing members
GPA	Shall provide all technical assistance	Not used	Translation of qualification documents and tenders	Developed Parties	Developing Parties

Source: Author's compilation

special emphasis is placed on developing country Members as recipients of technical assistance. Next, in the case of the CVA, the TRIPS Agreement, and the GPA, only developed country Members (or Parties) are required to provide technical assistance and only developing country Members (or Parties) can receive technical assistance. Finally, in the case of the GATS, DSU, and TPR Mechanism, the Secretariat is the provider of technical assistance and only developing country Members can be recipients, except in the case of the DSU where all Members can be beneficiaries.

The level of binding and specificity of technical assistance obligations seems to depend on who is the expected provider of technical assistance. When technical assistance is provided by the Secretariat, the obligations are binding and softening language such as "on mutually agreed terms and conditions" is not used. Moreover, required actions by the Secretariat are sometimes very specific, as in the case of the DSU, which requires the Secretariat to organize special training courses on dispute settlement. However, when technical assistance obligations fall on WTO Members, a strong term such as "shall provide technical assistance" is usually accompanied by softening language ("on mutually agreed terms and conditions") and the obligations become less binding. There are some agreements that include technical assistance obligations without such softening language. However, in these cases the technical assistance obligations are not required at the outset, and the scope is limited to the provision of advice and consideration (e.g., terms such as "shall advise," "shall consider," or "agree to facilitate" are used). With regard to the specificity of the obligation, the specific forms of technical assistance are always mentioned if the expected providers of technical assistance are developed country Members (CVA and TRIPS).[24] In contrast, the specific forms of technical assistance are usually not mentioned if the expected providers of technical assistance are all WTO Members (TBT).[25] Thus, the TRIPS Agreement is the only agreement that has binding and specific obligations on developed country Members in the form of a combination of a non-binding and non-specific obligation, and

---

[24] While the CVA uses the term "may include," the TRIPS Agreement uses "shall include" to spell out the possible forms of technical assistance.

[25] However, the SPS Agreement mentions specific forms of providing technical assistance.

a binding and specific obligation, although it mentions only training as a specific type of technical assistance.[26]

Based on the empirical analysis above, the technical assistance obligations of developed country Members under the WTO system are very limited, thereby supporting the argument that "the developing countries undertook to implement *bound* commitments in exchange for *unbound* commitments for assistance" (Finger and Winter, 2002, p. 51).[27]

6.5   Case Study: Technical Assistance under Japan–ASEAN EPAs

This section analyzes technical assistance obligations under FTAs, including additional, new area, and tailor-made obligations. Specifically, this section will examine technical assistance obligations under the economic partnership agreements (EPAs) between Japan and the Association of Southeast Asian Nations (ASEAN).

Japan–ASEAN EPAs are useful case studies for three reasons. First, substantial empirical studies on technical assistance under Asian economic agreements are lacking when compared with literature on technical assistance under agreements in Europe and North America.[28] Second, North–South FTAs generally have significant potential for technical assistance obligations (Hoekman and Schiff, 2002). Therefore, reviewing Japanese agreements with its Asian neighbors is relevant since such agreements are expected to include some technical assistance programs given Japan's level of development.[29] Finally, since Japan has signed bilateral EPAs with several ASEAN countries, a comparative analysis of these agreements

---

[26] In the case of the GPA, technical assistance providers are limited to its contracting Parties since the GPA is a plurilateral and not a multilateral agreement. The GPA imposes binding and specific obligations on Parties (non-specific and binding, and non-binding and specific).

[27] Also see Finger and Shuler (2002).

[28] See for example the discussion of Roffe *et al.* (2007) on technical assistance in the field of intellectual property under North–South FTAs in the Americas.

[29] Other North–South FTAs and EPAs in Asia, such as the EPA between Australia, New Zealand, and ASEAN, include substantial technical assistance obligations. Moreover, the agreement between China and ASEAN also includes some technical assistance, despite the fact that all parties are developing countries. Comparative analysis of technical assistance obligations under various FTAs and EPAs in Asia, especially South–South agreements (e.g., ASEAN–China), is an important topic for future research.

would be an interesting exercise. Specifically, it will be determined if the following proposition can be empirically supported: the lower the economic development of Japan's EPA partner, the greater the amount of technical assistance obligations included in the EPA between Japan and that country.

In the textual analysis below, underlines are supplied to highlight the difference in obligations across various agreements and articles.

6.5.1 Japan–Malaysia EPA (JMEPA)

Additional technical assistance under JMEPA. The SPS chapter (Chapter 6) in JMEPA includes binding and specific obligations of technical assistance. The chapter uses language such as "shall develop cooperation," while softening language such as "on mutually agreed terms and conditions" is not used. Strong language is also included such as "both countries shall cooperate . . . including capacity building, technical assistance, and exchange of experts" (Chapter 6, Article 70). Thus, JMEPA imposes binding and specific obligations on the contracting parties in terms of technical assistance in the area of SPS.

Meanwhile, the TBT chapter (Chapter 5) uses "shall cooperate" but also includes weaker words in determining the scope of technical assistance: "such cooperation may include: (a) joint studies, seminars, and symposia" (Article 64). Thus, while the requirements are specific, they are not binding. Likewise, the intellectual property chapter (Chapter 9) uses "shall cooperate" but also states that the forms of cooperation can be set forth in the Implementing Agreement. While some details are provided in the Implementing Agreement, it states that "the forms of cooperation may include . . . (ii) undertaking training and exchange of expert" (Implementing Agreement, Chapter 3, Article 10). Thus, technical assistance requirements regarding SPS and intellectual property are specific and not binding.

New area technical assistance under JMEPA. While investment, customs procedures, and competition are either not covered by a specific WTO agreement or are covered by only a very thin agreement without any technical assistance provisions, JMEPA includes technical assistance provisions in these fields. The customs procedures chapter (Chapter 4) uses the term "shall cooperate" while softening language, such as "on mutually agreed terms and conditions," is not included (Article 56). It also mentions specific modes of providing technical assistance or capacity building such as "exchange of experts." The chapter uses strong terms such as "the area of cooperation... shall include capacity building, such as training, technical assistance, and exchange of experts" (Article 57).[30] Thus, it can be said that JMEPA imposes binding and specific technical assistance obligations on the contracting parties in the area of customs procedures.

Meanwhile, the investment chapter (Chapter 7, Article 92) uses "shall cooperate," but also includes weaker language to limit the scope of activities: "through ways such as: (1) discussing effective ways on investment promotion activities and capacity building...." No further detailed stipulation on technical assistance in investment issues is provided in JMEPA or its Implementing Agreement, making it both non-binding and non-specific. In contrast, the chapter on controlling anti-competitive activities (Chapter 10) also uses "shall cooperate," with details provided in the Implementing Agreement. Article 13 (Technical Cooperation) of the Implementing Agreement says that "the Governments agree that it is in their common interest... to work together in technical cooperation activities." It also mentions the scope of activities using the term "may include... (a) exchange of implementing authorities' personnel for training purposes...." Thus, in the case of competition, JMEPA has a non-binding and specific obligation.

Tailor-made technical assistance under JMEPA. Chapter 12 of JMEPA focuses on cooperation. Article 139: Basic Principles says that the governments shall promote cooperation, while Article 140: Fields of Cooperation states that such cooperation shall include cooperation in eight areas: (i) agriculture, forestry, fisheries, and plantations; (ii) education and human resource development; (iii) information and communications technology; (iv) science and technology; (v) small and medium-sized enterprises;

---

[30]In the case of TBT (Chapter 5), it simply says that cooperation may include technical assistance and is thus not specific.

(vi) tourism; (vii) environment; and (viii) other fields to be mutually agreed upon by the government. The forms of cooperation are provided for in the Implementing Agreement. Chapter 6 of the Implementing Agreement focuses on cooperation, with each section of the chapter stipulating specific areas of cooperation by using the term "the area of cooperation under this section shall include..." and then listing the method of cooperation by using the term "forms of cooperation under this section may include...." For example, the exchange of experts and holding of seminars and workshops are mentioned as a form of cooperation. Accordingly, the obligations are binding and specific enough for the contracting parties (*c.f.* EPA between Japan and ASEAN countries other than Malaysia).[31] Table 6.3 provides a summary of cooperation under the seven fields specified in Article 140.

The chapter on trade in goods (Chapter 2) has a specific provision on cooperation in the automobile industry. Article 26: Cooperation in the Automobile Industry states that the two countries shall cooperate, with the participation of their respective automotive industries, to further enhance the competitiveness of the automotive industry in Malaysia. A technical assistance obligation that addresses a particular industry makes this EPA unique. The technical assistance mechanism also involves the private sectors in each country. At the same time, the assistance is not reciprocal as only Malaysia is the beneficiary of the technical assistance.

6.5.2 Japan–Indonesia EPA (JIEPA)

Additional technical assistance under JIEPA. JIEPA does not have chapters on TBT or SPS, two areas in which technical assistance plays an important role under WTO Agreements. Thus, no obligations can be found in JIEPA that go beyond those included in the WTO Agreements.

The intellectual property chapter (Chapter 9, Article 122) uses the term "shall cooperate," but it also states that the forms of cooperation can be set forth in the Implementing Agreement. Some details are provided in the Implementing Agreement such as "the forms of cooperation

---

[31] The term "the area of cooperation under this section may include" is used.

Table 6.3   Areas of cooperation under the implementing agreement for JMEPA

Sections	Areas of cooperation
Agriculture, Forestry, Fisheries, and Plantations	(i) sound development of food industries; (ii) efficient and sustainable utilization of natural resources; (iii) human resource development related to agriculture, forestry, fisheries, and plantations; (iv) development and promotion of technologies relating to agriculture, forestry, fisheries, and plantations; and food processing and distribution; and (v) development of rural areas
Education and Human Resource Development	(i) higher education, (ii) development of human resources with advanced knowledge and skills, (iii) technical and vocational training;, (iv) young people's mutual understanding, (v) occupational safety and health, and (vi) Japanese language education
Information and Communications Technology (ICT)	(i) next-generation internet, broadband networks, and ubiquitous networks; (ii) use of ICT-related services; (iii) electronic commerce, including procedures for accreditation of certification authorities for electronic signature; (iv) circulation of digital content over broadband networks; (v) human resource development relating to ICT, including skill standards; and (vi) collaboration on ICT research and development
Science and Technology	(i) science and technology suitable to provide a basis for industrial development, (ii) development of human resources with advanced knowledge and skills, and (iii) efficient utilization of natural resources
Small- and Medium-sized Enterprises (SMEs)	(i) strengthened management and competitiveness of SMEs, and (ii) human resource development relating to SMEs
Tourism	(i) tourism promotion, (ii) human resource development in the tourism sector, and (iii) sustainable development in the tourism sector
Environment	(i) conservation and improvement of the environment, and (ii) promotion of sustainable development

Source: Author's compilation

may include ... (ii) undertaking training and exchanging of experts ..."
(Implementing Agreement, Chapter 4, Article 10).

New area technical assistance under JIEPA. JIEPA includes a chapter on customs procedures that does not mention technical assistance. Likewise,

JIEPA includes an investment chapter but it does not mention technical assistance either. Thus, JIEPA does not impose technical assistance obligations in the fields of customs procedures or investment.

The competition chapter (Chapter 11) simply states that the parties shall cooperate on the promotion of competition (Article 127). The Implementing Agreement (Chapter 5: Competition, Article 15: Technical Cooperation) stipulates that the forms of technical cooperation in support of capacity building "shall be (a) exchange of personnel of the competition authorities for training purposes; (b) participation of personnel of the competition authorities as lecturers or consultants at training courses; and (c) assistance by the competition authority of a Party to the advocacy and educational campaign of the competition authority of the other Party for the consumers, business sector, and related agencies of its Country." Thus, JIEPA includes binding and specific technical assistance obligations with respect to competition.

Tailor-Made Technical Assistance under JIEPA. Chapter 13 of JIEPA focuses on cooperation. Article 134: Basic Principle states that "parties shall promote cooperation" in nine fields: (i) manufacturing industries; (ii) agriculture, forestry, and fisheries; (iii) trade and investment promotion; (iv) human resource development; (v) tourism; (vi) information and communications technology; (vii) financial services; (viii) government procurement; and (ix) environment. It also states that the forms of cooperation outlined in the chapter may be set forth in the Implementing Agreement (Article 135). The Implementing Agreement has a chapter on cooperation as well (Chapter 7) and each section stipulates "the area of cooperation under this section may include . . ." and then lists the forms of cooperation by using the term "forms of cooperation under this section may include . . .," with specific modes of supplying technical assistance being mentioned (c.f. JMEPA uses the following language: "the area of cooperation under this section shall include . . ."). Table 6.4 is the summary of specific areas of cooperation under the nine fields covered by the Implementing Agreement for JIEPA.

JIEPA calls for the establishment of an Initiative for Manufacturing Industry Development Center to enhance the competitiveness of Indonesian industries. The Joint Statement at the signing of the EPA between Japan and the Republic of Indonesia included the following

Table 6.4   Areas of cooperation under the implementing agreement for JIEPA

Sections	Areas of Cooperation
Manufacturing Industries	(i) strengthened competitiveness of manufacturing industries, including management, technology, research and development, and industrial standards; (ii) human resource development related to manufacturing industries; and (iii) improved manufacturing industry infrastructure
Agriculture, Forestry, and Fisheries	(i) efficient and sustainable utilization of natural resources; (ii) human resource development related to agriculture, forestry, and fisheries; (iii) development and promotion of technologies related to agriculture, forestry, and fisheries; (iv) improvement of market infrastructure, including the gathering and dissemination of market information related to agriculture and fisheries; (v) improvement of productivity and quality in the field of agriculture, forestry, and fisheries; and (vi) fostering the well-being of people in rural areas
Human Resource Development	(i) development of human resources with advanced knowledge and skills; and (ii) technical and vocational training
Tourism	(i) promotion of tourism, (ii) human resource development related to tourism, and (iii) sustainable development of tourism
Information Communications Technology (ICT)	(i) next-generation internet, and broadband and ubiquitous networks; (ii) use of ICT-related services; (iii) electronic commerce, including procedures for accreditation of certification authorities for electronic signatures; (iv) circulation of digital content over broadband networks; (v) further development of network infrastructure, including telecommunications centers, in rural areas; (vi) human resource development related to ICT; (vii) collaboration on ICT research and development; and (viii) disaster management using ICT, including tsunami warning systems
Financial Services	(i) implementation of sound prudential policies, and enhancement of effective supervision of financial institutions of a country operating in the other country; (ii) proper response to issues relating to globalization in financial services; (iii) maintenance of an environment that does not stifle legitimate financial market innovations; and (iv) supervision of global financial institutions to minimize systemic risks and limit contagion effects in the event of crises

(Continued)

Table 6.4   (*Continued*)

Sections	Areas of Cooperation
Environment	(i) conservation and improvement of the environment and (ii) promotion of sustainable development including measures to address climate change such as clean development mechanisms

Note: Trade and investment promotion, and government procurement are not mentioned in the Implementing Agreement for JIEPA
Source: Author's compilation

language:

> Especially, in the long-term framework of "Initiative for Manufacturing Industry Development Center," the two governments will jointly work to enhance the competitiveness of the Indonesian manufacturing industry in various sectors, namely, Metalworking, Tooling (Mold & Die) Technique, Welding Technique, Energy Conservation, Small and Medium-sized Enterprise Promotion Support, Export and Investment Promotion, Automotive/Auto parts, Electric/Electronic Equipment, Steel/Steel Products, Textile, Petrochemical, Oleo-chemical, Non Ferrous, and Food & Beverages. In order to implement cooperation projects, various schemes will be considered — Basic Study, Dispatchment of Expert, Provision of Equipment, Training, Seminar/Workshop, and Visiting Japanese Companies — based on the shared understanding of the two governments on the necessity and feasibility of projects in each sector.[32]

Thus, even though the main body of the Agreement does not mention technical assistance in specific industries the problem can be addressed in the negotiations on EPAs, and commitments on the provision of technical assistance can be mentioned in a political statement, which seems to be sufficient for developing countries seeking capacity building in a particular industry.

Chapter 8 of JIEPA is on energy and mining. Article 104: Cooperation states that both parties shall cooperate in the energy and mining sectors of Indonesia. It also says that areas of cooperation under this article shall include policy development, capacity building, and technology transfer. It is

---

[32]The Joint Statement is available at http://www.mofa.go.jp/region/asia-paci/indonesia/epa0708/joint.html

interesting to note that this article mentions technology transfer specifically, unlike in the case of technical assistance to the automobile industry in Malaysia under JMEPA.

Another example of sector-specific technical assistance under JIEPA can be found in the movement of natural persons. While the chapter on this subject (Chapter 7) does not include a stipulation on technical assistance, Annex 10: Specific Commitments for the Movement of Natural Persons states that "the Government of Japan shall notify the Government of Indonesia of the modalities and other related information on the training" (Section 6).[33] In practice, this has led to Japan organizing a 6-month course on the Japanese language for Indonesian applicants who satisfy the requirements for nurses and certified caregivers.

6.5.3   Japan–Philippines EPA (JPEPA)

Additional technical assistance under JPEPA. Just like in the case of JIEPA, JPEPA does not have chapters on TBT or SPS,[34] two areas in which technical assistance plays an important role under the relevant WTO Agreements.

The intellectual property chapter (Chapter 10) is the only chapter that includes the terms technical assistance or capacity building, with the exception of the chapter on cooperation. Chapter 10 states that parties shall develop and strengthen their cooperation in the field of intellectual property (Article 117) and specific modes of providing technical assistance are listed: "areas and forms of cooperation . . . may include, but not be limited to . . . (e) organizing international symposiums, workshops and fairs . . ." (Article 119). Thus, JPEPA has specific obligations related to intellectual property, but these are not binding.

New area technical assistance under JPEPA. JPEPA includes a chapter on customs procedures (Chapter 4), but the chapter does not mention technical assistance or capacity building. Likewise, JPEPA includes a chapter on investment (Chapter 8), but it also does not include any stipulation for technical assistance.

---

[33] In the case of JPEPA, the same words can be found in the Implementing Agreement for the EPA.

[34] The chapter on mutual recognition (Chapter 6) of JPEPA includes some elements of TBT-related issues. However, Chapter 6 does not mention technical assistance.

Chapter 12 of JPEPA covers competition and Article 136: Cooperation on Promoting Competition by Addressing Anti-Competitive Activities states that "the Parties shall . . . cooperate in the field of promoting
competition by addressing anti-competitive activities . . ." The details and
procedures of cooperation are provided in the Implementing Agreement,
which has an article on technical assistance in the field of competition
(Article 13) that lists specific modes of providing technical assistance that
can be utilized, such as exchange of personnel for training purposes (e.g.,
"technical cooperation activities . . . may include . . ."). Thus, JPEPA has
non-binding and specific requirements for technical assistance in the field
of competition.

Tailor-made technical assistance under JPEPA. Chapter 14 of the JPEPA
focuses on cooperation. Article 144: Basic Principle states that "Parties
shall promote cooperation" and it enumerates 10 areas for such cooperation: (i) human resource development, (ii) financial services, (iii) information and communications technology, (iv) energy and environment,
(v) science and technology, (vi) trade and investment promotion, (vii)
small and medium-sized enterprises, (viii) tourism, (ix) transportation,
and (x) road development. Avenues for cooperation are provided in Chapters 4–13 of the Implementing Agreement, with each chapter stipulating
"the area of cooperation under this section may include . . ." and then listing
the possible forms of cooperation by using the term "forms of cooperation
under this section may include . . .." The language is similar to that of JIEPA
and unlike JMEPA. Table 6.5 is the summary of the specific areas of cooperation under the 10 fields.

While the chapter on the movement of natural persons in JPEPA
(Chapter 9) does not include any stipulation on technical assistance, details
are provided in the Implementing Agreement. Specifically, Chapter 2,
Article 10: Movement of Natural Persons covers training by stating that
"the Government of Japan shall notify the Government of the Philippines
of the modalities and other related information on training." Just like in
the case of JIEPA,[35] Japan shall organize a six-month language and culture
course for Philippine applicants who satisfy the travel requirements.

---

[35]In the case of JIEPA, the same words can be found in the Annex of the EPA.

Table 6.5   Areas of cooperation under the implementing agreement for JPEPA

Sections	Areas of Cooperation
Human Resource Development	(i) language training and education on culture and social values, (ii) education and training, (iii) development of human resources with knowledge and skills at an advanced level, and (iv) harmonization of competency standards
Financial Services	(i) regulatory cooperation in the field of financial services, (ii) development of financial markets among the parties and in the Asian region, and (iii) improvement of financial market infrastructure among the parties including enhancing capabilities in monitoring financial and other relevant transactions arising from a liberalized trading environment
Information and Communications Technology (ICT)	(i) next-generation internet and broadband and ubiquitous networks, (ii) use of ICT and ICT-related services, (iii) electronic commerce including procedures of accreditation of certification authorities for electronic signatures, (iv) circulation of digital content over broadband networks, (v) human resource development relating to ICT including skill standards, (vi) promotion of information exchange on development of technology, and (vii) encouragement of research and development
Energy and Environment	(i) improvement of energy utilization and (ii) protection and management of environment
Science and Technology	(i) advanced science and technology; (ii) agriculture, forestry, fisheries, and management of natural resources; and (iii) human health and nutrition
Trade and Investment Promotion	(i) exchange of views and information on trade and investment; (ii) encouraging potential investors to use the JETRO Business Support Center in the Philippines, Invest Japan Business Support Centers, and other related facilities operated by JETRO, the Department of Trade and Industry of the Philippines, and its attached agencies; (iii) seminars and other events for further expansion of trade and investment; (iv) exchange of experts, specialists, trainees, and researchers, which may include government officials, to promote knowledge on trade and investment; (v) information exchanges on the investment environment and laws and regulations related to business to promote further trade and investment and relevant business operations between the parties; and (vi) contacts between relevant government agencies and entities to maximize the benefits of cooperation
Small and Medium-sized Enterprises (SMEs)	(i) strengthened management and competitiveness of SMEs, and (ii) human resource development relating to SMEs

(*Continued*)

Table 6.5 (*Continued*)

Sections	Areas of Cooperation
Tourism	(i) promotion and development of tourism, and (ii) human resource development
Transportation	(i) improvement of technology of transportation, and (ii) human resource development
Road Development	(i) improvement of the technology of road development, and (ii) human resource development

JETRO = Japan External Trade Organization
Source: Author's compilation

6.5.4   *Japan–Singapore EPA (JSEPA)*

Additional technical assistance under JSEPA. The scope of JSEPA is limited and it does not have a chapter on SPS or TBT,[36] two areas in which technical assistance plays an important role under WTO Agreements.

JSEPA's chapter on intellectual property (Chapter 10) has specific stipulations on technical assistance. Article 96: Areas and Forms of Cooperation lists possible forms of cooperation such as training and the exchange of experts. Because it uses the term "the form of cooperation...may include...," the requirement is non-binding.

New area technical assistance under JSEPA. While JSEPA has a chapter on customs procedures (Chapter 4), technical assistance is not mentioned. JSEPA includes two chapters on investment, Chapters 8 (investment) and 17 (trade and investment promotion). However, neither makes any mention of technical assistance in the field of investment policies.

The chapter on competition (Chapter 12) states that the parties shall cooperate in controlling anti-competitive activities (Article 104), with the details set forth in the Implementing Agreement. The Implementing Agreement includes an article on technical assistance in the field of competition policies (Chapter 5, Article 19), which states that "each party may render technical assistance to the other party for the effective management and

---

[36]The chapter on mutual recognition (Chapter 6) of JSEPA includes some elements of TBT-related issues. However, Chapter 6 does not mention technical assistance.

adoption of laws and regulations controlling anti-competitive activities." However, this is not a binding requirement and no specific mode of technical assistance is mentioned.

Tailor-made technical assistance under JSEPA. What is unique in JSEPA is that the Agreement has a chapter on human resource development (Chapter 16). While Agreements between Japan and other ASEAN economies have a chapter on cooperation that includes various items, including human resource development, JSEPA has a chapter specifically focusing on how to develop human resources in the two countries' research and government sectors, putting emphasis on mutual assistance. Article 124 in Chapter 16 states "the parties shall promote exchanges of their government officials with a view to mutual understanding of the policies of their respective governments." While the requests for action are specific, they are not binding.

6.5.5   *Japan–Thailand EPA (JTEPA)*

Additional technical assistance under JTEPA. JTEPA does not include chapters on TBT or SPS,[37] two areas in which technical assistance is common under WTO Agreements. JTEPA has a substantial chapter on intellectual property (Chapter 10), which has 23 articles in total. However, technical assistance is not mentioned.

New area technical assistance under JTEPA. JTEPA includes a chapter on customs procedures (Chapter 4), although technical assistance is not mentioned. However, the Implementing Agreement (Chapter 1, Article 1) states that "the Parties shall cooperate through their customs authorities, when necessary and appropriate, in the area of research, development, and testing of new customs procedures and new enforcement aids and techniques, training activities of customs officers and exchange of personnel between them." Thus, binding and specific obligations are imposed on the contracting parties by JTEPA. Although the term "when appropriate" is used, the level of obligation is high.

Investment and competition are covered in JTEPA. However, the investment chapter (Chapter 8) and the competition chapter (Chapter 12)

---

[37]The chapter on mutual recognition (Chapter 6) of JTEPA includes some TBT-related issues. However, Chapter 6 does not mention technical assistance.

of JTEPA do not make any mention of technical assistance or capacity building.

Tailor-made technical assistance under JTEPA. Chapter 13 of JTEPA focuses on cooperation. Article 152: Basic Principles states that "the Parties shall promote cooperation between the Governments of the Parties" and enumerates nine fields: (i) agriculture, forestry, and fisheries; (ii) education and human resource development; (iii) enhancement of the business environment; (iv) financial services; (v) information and communications technology; (vi) science, technology, energy and the environment; (vii) small and medium-sized enterprises; (viii) tourism; and (ix) trade and investment promotion. Nine chapters in the Implementing Agreement (Chapters 5–13) provide details on cooperation in the aforementioned fields. Each section stipulates "the areas of cooperation under this section include..." and then the "forms of cooperation under this section include...." Neither "may" nor "shall" is used before the word "include." For example, the exchange of experts and holding of seminars and workshops are mentioned as forms of cooperation. Accordingly, the obligations are binding and specific for the contracting parties. Table 6.6 provides a summary of the specific areas of cooperation provided for in the Implementing Agreement.

6.5.6   *Japan–Vietnam EPA (JVEPA)*

Additional technical assistance under JVEPA. The chapter on TBT (Chapter 6) in JVEPA includes an article on cooperation (Article 53), which states that parties shall cooperate in the field of TBT. The article also mentions seminars and exchange of officials as possible forms of cooperation by using the term "the forms of cooperation . . . may include . . . ." Thus, the TBT chapter in JVEPA imposes specific but non-binding obligations. In contrast, the chapter on SPS (Chapter 5) does not include an article on cooperation nor does it mention technical assistance.

JVEPA includes a chapter on intellectual property (Chapter 9), in which where there is an article on cooperation (Article 96). However, it simply says that the two countries shall cooperate in the field of intellectual property. The Implementing Agreement sets out the details in Article 6, stating that "Parties shall endeavor to promote through seminars and training courses,

Table 6.6   Areas of cooperation under the implementing agreement for JTEPA

Sections	Areas of Cooperation
Agriculture, Forestry, and Fisheries	(i) sound development of food industries covering all stages, from farm to market, including food distribution systems such as cold chain and packaging; (ii) human resource development; (iii) development and promotion of new technologies; (iv) quality control, inspection, and certification systems; (v) application of risk analysis; (vi) development of rural areas; (vii) human resource development; (viii) development of technical know-how and promotion of technology transfer; and (ix) promotion of joint investment leading to mutual benefits for relevant entities in both countries
Education and Human Resource Development	(i) enhancement of mutual understanding of policies of the respective parties, (ii) promotion of technical and vocational training including mould and die technologies, (iii) collaboration on academic research and institutional networking in areas of mutual interest, (iv) improvement of educational standards including those for management and development of educational institutions, (v) information and communications technology for education, (vi) promotion of technology transfer of educational tools and methods at all levels of education, (vii) Japanese and Thai language and cultural studies, (viii) joint third country training in areas of mutual interest based on the need of recipient countries, (ix) close cooperation between the educational and research institutions of the countries, and (x) promotion and facilitation of access to academic programs in both countries
Information and Communications Technology (ICT)	(i) advanced telecommunications networks including a next-generation Internet and broadband network between Southeast Asia and Northeast Asia through the Asia Broadband Program; (ii) promotion of consumer, public, and private use of ICT-related services including newly emerging services such as interactive broadband multimedia services; (iii) promotion of electronic commerce and development of relating legislation and guidelines including cooperation for facilitation of procedures of accreditation or recognition of certification authorities; (iv) promotion of circulation of digital content over broadband platform; and (v) human resource development relating to ICT including skill standards

(Continued)

Table 6.6 (*Continued*)

Sections	Areas of Cooperation
Science, Technology, Energy, and Environment	(i) science and technology suitable to provide a basis for industrial development; (ii) life sciences including biotechnology; (iii) advanced technology including material technology and engineering, nanotechnology, and biomass; (iv) standardization and certification; (v) energy including solar energy; (vi) natural resource management and environmental conservation and protection; and (vii) natural disaster risk reduction including early warning systems
Small and Medium-Sized Enterprises (SMEs)	(i) capacity building for SMEs; (ii) promotion of business collaboration and marketing development; (iii) strengthening of SMEs' management, competitiveness, and technological capability; (iv) improvement of financial access for SMEs; and (v) exchange of information on SMEs policies and best practices.
Tourism	(i) facilitation of tourism and enhanced travel connections; (ii) facilitation of application procedures for visas to promote tourism; (iii) mutual cooperation in tourism marketing and promotion including long stay, Thai spas, and Japanese hot springs (*onsen*), as well as marine tourism and ecotourism; and (iv) human resources development
Trade and Investment Promotion	(i) trade and investment promotion for Kitchen of the World project, (ii) Japan–Thailand Steel Industry Cooperation program, (iii) Automotive Human Resource Development Institute project, (iv) energy conservation, (v) value creation economy, (vi) public– private partnership, and (vii) textile and apparels cooperation

Note: Areas of cooperation under Enhancement of Business Environment and Financial Services are not provided for in the Implementing Agreement
Source: Author's compilation

effective enforcement of border measures . . ." The obligation is not binding, although it is specific.

New area technical assistance under JVEPA. Although JVEPA includes a chapter on customs procedures (Chapter 4), technical assistance is not mentioned there. However, the Implementing Agreement (Chapter 2, Article 2) states that "the Parties shall cooperate through their customs authorities, when necessary and appropriate, in the area of research, development, and testing of new customs procedures and new enforcement aids and techniques, training activities of customs officers, and exchange of personnel between customs authorities." (This language is very similar to that found in the Implementing Agreement for JTEPA). Thus, binding and specific obligations are imposed on the contracting parties by JVEPA. Although the term "when appropriate" is used, the level of obligation is high.

JVEPA does not include a chapter on investment, while it does include a chapter on competition (Chapter 10). Article 102: Technical Cooperation states that "the Parties agree that it is in their common interest . . . to work together in technical cooperation activities related to strengthening competition policy . . . ." No further detail on competition is provided either in this chapter or in the Implementing Agreement.

Tailor-made technical assistance under JVEPA. Chapter 12 of JVEPA focuses on cooperation. Article 111: Basic Principles states that "the Parties shall promote cooperation between the Governments of the Parties" and enumerates eight fields: (i) agriculture, forestry, and fisheries; (ii) trade and investment promotion; (iii) small and medium-sized enterprises; (iv) human resource management and development; (v) tourism; (vi) information and communications technology; (vii) environment; and (viii) transportation. Eight chapters in the Implementing Agreement (Chapters 4–11) provide the modalities of cooperation in these fields in detail. Each section stipulates "the area of cooperation under this Chapter may include . . . " and then lists the forms of cooperation by using the term "forms of cooperation under this Chapter may include . . . ." For example, the exchange of experts and holding of seminars and workshops are mentioned as forms of cooperation. Accordingly, the obligations are nonbinding and specific. Table 6.7 is the summary of the areas of cooperation under the Implementing Agreement.

6.5.7   Comparative analysis of Japan–ASEAN EPAs

The depth of technical assistance requirements set by EPAs varies in terms of both the level of binding and specificity. While technical assistance plays an important role in the WTO Agreements covering TBT and SPS issues, most EPAs do not have chapters on TBT or SPS, and a minority of the EPAs analyzed in this chapter impose additional technical assistance obligations

Table 6.7   Areas of cooperation under the implementing agreement for JVEPA

Sections	Areas of Cooperation
Agriculture, Forestry, and Fisheries	(i) human resource development related to agriculture, forestry, and fisheries
Small- and Medium-sized Enterprises (SMEs)	(i) strengthening of management and competitiveness of SMEs, (ii) human resource development related to SMEs, and (iii) development of supporting industries
Human Resource Management and Development	(i) language training and education on culture and social values, (ii) education and training, (iii) human resource management and development with knowledge and skills at an advanced level, and (iv) harmonization of competency standards
Tourism	(i) promotion and development of tourism, and (ii) human resource development related to tourism
Information and Communications Technology (ICT)	(i) human resource development related to ICT including skill standards; (ii) next-generation IP-based network, broadband networks, and ubiquitous networks; (iii) mobile communications technology; (iv) promotion of information exchanges on development technology; (v) circulation of digital content over broadband networks; and (vi) research and development
Environment	(i) conservation and improvement of the environment and (ii) promotion of sustainable development including measures to address climate change (e.g., Clean Development Mechanism and the co-benefit approach)
Transportation	(i) human resource development related to transportation

Note: Specific areas of cooperation in Trade and Investment Promotion are not included in the Implementing Agreement
Source: Author's compilation

in these two fields (Table 6.8). Among them, JMEPA is unique in the sense that it sets binding and specific obligations of technical assistance in the field of SPS.

Intellectual property is the only area where Japan's EPAs with ASEAN member countries have significant additional technical assistance obligations *vis-à-vis* those under the WTO. While the TRIPS Agreement states that Members shall furnish technical and financial assistance (and highlights training) by using the term "shall include," the level of specificity of the mode of providing technical assistance is not high. Though

Table 6.8   Summary of additional technical assistance

	TBT	SPS	IPR
JMEPA	Additional TA (non-binding and specific)	Additional TA (binding and specific)	Additional TA (non-binding and specific)
JIEPA	No chapter	No chapter	Additional TA (non-binding and specific)
JPEPA	No chapter	No chapter	Additional TA (non-binding and specific)
JSEPA	No chapter	No chapter	Additional TA (non-binding and specific)
JTEPA	No chapter	No chapter	No TA mentioned
JVEPA	Additional TA (non-binding but specific)	No TA mentioned	Additional TA (non-binding and specific)

Source: Author's compilation

the technical assistance obligations in this field under the EPAs are not binding, the intellectual property chapters of JMEPA, JIEPA, JPEPA, JSEPA, and JVEPA offer specific methods of providing technical assistance including seminars, trainings, staff exchanges, fairs, and symposiums, thereby exceeding the stipulations in the TRIPS Agreement in terms of specificity.

Investment and competition (i.e., Singapore issues) are two areas where there are either no WTO agreements or only thin agreements without technical assistance provisions, but the technical assistance obligations under the Japan–ASEAN EPAs in those two areas vary widely (Table 6.9). In the case of investment, most EPAs do not set technical assistance obligations, with the only exception being JMEPA, which mandates only slightly deeper obligations than the WTO. In contrast, in the case of competition most EPAs include technical assistance provisions. For example, JIEPA imposes binding and specific technical assistance obligations on contracting parties, such as the exchange of personnel and their participation as lecturers in training courses. In the field of customs procedures, which is another Singapore issue, JMEPA, JTEPA, and JVEPA impose binding and specific technical assistance obligations.

Table 6.9   Summary of new area technical assistance

	Customs Procedures	Investment	Competition
JMEPA	TA mentioned (binding and specific)	TA mentioned (non-binding and non-specific)	TA mentioned (non-binding and specific)
JIEPA	No TA mentioned	No TA mentioned	TA mentioned (binding and specific)
JPEPA	No TA mentioned	No TA mentioned	TA mentioned (non-binding and specific)
JSEPA	No TA mentioned	No TA mentioned	TA mentioned (non-binding and non-specific)
JTEPA	TA mentioned (binding and specific)	No TA mentioned	No TA mentioned
JVEPA	TA mentioned (binding and specific)	No chapter	No TA mentioned

Source: Author's compilation

One of the distinctive features of EPAs between Japan and ASEAN member countries is the inclusion of a chapter dedicated to cooperation (except JSEPA, which can be regarded as a North–North agreement). The cooperation chapter in each EPA usually lists the fields in which cooperation is required and the specific forms of assistance are usually stated in the respective Implementing Agreements (Table 6.10). Furthermore, industry-specific technical assistance obligations are also included in some of the EPAs. In the case of JMEPA, technical assistance to Malaysia's automobile industry is a binding obligation. Likewise, JIEPA imposes binding obligations on Japan to provide technical assistance to Indonesia's mining and energy sectors. JIEPA and JPEPA oblige the Japanese government to sponsor Japanese language training for Indonesian and Philippine applicants for nurses. Thus, as far as countries have a clear idea of their industrial development policies, EPAs can be an effective tool in upgrading specific industries.

The assumed negative correlation in Japan–ASEAN EPAs between developmental level and the number of technical assistance provisions does not seem to be valid. Japan's EPAs with lower income countries in

Table 6.10   Summary of tailor-made technical assistance

	Cooperation	Industry Specific
JMEPA	TA mentioned (binding and specific)	Automobile: TA mentioned (binding and specific)
JIEPA	TA mentioned (non-binding and specific)	Energy and Mining: TA mentioned (binding and specific) Nursing: TA mentioned (binding and specific)
JPEPA	TA mentioned (non-binding and specific)	Nursing: TA mentioned (binding and specific)
JSEPA	No chapter	No TA mentioned
JTEPA	TA mentioned (binding and specific)	No TA mentioned
JVEPA	TA mentioned (non-binding and specific)	No TA mentioned

Source: Author's compilation

ASEAN do not necessarily cover more technical assistance or coopera-
tion issues. For example, Japan's EPA with Malaysia, which is a middleincome country, has the most comprehensive technical assistance programs
of any of Japan's EPAs with ASEAN member countries. This is perhaps
because of Malaysia's needs to upgrade its regulatory framework in several
areas. In contrast, the issues covered in both JIEPA and JPEPA are limited
as neither has a chapter on TBT, for example. At the same time, JVEPA
includes more technical assistance obligations than JIEPA, JPEPA, and
JTEPA.

6.6   Policy Implications: The Developmental Perspective
of Regionalism Debates

Based on a comparative analysis of technical assistance obligations under
the WTO and EPAs between Japan and ASEAN countries, the latter include
several examples of technical assistance obligations that can be considered
WTO-plus. With regard to obligations in fields where the WTO already
imposes obligations on (some) Members, most Japan–ASEAN EPAs have
additional specific technical assistance obligations, particularly in the field
of intellectual property. Some of them also include additional technical
assistance obligations in the fields of TBT and SPS.

With regard to new area technical assistance obligations covering three of the four Singapore Issues — customs procedure and trade facilitation, investment, and competition — the level of technical assistance obligations under the Japan–ASEAN Epas are not homogeneous. While the majority of agreements set non-binding but very specific technical assistance obligations in the field of competition, only one agreement (JMEPA) has a chapter on investment that mentions the technical assistance obligations (non-binding and non-specific). However, one should not overlook the possibility that technical assistance is provided to ASEAN countries by Japan in the field of competition under respective EPas, because those EPas impose obligations of implementing effective competition policies on counterpart ASEAN countries. While this research focuses on WTO-plus elements in technical assistance obligations, further research is needed on the relation between WTO-plus general obligations and WTO-plus technical assistance obligations in the field of competition.[38]

In addition, all Japan–ASEAN Epas, except JSEPA, include a chapter on cooperation that covers various types of tailor-made technical assistance programs. Moreover, some EPas include concrete technical assistance measures targeting a specific industry, for example, in the automobile sector under JMEPA and in the energy and mining sectors under JIEPA. Thus, the tailor-made technical assistance obligations under a number of Japan–ASEAN Epas are substantial.

From the perspective of the regionalism–multilateralism debate, meaningful regional agreements that deliver tangible benefits to members pose the succeeding fundamental question of whether or not such agreements contribute to the multilateral economic system. In this sense, the obligation to provide meaningful technical assistance under FTAs is not an exception. The more substantial the technical assistance mechanisms under an FTA are, the more serious its systemic implications become. How can we consider that technical assistance mechanisms under Asian FTAs contribute to the sound development of the multilateral system? In tackling this regionalism–multilateralism question on technical assistance, two issues arise.

---

[38]There is a possibility that ASEAN countries undertook to implement binding commitments in exchange for binding commitments of technical assistance in the field of competition policy. See the caveat in Section 6.3 of this chapter.

First, the implications on capacity building of technical assistance under FTAs should be considered. In Section 6.3 we discussed the relationship between WTO-plus technical assistance obligations on developed countries and WTO-plus general obligations on developing countries. The argument proposed was that there is a high probability that technical assistance obligations under FTAs that build specific capacities contribute to the enhancement of developing countries' capability in drawing up policies in general. In fact, the forms of technical assistance mentioned in the Japan–ASEAN EPAs are training, seminars, and exchanges of staff, which all contribute to the general capacity of trade policy making in the recipient countries. Thus, the beneficiaries of the establishment of a proper regulatory framework through technical assistance under an FTA are not limited to FTA members.

Second, we should consider why technical assistance should be limited to FTA partners. A high degree of technical assistance commitments under FTAs is beneficial to developing country members, but we should not rule out the possibility of negative impacts on non-members. More specifically, there is the risk of crowding out effects. For example, Japan's provision of a large amount of technical assistance to ASEAN countries under Japan–ASEAN EPAs may lead to a reduction in Japan's technical assistance to African countries. In considering this issue, the stipulation in JTEPA on human resource development is helpful: "joint third country training in areas of mutual interest based on the need of recipient countries."[39] This is known as third-country training, where officials from countries other than Japan and Thailand are trained. Thus, we can say that Japan and Thailand have attempted to multilateralize the technical assistance obligations under their EPA to a certain degree.[40]

6.7   Summary

There is wide consensus that technical assistance is needed for developing countries to participate fully in international trade activities. However,

---

[39] Implementing Agreement for JTEPA, Chapter 6: Cooperation in the Field of Education and Human Resource Development.

[40] In the case of Singapore the Japan–Singapore Partnership Programme for the 21st Century, which was launched in 1994 and included third-country training, is linked to the current JSEPA. See Joint Announcement of the Prime Ministers of Singapore and Japan at the Signing of the Agreement Between the Republic of Singapore and Japan. Available at http://www.fta.gov.sg/jsepa/fta_jsepa_ jointannouncement.pdf

there are also situations in which developing countries undertake to implement bound commitments in exchange for unbound commitments of assistance from developed countries under the WTO system (Finger and Winter, 2002). The multilateral governance on developmental issues under the WTO system is very weak. In particular, it is too optimistic for developing countries to expect that technical assistance is automatically rendered by developed countries under the WTO rules.

FTAs have the potential to become a powerful avenue for the provision of technical assistance to developing countries. In fact, all Asian FTAs analyzed in this chapter include various types of technical assistance obligations, some of which are binding as well as specific. In some cases, industry-specific capacity building programs are also included in FTAs. It is critically important for developing countries to use FTAs as a tool to secure the provision of technical assistance by developed countries. It is mainly technical assistance that developing countries can gain from FTA negotiations as far as a tangible output is concerned.

The benefits of technical assistance under FTA may have significant multilateral implications. In other words, the impact of technical assistance conducted under a certain FTA goes beyond the trade between the contracting parties. Capacity building through technical assistance under FTAs contributes to the enhancement of developing countries' trade-related policy making in general. Furthermore, the beneficiaries of technical assistance can also include non-members of FTAs when joint third-country training is included in an EPA as is the case with some Japan–ASEAN EPAs. Thus, technical assistance under a regional scheme can assist capacity building in both a regional and multilateral context.

Appendix 6.1

Technical Assistance Provisions in WTO Agreements

Technical Barriers to Trade (TBT)

Article 11 Technical Assistance to Other Members

11.1 Members shall, if requested, advise other Members, especially the developing country Members, on the preparation of technical regulations.

11.2 Members shall, if requested, advise other Members, especially the developing country Members, and shall grant them technical assistance on mutually agreed terms and conditions regarding the establishment of national standardizing bodies, and participation in the international standardizing bodies, and shall encourage their national standardizing bodies to do likewise.

11.3 Members shall, if requested, take such reasonable measures as may be available to them to arrange for the regulatory bodies within their territories to advise other Members, especially the developing country Members, and shall grant them technical assistance on mutually agreed terms and conditions regarding:

    11.3.1 the establishment of regulatory bodies, or bodies for the assessment of conformity with technical regulations; and

    11.3.2 the methods by which their technical regulations can best be met.

11.4 Members shall, if requested, take such reasonable measures as may be available to them to arrange for advice to be given to other Members, especially the developing country Members, and shall grant them technical assistance on mutually agreed terms and conditions regarding the establishment of bodies for the assessment of conformity with standards adopted within the territory of the requesting Member.

11.5 Members shall, if requested, advise other Members, especially the developing country Members, and shall grant them technical assistance on mutually agreed terms and conditions regarding the steps that should be taken by their producers if they wish to have access to systems for conformity assessment operated by governmental or non-governmental bodies within the territory of the Member receiving the request.

11.6 Members which are members or participants of international or regional systems for conformity assessment shall, if requested, advise other Members, especially the developing country Members, and shall grant them technical assistance on mutually agreed terms and conditions regarding the establishment of the institutions and legal framework which would enable them to fulfil the obligations of membership or participation in such systems.

11.7 Members shall, if so requested, encourage bodies within their territories which are members or participants of international or regional systems for conformity assessment to advise other Members, especially the developing country Members, and should consider requests for technical assistance from them regarding the establishment of the institutions which would enable the relevant bodies within their territories to fulfil the obligations of membership or participation.

11.8 In providing advice and technical assistance to other Members in terms of paragraphs 1 to 7, Members shall give priority to the needs of the least-developed country Members.

Sanitary and Phytosanitary (SPS)

Article 9 Technical Assistance

1. Members agree to facilitate the provision of technical assistance to other Members, especially developing country Members, either bilaterally or through the appropriate international organizations. Such assistance may be, *inter alia*, in the areas of processing technologies, research and infrastructure, including in the establishment of national regulatory bodies, and may take the form of advice, credits, donations and grants, including for the purpose of seeking technical expertise, training and equipment to allow such countries to adjust to, and comply with, sanitary or phytosanitary measures necessary to achieve the appropriate level of sanitary or phytosanitary protection in their export markets.

2. Where substantial investments are required in order for an exporting developing country Member to fulfil the sanitary or phytosanitary

requirements of an importing Member, the latter shall consider providing such technical assistance as will permit the developing country Member to maintain and expand its market access opportunities for the product involved.

Customs Valuation Agreement (CVA)

PART III SPECIAL AND DIFFERENTIAL TREATMENT

Article 20

3. Developed country Members shall furnish, on mutually agreed terms, technical assistance to developing country Members that so request. On this basis developed country Members shall draw up programmes of technical assistance which may include, *inter alia*, training of personnel, assistance in preparing implementation measures, access to sources of information regarding customs valuation methodology, and advice on the application of the provisions of this Agreement.

Agreement on Preshipment Inspection (PSI)

Article 3 Obligations of Exporter Members

3. Exporter Members shall offer to provide to user Members, if requested, technical assistance directed towards the achievement of the objectives of this Agreement on mutually agreed terms.[5]

> 5. It is understood that such technical assistance may be given on a bilateral, plurilateral or multilateral basis.

General Agreement on Trade in Services (GATS)

Article XXV Technical Cooperation

1. Service suppliers of Members which are in need of such assistance shall have access to the services of contact points referred to in paragraph 2 of Article IV.
2. Technical assistance to developing countries shall be provided at the multilateral level by the Secretariat and shall be decided upon by the Council for Trade in Services.

Trade Related Intellectual Properties (TRIPS)

Article 67 Technical Cooperation

In order to facilitate the implementation of this Agreement, developed country Members shall provide, on request and on mutually agreed terms and conditions, technical and financial cooperation in favour of developing and least-developed country Members. Such cooperation shall include assistance in the preparation of laws and regulations on the protection and enforcement of intellectual property rights as well as on the prevention of their abuse, and shall include support regarding the establishment or reinforcement of domestic offices and agencies relevant to these matters, including the training of personnel.

Understanding on Rules and Procedures Governing the Settlement of Disputes (DSU)

Article 27 Responsibilities of the Secretariat

1. The Secretariat shall have the responsibility of assisting panels, especially on the legal, historical and procedural aspects of the matters dealt with, and of providing secretarial and technical support.
2. While the Secretariat assists Members in respect of dispute settlement at their request, there may also be a need to provide additional legal advice and assistance in respect of dispute settlement to developing country Members. To this end, the Secretariat shall make available a qualified legal expert from the WTO technical cooperation services to any developing country Member which so requests. This expert shall assist the developing country Member in a manner ensuring the continued impartiality of the Secretariat.
3. The Secretariat shall conduct special training courses for interested Members concerning these dispute settlement procedures and practices so as to enable Members' experts to be better informed in this regard.

Trade Policy Review Mechanism (TPR)

D. Reporting

... Particular account shall be taken of difficulties presented to least-developed country Members in compiling their reports. The Secretariat shall make available technical assistance on request to developing country Members, and in particular to the least-developed country Members. ...

Agreement on Government Procurement (GPA)

Article V Special and Differential Treatment for Developing Countries

Technical Assistance for Developing Country Parties

8. Each developed country Party shall, upon request, provide all technical assistance which it may deem appropriate to developing country Parties in resolving their problems in the field of government procurement.

9. This assistance, which shall be provided on the basis of non-discrimination among developing country Parties, shall relate, *inter alia*, to:

   — the solution of particular technical problems relating to the award of a specific contract; and

   — any other problem which the Party making the request and another Party agree to deal with in the context of this assistance.

10. Technical assistance referred to in paragraphs 8 and 9 would include translation of qualification documentation and tenders made by suppliers of developing country Parties into an official language of the WTO designated by the entity, unless developed country Parties deem translation to be burdensome, and in that case explanation shall be given to developing country Parties upon their request addressed either to the developed country Parties or to their entities.

CHAPTER 7

Conclusion: Counter-intuitive Policy Implications for WTO-Compatible FTAs

The conclusion chapter has two main tasks. First, we will summarize the main empirical findings of this study in terms of the overarching research question. We examined the relationship between FTAs and WTO from various angles, and there are many interesting findings and observations, which are uncommon in existing studies. Second, we will consider policies that make FTAs compatible with WTO. Since at the end of each empirical chapter, we have already considered policy issues relating to the WTO compatibility of regional initiatives in a particular field, the discussion here will focus on "counter-intuitive" policy implications of this study. What is widely considered as a standard policy to enhance the WTO compatibility of FTAs in conventional studies may need to be revised, given that recent FTAs cover various issue areas in addition to preferential tariff liberalization.

7.1   Summary of Important Empirical Findings

It seems that our findings are mixed in light of the overarching research question: whether Asian FTAs covering various issue areas are WTO-compatible or not. Since comparing the absolute level of WTO compatibility of regionalism in various issue areas is challenging, we will consider the level of WTO compatibility of each issue area in comparison with conventional views regarding the matter. In some fields, FTAs seem to be more compatible with the WTO than widely thought; but in other fields, FTAs do not seem to be that WTO-compatible. Thus, we can neither be too pessimistic nor too optimistic. It is important to properly design FTAs so that they will be not only legally consistent to WTO rules but they will also contribute to non-members' welfare and the multilateral trade liberalization.

Regional initiatives in two fields examined in this study seem to be *less* WTO-compatible than widely thought. First, it is wrong to assume that Asian FTAs in trade in goods are highly WTO-compatible. Above all, the majority of intra-Asian FTAs are based on the Enabling Clause, not on GATT Article XXIV. Thus, naturally, those FTAs may not satisfy the requirements of FTAs stipulated in GATT Article XXIV and their external effect may be more unfavorable than FTAs based on GATT Article XXIV. This situation is not necessarily problematic in terms of WTO consistency because developing countries are allowed to sign Enabling Clause-based FTA among themselves. The problem is that outside Asia, Enabling Clause-based FTAs attempt to reduce their negative external effects by adopting open membership policy. Non-Asian Enabling Clause-based FTAs are usually plurilateral agreement and they usually welcome neighboring countries to join the group. When non-Asian developing countries sign bilateral FTAs, those are usually based on GATT Article XXIV, not the Enabling Clause, despite the fact that they are entitled to use the latter. However, in Asia, the Enabling Clause is used to sign bilateral FTAs that do not have accession clause. It is recommended that Asian developing countries sign either bilateral FTAs based on GATT Article XXIV or plurilateral FTAs based on the Enabling Clause that have the accession clause, not bilateral FTAs based on the Enabling Clause. In this regard, there are some concerns regarding the current proliferation of bilateral FTAs based on the Enabling Clause in Asia because they are not as compatible to WTO as non-Asian FTAs, especially in terms of WTO friendliness.

It has been widely considered that trade facilitation seldom becomes exclusive and thus including various types of trade facilitation measures in FTAs enhance their WTO compatibility. However, the empirical findings of this study suggest that such a simple claim is not plausible. It is wrong to assume that trade facilitation measures are always non-exclusive. Policymakers should realize that there are many exclusive/discriminatory trade facilitation measures under FTAs. In short, we cannot be optimistic about the WTO compatibility of FTAs just because they include various trade facilitation measures. Moreover, discriminatory trade facilitation measures exclusive to FTA partners seem to be more harmful than discriminatory tariff treatment exclusive to FTA partners. This is because the former is less transparent than the latter and it is difficult to examine the impact of the former unlike the latter.

Regional initiatives in two fields examined in this study seem to be *more* WTO-compatible than widely thought. A certain type of regional services agreement seems to be highly WTO-compatible. In particular, when a regional services agreement brings enhanced non-discriminatory market access both to its members and non-members (GATS-plus commitments with non-discriminatory market access enhancement), such an agreement is certainly WTO-compatible. But the frequency of this scenario may not be that high. Moreover, there is a possibility that new discriminatory regulation is introduced under this scenario. When a regional services agreement brings enhanced discriminatory market access only to its members, maintaining the restrictive market access to the other parties (GATS-plus commitments with discriminatory market access enhancement), such a situation does not seem to be desirable in terms of WTO compatibility. Services sector regulations that discriminate services suppliers depending on their origin is a result of poor regulatory framework. Regulatory framework would become largely fragmented by the introduction of discriminatory regulations for regional members and it would eventually become non-manageable.

In contrast, a regional services agreement that has GATS-plus commitments without new market access may be useful, especially when there is a policy space (actual regulation is more liberal than preferential binding). This type of services commitments seem to be beneficial to non-members in terms of the lock-in effects because, under this scenario, it is reasonable to consider that a country tends to introduce tighter regulations in future within a regional policy space in a non-discriminatory manner, rather than introducing either discriminatory regulations that are tighter than the regional commitment and applicable only to non-members, or non-discriminatory regulations that are tighter than the regional commitment and subject to compensation being offered to regional members. The regional policy space seems to function as a buffer by creating an incentive for countries to avoid discriminatory measures. Thus, the benefit of lock-in effects of regulations brought about by this type of regional commitments can also be enjoyed by non-members (non-regional members can free ride on GATS-plus commitments in others' services agreements). In short, a GATS-plus regional commitment without new market access has two inter-related positive effects: (i) incentives for countries to introduce regulations in the context of regional policy space in a non-discriminatory manner, and (ii) confidence-building for non-members due to the lock-in effects of regional commitments. Modest regional services agreement seems to be highly WTO-compatible. Regional services agreements should lead to long-term reform rather than one-off market opening.

Second, economic cooperation provisions under FTA, especially those relating to capacity building seems to be a useful contributor to the WTO compatibility of FTAs. FTAs have the potential to become a powerful avenue for the provision of technical assistance to developing countries. FTAs can include various types of technical assistance obligations, some of which are binding as well as specific. In some cases, industry-specific capacity building programs targeting at the removal of supply side constraints are also included in FTAs. It is mainly technical assistance that developing countries can gain from FTA negotiations as far as a tangible output is concerned. The benefits of technical assistance under FTA may have significant multilateral implications. The impact of technical assistance conducted under a certain FTA goes beyond the trade between the contracting parties. Capacity building through technical assistance under FTAs contributes to the enhancement of developing countries' trade-related policy making in general. Thus, technical assistance under a regional scheme can assist capacity building in both regional and multilateral context.

7.2   Counter-intuitive Policy Implications

Finally, it is useful to draw several policy implications based on the empirical findings of this study regarding the WTO compatibility of FTAs. The main purpose here is to extract some policy-oriented lessons that contribute to the making of WTO-compatible FTAs. Counter-intuitive policy implications are very useful to make FTAs truly WTO-compatible, avoiding false WTO-compatible FTAs. Conscious effort to design open and outward-oriented FTAs is necessary to ensure that FTAs are WTO-compatible. There are at least six important counter-intuitive policy implications:

- Counter-intuitive policy implication 1: While some tend to think that FTAs that satisfy rules and conditions of forming FTAs set by WTO are WTO-compatible, in reality, WTO-consistent FTAs are not necessarily WTO-compatible FTAs.

There are three interrelated concepts regarding WTO compatibility: (i) Consistency with WTO (legal issue); (ii) Friendliness to the WTO system (political scientific issue[1]); and (iii) Friendliness to other WTO Members, which are non-members of the FTA (economic issue). FTA compatible with WTO should satisfy the three criteria. In other words, FTA that is legally consistent with WTO rules and conditions and that brings overall positive effects on non-members and contributes to the multilateral trade liberalization is truly WTO-compatible FTA. It is misleading to overemphasize the legal consistency of FTAs *vis-à-vis* WTO rules in considering the WTO compatibility of FTAs.

- Counter-intuitive policy implication 2: While some tend to emphasize GATT Article XXIV in discussing the relation between WTO and FTA (in trade in goods), in reality, GATT Article XXIV centric argument is less convincing in Asia because the majority of Asian FTAs is formed based on the Enabling Clause, not GATT Article XXIV.

It is true that almost all FTAs signed before 2000 are based on GATT Article XXIV, with some notable exceptions. The contracting parties of most FTAs before 2000 are non-Asians. In Asia, trade regionalism surged after 2000 and the majority of FTAs are based on the Enabling Clause. While it is possible to argue that it is a desirable best practice if Enabling Clause-based FTAs also satisfy the conditions set by GATT Article XXIV, in reality there is no guarantee that will be possible.

Given that Enabling Clause-based FTAs are unlikely to satisfy GATT Article XXIV conditions and they may have some negative impacts on non-members, Enabling Clause-based FTAs outside Asia attempt to reduce their negative effects by adopting an open membership policy. Thus, rather than expecting that Enabling Clause-based FTAs in Asia satisfy GATT Article XXIV conditions, encouraging them to adopt open membership policy is more useful to make them WTO-compatible.

- Counter-intuitive policy implication 3: While some argue that the inclusion of WTO-plus elements in FTAs is a kind of best practice, in reality, they could be a source of concern in terms of WTO compatibility.

---

[1]This point was initially emphasized by trade economist like Bhagwati. For the details, see Chapter 1 (Section 1.2).

WTO-plus elements in FTAs do not automatically lead to their WTO-compatible status. Rather, it is critically important to assess whether the WTO-plus elements are discriminatory in both *de jure* and *de facto* senses. FTAs' WTO-plus elements are just the start of the discussion regarding the WTO compatibility of FTAs, and we should carefully examine the nature and degree of WTO-plus elements, especially their exclusiveness to non-members. Only when WTO-plus elements of FTAs do not have serious negative effects on non-members, we can say that they contribute to the WTO compatibility of FTAs. In short, we should bear in mind that WTO-plus elements could be harmful.

- Counter-intuitive policy implication 4: While some argue that regional initiatives in various fields such as trade facilitation tend to be WTO-compatible, in reality, we cannot be very optimistic about the WTO compatibility of regional initiatives in the field widely considered to be WTO-compatible.

It is widely said that the inclusion of trade facilitation measures in FTAs is good because they tend to facilitate trade with non-members, too. However, we should not forget that such an argument implicitly assumes either (i) trade facilitation measures cannot be exclusive from the beginning; or (ii) trade facilitation measures applicable to FTA partners are extended to non-member on a *de facto* basis, which are not necessarily always the case. There are many regional trade facilitation measures that are exclusive to the members.

In terms of WTO compatibility, discriminatory trade facilitation measures at regional level (discriminatory trade facilitation measures of FTAs) could be more harmful than discriminatory (preferential) tariff treatment. This is because (i) discriminatory trade facilitation measures could be less transparent; (ii) the magnitude of discriminatory effects of regional trade facilitation measures is unclear. Thus, although introduction of discriminatory trade facilitation measure is allowed, this should be discouraged. If countries want to give preferential treatment to partners, this should be done in the form of discriminatory (preferential) tariff, not with the introduction of discriminatory trade facilitation measures.

- Counter-intuitive policy implication 5: While some emphasize FTA's lock-in effect of *past* reform, in reality, they should be rather used as a trigger of long-term reforms in *future*.

What is widely said is that FTAs has a lock-in effect of past (one-off) reforms. Moreover, countries decide to sign FTAs expecting that international communities consider that the past reform effort was real. While it seems true that FTAs have some lock-in effects, one important question is multilateral commitments at the WTO is much powerful in terms of credibility of locking in past reforms. The only advantage of locking-in the past reforms at FTAs *vis-à-vis* multilateral is that the compensation of breach of commitment is smaller. However, this is exactly the reasons why lock-in effects of FTAs is smaller than WTO. Lock-in effect at FTAs should be a transitory devise to the commitment at the multilateral level.

Rather, countries should use FTAs as a trigger of long-term reforms in future. Reform is unilateral and there is no problem that reform conducted recently is not bound in the FTA. Only when countries feel confident about the past reform can they be bound for the international commitments. The ideal sequence would be: recent reform at home, which is a unilateral initiative triggered by FTA negotiations is first bound at the regional level (because binding at the multilateral level at the outset is risky) and then bound at the multilateral level once countries feel confident. This is a forward looking way of using FTAs.

- Counter-intuitive policy implication 6: While some tend to consider that North–South FTAs are not beneficial to the developing contracting parties, in reality, it is not South–South FTAs but North–South FTAs that have a huge potential for economic development.

In order to increase trade, especially export, not only trade liberalization but also the capacity building is necessary for developing countries. Capacity building of both public sectors and private sectors are equally important for economic development. While South–South FTAs are good to enhance the trade/export opportunity among developing countries, the impact on capacity development of this type of FTAs seems to be limited. In contrast, North–South FTAs can be a useful avenue for the capacity development of the developing contracting parties, if technical cooperation provisions are properly crafted. In short, it is totally wrong to underestimate the benefit of North–South FTAs from the developing country perspective. While South–South FTAs enhance opportunity to trade, North–South FTAs enhance not only opportunity to trade but also capacity to trade.

References

Abbott, K.W., R.O. Keohane, A. Moravcsik, A.-M. Slaughter, and D. Snidal (2000). The concept of legalization. *International Organization*, 54(3), 17–35.

Acharya, A. (1997). Ideas, identity, and institution-building: From the "ASEAN way" to the "Asia-Pacific way"? *The Pacific Review*, 10(3), 319–46.

ADB [Asian Development Bank] (2011). OREI: Office of Regional Economic Integration. Available at http://www.adb.org/publications/office-regional-economic-integration-brochure.

ADB and ESCAP [United Nations Economic and Social Commission for Asia and the Pacific] (2009). Designing and Implementing Trade Facilitation in Asia and the Pacific. Available at http://www.aric.adb.org/.

Adlung, R. (2006). Services negotiations in the Doha round: Lost in flexibility? *Journal of International Economic Law*, 9(4), 865–893.

Adlung, R. and S. Miroudot (2012). Poison in the wine? Tracing GATS-minus commitments in regional trade agreements. *Staff Working Paper ERSD*, No. 2012-04.

Adlung, R. and M. Molinuevo (2008). Bilateralism in services trade: Is there fire behind the (bit) smoke? *Journal of International Economic Law*, 11(2), 365–409.

Alam, Q., M.A. Yusuf and K.A. Coghill (2010). Unilateral liberalisation and WTO GATS commitments: The telecommunications sector in selected countries. *Asian-Pacific Economic Literature*, 24(1), 43–64.

Anderson, J.E. and E. van Wincoop (2004). Trade cost. *Journal of Economic Literature*, 42(3), 691–751.

APEC [Asia-Pacific Economic Cooperation] (1995). Selected APEC documents 1995. APEC Secretariat.

Arunanondchai, J. and C. Fink (2007). Trade in health services in the ASEAN region. *World Bank Policy Research Working Paper*, No. 4147.

Arup, C. (2008). Services and investment in Free Trade Agreements: Liberalization, regulation, and law. In Buckle, R., L.V. Lo, and L. Boulle (eds.), *Challenges to Multilateral Trade: The Impact of Bilateral, Preferential, and Regional Agreements. Kluwer Global Trade Law Series* No. 14.

ASEAN [Association of Southeast Asian Nations] Secretariat (2011). *ASEAN Integration in Trade in Services: Development, Challenges, and Way forward*. Presentation at ADBI-PECC Conference on Trade and Investment in Services. June 1–3, Hong Kong, China. Available at www.pecc.org/.../

1716-asean-integration-in-trade-in-services-development-challenges-and-way-forward-presentation.

ASEAN Secretariat (2009). *ASEAN Integration in Services*. Available at www.asean.org/publications/AFAS-2009.pdf.

Baldwin, R. (2006). Multilateralising regionalism: Spaghetti bowls as building blocs on the path to global free trade. *The World Economy*, **29**(11), 1451–1518.

Baldwin, R. (1993). A domino theory of regionalism. *Working Paper, No. 4465*, Cambridge, USA: National Bureau of Economic Research.

Baldwin, R. and T. Carpenter (2011). Regionalism: Moving from fragmentation toward coherence. In Cottier, T. and P. Delimatsis (eds.), *The Prospects of International Trade Regulation: From Fragmentation to Coherence.* Cambridge, UK: Cambridge University Press.

Baldwin, R., S. Evenett, and P. Low (2009). Beyond Tariff: Multilateralizing Non-Tariff RTA Commitments, In Baldwin, R. and P. Low (eds.), *Multilateralizing Regionalism: Challenges for the Global Trading System.* Cambridge, UK: Cambridge University Press.

Baldwin, R. and P. Low (eds.) (2009a). *Multilateralizing Regionalism: Challenges for the Global Trading System.* Cambridge, UK: Cambridge University Press.

Baldwin R. and P. Low (2009b). Introduction. In Baldwin, R. and P. Low (eds.), *Multilateralizing Regionalism: Challenges for the Global Trading System.* Cambridge, UK: Cambridge University Press.

Bartels, L. (2005). The legality of the EC mutual recognition clause under WTO law. *Journal of International Economic Law*, **8**(3), 691–720.

Bin, P. (2008). *Trade Facilitation Provisions in Regional Agreements in Asia and the Pacific*. Available at http://www.unescap.org/tid/publication/swp108.pdf.

Bergsten, C.F. (1997). Open regionalism. *Institute for International Economics Working Paper.* Washington, DC: Institute for International Economics.

Bergsten, C.F. (1998). Reviving the Asian Monetary Fund. *The International Economy*, November–December.

Bergsten, C.F. (1994). APEC and world trade: A force for worldwide liberalization. *Foreign Affairs*, **73**(3), 20–26.

Bergsten C.F., N.R. Lardy, and D.J. Mitchell (2008). *China's Rise: Challenges and Opportunities*. Washington, DC: Peterson Institute for International Economics and Center for Strategic and International Studies.

Bhagwati, J. (1995). US trade policy: The infatuation with free trade areas. In Bhagwati, J. and A.O. Kruger (eds.), *The Dangerous Drift to Preferential Trade Agreements*. American Enterprise Institute for Public Policy Research.

Bhagwati, J. (1993). Regionalism and multilateralism: An overview. In Melo, J. and A. Panagariya (eds.), *New Dimensions in Regional Integration*. Cambridge, UK: Cambridge University Press.

Bhagwati, J. (1991). *The World Trading System at Risk.* Princeton, NJ: Princeton University Press and Harvester Wheatsheaf.

Bhagwati, J. and A. Panagariya (1996). Preferential trading areas and multilateralism: Strangers, friends, or foes? *Columbia University Discussion Paper Series* No. 9596-04.

Bolhöfer, C.E. (2007). Trade facilitation — WTO law and its revision to facilitate global trade in goods. *Global Trade and Customs Journal,* 2(11/12), 385–391.

Bosworth, M. and R. Trewin (2008). The domestic dynamics of preferential services liberalization: The experience of Australia and Thailand. In Marchetti, J. and R. Martin (eds.), *Opening Markets for Trade in Services: Countries and Sectors in Bilateral and WTO Negotiations.* Cambridge, UK: Cambridge University Press.

Bowie, R.R. and R.H. Immerman (1998). *Waging Peace: How Eisenhower Shaped an Enduring Cold War Strategy.* Oxford, UK: Oxford University Press.

Capie, D. and P. Evans (2002). *The Asia-Pacific Security Lexicon.* Singapore: Institute of Southeast Asian Studies.

Caporaso, J.A. (1992). International relations theory and multilateralism: The search for foundations. *International Organization,* 46(3), 599–632.

Carpenter, T. (2009). A historical perspective on regionalism. In Baldwin, R. and P. Low (eds.), *Multilateralizing Regionalism: Challenges for the Global Trading System.* Cambridge, UK: Cambridge University Press.

Chase, K. (2005). Multilateralism compromised: The mysterious origins of GATT Article XXIV. *World Trade Review 2006,* 5(1), 1–30.

Chia, S.Y. (2010). Trade and investment policies and regional economic integration in East Asia. *ADBI Working Paper* Series 210. Tokyo, Japan: ADBI.

Chirathivat, S. and S. Mallikamas (2004). Thailand's FTA strategy current development and future challenges. *ASEAN Economic Bulletin,* 21(1), 37–53.

Cohen, B.J. (1998). *The Geography of Money.* Ithaca, USA: Cornell University Press.

Committee on Trade in Services (2006). Report by the Chairman to the Trade Negotiations Committee. TN/S/20, World Trade Organization.

Cooper, R. (1993). Round table discussion. In Melo, J. and A. Panagariya (eds.), *New Dimensions in Regional Integration.* Cambridge, UK: Cambridge University Press.

Cornish, M. and C. Findlay (2010). *Services Liberalization in the "ASEAN Plus" Free Trade Agreements.* In Findlay, C. (eds.), *ASEAN +1 FTAS and Global Value Chains in East Asia,* ERIA Research Project Report 2010-29. Jakarta: ERIA.

Crawford, J.-A. and L. Chin-Leng (2011). Cast light and evil will go away: The first transparency mechanism for regulating regional trade agreements three years after. *Journal of World Trade,* 45(2), 375–400.

Crawford, J.-A. and R. Fiorentino (2005). Changing landscape of regional trade agreements. *WTO Discussion Paper* No. 8. Geneva: World Trade Organization.

Davey, W. (2011). A model Article XXIV: Are there realistic possibilities to improve it? In Bagwell, K. and P. Mavroidis (eds.), *Preferential Trade Agreements: Law, Policy, and Economics.* Cambridge, UK: Cambridge University Press.

De Bardeleben, J. (ed.) (2005). *Soft or Hard Borders? Managing the Divide in an Enlarged Europe.* Burlington, VT, USA: Ashgate.

Dee, P. (2012). *ASEAN Economic Community Mid-term Review — Services Liberalization: Impact and Way forward.* Jakarta: ASEAN.

Dee, P. (2010). Deepening East Asian economic integration in services. *ERIA Policy Brief.* No. 2010-01.

Dee, P. and A. McNaughton (2011). Promoting domestic reforms through regionalism. *ADBI Working Paper* No. 312. Tokyo: Asian Development Bank Institute.

Dee, P. and C. Findlay (2006). Trade facilitation: What, why, how, where and when? IDB publications from Inter-American Development Bank No. 47578.

Deere, C. (2005). International trade technical assistance and capacity building. *Human Development Report Office Occasional Paper* No. 2005/5. New York: UNDP.

Delimatsis, P. (2010). Concluding the WTO services negotiations on domestic regulation — Hopes and fears. *World Trade Review,* 9(4), 643–673.

Dent, C.M. (2008). The Asian development bank and developmental regionalism in East Asia. *Third World Quarterly,* 29(4), 767–786.

Dietrich, D., J. Finke, and C. Tietje (2010). Liberalization and rules on regulation in the field of financial services in bilateral trade and regional integration agreements. *Heft 97.* Institute of Economic Law. Available at http://www.wirtschaftsrecht.uni-halle.de/sites/default/files/altbestand/Heft_97.pdf.

Drake-Brockman, J. (2011). Access through presence: Australian perspectives on measuring mode 3 trade. In Sauvé, P., G. Pasadilla, and M. Mikic (eds.), *Service Sector Reforms: Asia-Pacific Perspectives.* ADBI Institute and ARTNeT.

Drysdale P. (2006). APEC then and now: The catalytic role of the APEC process: Behind the border, beyond the APEC goals. Presented at the *APEC International Symposium. Catalytic Role of the APEC Process: Behind the Border, Beyond the Bogor Goals,* March 14–15, Chiba, Japan. Available at http://www.apec.org.au/docs/06_apec_perspect.pdf

Drysdale P. and A. Elek (1996). The APEC experiment: An open economic association in the Asia Pacific. *International Journal of Social Economics,* 23(4/5/6), 164–187.

Drysdale, P., A. Elek and H. Soesastro (1998). Open regionalism: The nature of Asia Pacific integration. In Drysdale, P. and D. Vines (eds.), *Europe, East Asia, and APEC: A Shared Global Agenda?* Cambridge, UK: Cambridge University Press.

Drysdale, P., D. Vines, and B. House (1998). Europe and East Asia: A shared global agenda? In Drysdale, P. and D. Vines (eds.), *Europe, East Asia, and APEC: A Shared Global Agenda?* Cambridge, UK: Cambridge University Press.

Duval, Y. (2011). Trade facilitation in regional trade agreements: Recent trends in Asia and the Pacific. *Working Paper Series* No. 211, United Nations Economic and Social Commission for Asia and the Pacific (ESCAP).

Duval, Y. and C. Utoktham (2009). Behind the border trade facilitation in Asia-Pacific: Cost of trade, credit information, contract enforcement and regulatory coherence. *Trade and Investment Division, Staff Working Paper.* No. 02/09. Bangkok: United Nations Economic and Social Commission for Asia and the Pacific.

Ekins, P. and R. Vanner (2009). Reducing the impacts of the production and trade of commodities. In Ekins, P. and T. Voituriez (eds.), *Trade, Globalization and Sustainability Impact Assessment.* MapSet.

El-Agraa, A.M. (2002). The UTR versus CU formation analysis and Article XXIV. *Applied Economics Letters,* 9, 621–624.

Elek, A. (1995). APEC beyond bogor: An open economic association in the Asian-Pacific region. *Asian-Pacific Economic Literature,* 9(1), 1–16.

Elek, A. (1992). Trade policy options for the Asia-Pacific region in the 1990's: The potential of open regionalism. *American Economic Review,* 82(2), 74–78.

ESCAP [United Nation Economic and Social Commission for Asia and the Pacific] (2005). Multilateralizing regionalism: Towards an integrated and outward-oriented Asia-Pacific economic area. Paper presented at the *Conference on Delivering on the WTO Doha Round: A High-level Government–Business Dialogue for Development,* October 4–6, Macao.

Estevadeordal, A., J. Harris, and K. Suominen (2009). Harmonizing preferential rules of origin regimes around the world. In Baldwin, R. and P. Low (eds.), *Multilateralizing Regionalism: Challenges for the Global Trading System.* Cambridge, UK: Cambridge University Press.

Estevadeordal, A., C. Freund, and E. Ornelas (2008). Does regionalism affect trade liberalization toward non-members? *World Bank Policy Research Working Paper* No. 4751. Washington, D.C.: World Bank.

Findlay, C. (2003). Plurilateral agreements on trade in air transport services: The US model. *Journal of Air Transport Management,* 9, 211–220.

Finger, J. M. and P. Schuler (2002). Implementation of WTO commitments: The development challenge. In Hoekman, B., A. Mattoo, and P. English (eds.), *Development, Trade, and WTO: A Handbook.* Washington D.C.: World Bank.

Finger, J. M. and A. Winters (2002). Reciprocity in the WTO. In Hoekman, B., A. Mattoo, and P. English (eds.), *Development, Trade, and the WTO: A Handbook.* Washington D.C.: World Bank.

Fink, C. (2008). PTAs in services: Friends or foes of the multilateral trading system? In Marchetti, J. and R. Martin (eds.), *Opening Markets for Trade in Services:*

Countries and Sectors in Bilateral and WTO Negotiations. Cambridge, UK: Cambridge University Press.

Fink, C. and M. Molinuevo (2008). East Asian free trade agreements in services: Key architectural elements. *Journal of International Economic Law,* 11(2), 263–311.

Fink, C. and M. Jansen (2007). Services provisions in regional trade agreements: stumbling blocks for multilateral liberalization? Paper presented at the *Conference on Multilateralizing Regionalism* organized by WTO and CEPR.

Fink, C. and D. Nikomboriak (2007). Rules of origin in services: A case study of five ASEAN countries. *World Bank Policy Research Working Paper* No. 4130.

Fiorentino, R., L. Verdeja, and C. Toqueboeuf (2007). The changing landscape of regional trade agreements: 2006 update. *Discussion Paper* No. 12. Geneva: WTO Publications.

Fon, V. and F. Parisi (2005). Formation and accession to international treaties. *George Mason University Law and Economics Working Paper Series* No. 05-33 Fairfax, USA: George Mason University.

Footer, M. and C. George (2005). The general agreement on trade in services. In Macrory, P., A.E. Appleton, and M. Plummer (eds.), *The World Trade Organization: Legal, Economic, and Political Analysis.* New York: Springer.

Francois, J. and B. Hoekman. (2010). Services trade and policy. *Journal of Economic Literature,* 48, 642–692.

Funabashi, Y. (1995). *Asia Pacific Fusion: Japan's Role in APEC.* Washington, D.C.: Institute for International Economics.

Gamble, A. and A. Payne (1996). Introduction: The political economy of regionalism and world order. In Gamble, A. and A. Payne (eds.), *Regionalism and World Order.* Basingstoke, UK: Macmillan.

Gao, H. (2008). The RTA strategy of China: Critical visit. In Buckelry, R., V. I. Lo, and L. Boulle (eds.), *Challenges to Multilateral Trade: The Impact of Bilateral, Preferential, and Regional Agreements. Kluwer Global Trade Law Series* No. 14.

Garnaut, R. (2005). Australia, the US, and China: Open regionalism in an era of bilateral FTAs. Paper presented at a Public Lecture, Asialink, Melbourne, March 22.

Garnaut, R. (2004). A new open regionalism in Asia and the Pacific. Paper presented at the *International Conference on World Economy,* November 25, Colima, Mexico.

Garnaut, R. (1996). *Open Regionalism and Trade Liberalization: An Asia-Pacific Contribution to the World Trade System.* Singapore: ISEAS.

Garnaut, R. (1994). Open regionalism: Its analytic basis and relevance to the international system. *Journal of Asian Economics,* 5(2), 273–290.

Garnaut R. and D. Vines (2007). Regional free trade areas: Sorting out the tangled spaghetti. *Oxford Review of Economic Policy,* 23(3), 508–527.

Ghosh, A. (2010). Developing countries in the WTO trade policy review mechanism. *World Trade Review,* 9(3), 419–455.

Gobbi, A.T. and G.N. Horlick (2006). Mandatory abolition of anti-dumping, countervailing duties and safeguards in customs unions and free trade areas constituted between WTO members: Revisiting a long-standing discussion in light of the appellate body's Turkey-textile ruling. In Bartels, L. and F. Ortino (eds.), *Regional Trade Agreements and the WTO Legal System*. Oxford, UK: Oxford University Press.

Goldstein, J.L., D. Rivers, and M. Tomz (2007). Institutions in international relations: Understanding the effects of the GATT and the WTO on world trade. *International Organization*, 61(1), 37–67.

Haas, D.A. (1994). Out of others' shadows: ASEAN moves toward greater regional cooperation in the face of the EC and NAFTA. *American University International Law Review*, 9(3), 809–867.

Haggard, S. (1997). Regionalism in Asia and the Americas. In Mansfield, E. and H. Milner (eds.), *The Political Economy of Regionalism*. New York, NY: Columbia University Press.

Hamanaka, S. (2013a). On the use of FTAs: A review of research methodologies. *ADB Working Paper on Regional Economic Integration* No. 113. Manila, Philippines: ADB.

Hamanaka, S. (2013b). Study of non-notified trade agreement to the WTO: The case of Asia-Pacific. *Working Paper on Regional Economic Integration* (forthcoming).

Hamanaka, S. (2012a). Evolutionary paths toward a region-wide economic agreement in Asia. *Journal of Asian Economics*, 23, 383–394

Hamanaka, S. (2012b). Unexpected usage of enabling clause? Proliferation of bilateral trade agreement in Asia. *Journal of World Trade*, 46(6).

Hamanaka, S. (2011a). Asian financial cooperation in the 1990s: The politics of membership. *Journal of East Asian Studies*, 11(1).

Hamanaka, S. (2011b). Japan's foreign direct investment in services in ASEAN: The implications of services and investment agreements. *Journal of World Investment and Trade*, 12(3), 351–376.

Hamanaka, S. (2009). *Asian Regionalism and Japan: The Politics of Membership in Regional Diplomatic, Financial and Trade Groups*. London, UK: Routledge.

Hamanaka, S., A. Tafgar, and D. Lazaro (2010). Trade facilitation measures under free trade agreements: Are they discriminatory against non-members? *ADB Working Paper on Regional Economic Integration* No. 55. Manila, Philippines: ADB.

Harris, S. (1994). Policy networks and economic cooperation: Policy coordination in the Asia-Pacific region. *Pacific Review*, 7(4), 381–395.

Henning, C.R. (2002). *East Asian Financial Cooperation*. Washington, D.C.: Peterson Institute for International Economics.

Higgott, R. and R. Stubbs (1995). Competing conceptions of economic regionalism: APEC versus EAEC in the Asia Pacific. *Review of International Political Economy*, 2(3), 516–535.

Hill, H. and J. Menon (2013). Financial safety nets in Asia: Genesis, evolution, adequacy, and way forward. *ADBI Working Paper* Series No. 395. Tokyo, Japan: ADBI.

Hoekman, B. (1995). Assessing the general agreement on trade in services. *World Bank Discussion Paper* No. 307.

Hoekman, B. and A. Mattoo (2011). Services trade liberalization and regulatory reform: Re-invigorating international cooperation. *World Bank Policy Research Working Paper* No. 5517.

Hoekman, B. and A. Winters (2009). Multilateralizing preferential trade agreements: A developing country perspective. In Baldwin, R. and P. Low (eds.), *Multilateralzing Regionalism: Challenges for the Global Trading System*. Cambridge, UK: Cambridge University Press.

Hoekman, B., A. Mattoo, and A. Sapir (2007). The political economy of services trade liberalization: A case for international regulatory cooperation? *Oxford Review of Economic Policy*, **23**(3), 367–391.

Hoekman, B. and M. Schiff (2002). Benefiting from regional integration. In Hoekman, B., A Mattoo, and P English (eds.), *Development, Trade, and the WTO: A Handbook*. Washington, D.C.: World Bank.

Hooker, N. and J. Caswell (1999). A framework for evaluating non-tariff barriers to trade related to sanitary and phytosanitary regulation. *Journal of Agricultural Economics*, **50**(2), 23–46.

Hormats, R.D. (1994). Making regionalism safe. *Foreign Affairs*, **73**(2), 97–108.

Hurrell, A. (1995). Regionalism in theoretical perspective. In Fawcett, L. and A. Hurrell (eds.), *Regionalism in World Politics: Regional Organization and International Order*. Oxford, UK: Oxford University Press.

Irish, M. (2008). Regional trade, the WTO, and the NAFTA model. In Buckelry, R., V. I. Lo, and L. Boulle (eds.), *Challenges to Multilateral Trade: The Impact of Bilateral, Preferential, and Regional Agreements*. Kluwer Global Trade Law Series No. 14.

Ishido, H. (2011). Liberalization of trade in services under ASEAN+n: A mapping exercise. *ERIA Discussion Paper Series* No. 2011-2.

Ishido, H. and Y. Fukunaga (2012). Liberalization of trade in services: Toward a harmonized ASEAN++ FTA. *ERIA Policy Brief* No. 2012-02. Economic Research Institute for ASEAN and East Asia (ERIA).

Jones, E., C. Deere-Birkbeck, and N. Woods (2009). *Manouevring at the Margins: Constraints Faced by Small States in International Trade Negotiations*. London: Commonwealth Secretariat.

Katada, S. N. and M. Solis (2011). Cross regional trade agreements: Understanding permeated regionalism in East Asia. *The Political Economy of the Asia-Pacific*. Springer.

Katsuri, D. (2007). GATS 2000 negotiations and India: Evolution and state of play. *Journal of World Trade*, **41**, 1185–1236.

Katzenstein, P.J. and T. Shiraishi (1997). *Network Power: Japan and Asia.* Ithaca, US: Cornell University Press.

Kelley, J. (2010). The Role of Membership Rules in Regional Organizations. *ADB Working Paper Series on Regional Economic Integration* No. 53. Manila, Philippines: ADB.

Kemp, M.C. and H.V. Wan, Jr. (1976). An Elementary Proposition Concerning the Formation of Customs Unions, *Journal of International Economics,* 6(1), 95–97.

Keohane, R.O. (1990). Multilateralism: An agenda for research. *International Journal,* 45, 731–764.

Keohane, R.O. (1984), *After Hegemony: Cooperation and Discord in the World Political Economy.* Princeton, US: Princeton University Press.

Khadiagala, G.M. (2011). Institution building for African regionalism. *ADB Working Paper Series on Regional Economic Integration* No. 85. Manila Philippines: ADB.

Kim, W.-H. (2008). The next APEC membership from Latin America: A contextual approach. *APEC Study Series* No. 08-03. Seoul, Republic of Korea: Korea Institute for International Economic Policy.

Kim, J.B. (2006). Legal review of FTA tariff negotiations. Paper presented at RIETI on August 7, 2007 at the Research Institute of Economy, Trade and Industry (RIETI), Tokyo.

Kostecki, M. (2001). Technical assistance services in trade policy: A contribution to the discussion on capacity-building in the WTO 6. *ICTSD Resource Paper No. 2.*

Krauss, E. and T.J. Pempel (2007). *Beyond Bilateralism: US–Japan Relations in the New Asia-Pacific.* Stanford, Stanford University Press.

Krueger, A.O. (1997). Free trade agreements versus customs unions. *Journal of Development Economics,* 54, 169–187.

Krueger, A.O. (1995). The role of the NAFTA debate in US trade policy. *Australian Economic Papers,* 34, 5–16.

Lamy, P. (2002). Stepping stones or stumbling blocks? The EU's approach towards the problem of multilateralism vs. regionalism in trade policy. *World Economy,* 25, 1399–1413.

Lee, Y.-S. (2006). *Reclaiming Development in the World Trading System.* Cambridge, UK: Cambridge University Press.

Lewis, M.K. (2010). TPP & selected aspects of the P4 exchange. *The Trans-Pacific Partnership Digest.* Available at http://tppdigest.org/index.php?option=com_content&view=article&id=99:tpp-and-p4-legal-texts&catid=42:the-discussion-papers&Itemid=55.

Lim, C.L. (2007). Free trade agreements in Asia and some common legal problems. In Taniguchi, Y., A. Yanovich, and J. Bohanes (eds.), *The WTO in the Twenty-First Century: Dispute Settlement, Negotiations, and Regionalism in Asia.* Cambridge, UK: Cambridge University Press.

Lloyd, P. (2002). New bilateralism in the Asia-Pacific. *The World Economy*, 25(9), 1279–1296.

Lucenti, K. (2003). Is there a case for further multilateral rules on trade facilitation? In State Secretariat of Economic Affairs and S. Evenett (eds.), *The Singapore Issues and the World Trading System: The Road to Cancùn and Beyond.*

Mansfield, E.D. and H.V. Milner (1999). The new wave of regionalism. *International Organization*, 53(3), 589–627.

Marchetti, J. and R. Martin (2008). Services liberalization in the WTO and PTAs. In Marchetti, J. and M. Roy (eds.), *Opening Markets for Trade in Services Countries and Sectors in Bilateral and WTO Negotiations.* Cambridge, UK: Cambridge University Press.

Mattoo, A. and P. Sauvé (2010). The preferential liberalization of services trade. *NCCR Working Paper* No. 2010/13. Bern: World Trade Institute.

Mattoo, A. and P. Sauvé (2008). Regionalism in services trade. In Mattoo, A., R.M. Stern, and G. Zanini (eds.), *A Handbook of International Trade in Services.* Oxford, UK: Oxford University Press.

Mattoo, A. and C. Fink (2004). Regional agreements and trade in services: Policy issues, *Journal of Economic Integration*, 19(4), 742–779.

Maur, J.-C. (2011). Trade facilitation. In Chauffour, J.P. and J.C. Maur (eds.), *Preferential Trade Agreement Policies for Development: A Handbook.* Washington D.C.: World Bank.

Maur, J.-C. (2008). Regionalism and trade facilitation: A primer. *Policy Research Working Paper* No. 4464. Washington, D.C.: World Bank.

Maur, J.-C. (2005). Exporting Europe's trade policy. *The World Economy*, 28(11), 1565–1590.

Maur, J.-C. and B. Shepherd (2011). Regional integration and trade facilitation. Discussion Forum, World Trade Report 2011. Available at http://www.wto.org/english/res_e/publications_e/wtr11_forum_e.htm

Maurer, A. and J. Magdeleine (2011). Measuring trade in services in mode 4. In Sauvé, P., G. Pasadilla, and M. Mikic (eds.), *Service Sector Reforms: Asia–Pacific Perspectives.* ADBI Institute and ARTNeT.

Mathis, J.H. (2002). *Regional Trade Agreements in the GATT/WTO: Article XXIV and the Internal Trade Requirement.* The Hague: T.M.C. Asser Press.

McMillan, J. (1993). Does regional integration foster open trade? Economic theory and GATT's Article XXIV. In Anderson, K. and R. Blackhurst (eds.), *Regional Integration and the Global Trading System.* London: Harvester Wheatsheaf.

Menon, J. (2009). Dealing with the proliferation of bilateral free trade agreements. *The World Economy*, 32(10), 1381–1407.

Menon, J. (2007). Bilateral trade agreements. *Asian-Pacific Economic Literature*, 21(2), 29–47.

Menon, J. (2005). Building blocks or stumbling blocks? Regional cooperation arrangements in Southeast Asia. *ADB Institute Discussion Paper* No. 41. Tokyo: ADBI.

Miroudot, S., J. Sauvage, and M. Sudreau (2010). Multilateralising regionalism: How preferential are services commitments in regional trade agreements? *OECD Trade Policy Working Paper* No. 106. Paris: OECD Trade and Agriculture Directorate.

MITI [Ministry of International Trade and Industry of Malaysia] (2011), *Liberalization of Services under ASEAN Framework Agreement on Services (AFAS)*, March 17, 2011. Available at www.mfea.org.my/admin/FileStorage/mfeaorgmy/.../Afas.pdf.

Moïsé, E. (2006). Special and differentiated treatment in the area of trade facilitation. *OECD Trade Policy Working Paper* No. 32 TD/TC/WP(2006)9/FINAL.

Moïsé, E. (2002). The relationship between regional trade agreements and multilateral trading system: Trade facilitation, working party of the trade committee. TD/TC/WP(2002)17/FINAL. Paris: Organization for Economic Co-operation and Development.

Nartova, O. (2008). GATS Article XXV. In Wolfrum, R., P.-T. Stroll, and C. Feinaugle (eds.), *WTO–Trade in Services*. Martinus Nijhoff.

Nesadurai, H.E.S. (2003). Attempting developmental regionalism in AFTA: The domestic sources of regional governance. *Third World Quarterly*, 24(2), 235–53.

Ng, F. and A.J. Yeats (2003). Export profiles of small landlocked countries: A case study focusing on their implications for lesotho. *World Bank Policy Research Working Paper* No. 3085. Washington, D.C.: World Bank.

Nicolaïdis, K. (2000). Non-discriminatory mutual recognition: An oxymoron in the new WTO lexicon? In Cottier, T., P.C. Mavroidis, and P. Blatter (eds.), *Regulatory Barriers and the Principle of Non-discrimination in World Trade Law: Past, Present, and Future (Studies in International Economics)*. University of Michigan Press.

Ochiai, R., P. Dee, and C. Findlay (2009). Services in free trade agreements. In Findlay, C. and S. Urata (eds.), *Free Trade Agreements in the Asia-Pacific*, Singapore: World Scientific.

OECD [Organisation for Economic Co-operation and Development] (2005). Looking Beyond Tariffs: The Role of Non-Tariff Barriers in World Trade, OECD Trade Policy Studies, Paris.

OECD (2002). Business benefits of trade facilitation. Working Party of the Trade Committee, TD/TC/WP(2001)21/FINAL.

Onguglo, B. (2005). Issues regarding notification to the WTO of a regional trade agreement. In Mashayekhi, M. and T. Ito (eds.), *Multilateralism and Regionalism: The New Interface*. Geneva: UNCTAD.

Panagariya, A. (1999). The regionalism debate: An overview. *World Economy*, 22(4), 477–511.

Park, I. and S. Park (2011). Best practices for regional trade agreements. *Review of World Economics*, 147(2), 249–268.

Park, S.-H. (2006). *Increasing Sub-regionalism within APEC and the Bogor Goals.* Presented at the APEC Study Center Consortium Conference at the PECC Trade Forum. Seoul. May 22–25. Available at http://www.apec.org.au/docs/06_apec_perspect.pdf.

Park, S.-H. (2002). Regionalism, open regionalism, and Article XXIV GATT: Conflicts and harmony. In Francis, S. (ed.), *Regional and Global Regulation of International Trade: Studies in European Law and Integration.* Oxford, UK: Hart Publishing.

Park, S.-H and J.Y. Lee (2009). APEC at a crossroads: Challenges and opportunities, *Asian Perspective*, 33(2), 97–124.

Pauwelyn, J. (2009). Multilateralizing regionalism: What about an MFN clause in preferential trade agreements? *Proceedings of the Annual Meeting of the American Society of International Law*, 103, 122–124.

Pempel, T.J. (2006). *Firebreak: East Asia Institutionalize Its Finances.* Presented at a Conference on Northeast Asia's Economic and Security Regionalism: Old Constraints and New Prospects. Los Angeles. March 3–4.

Pempel, T.J. (2005). Conclusions: Tentativeness and tensions in the construction of an Asian region. In Pempel, T.J. (ed.), *Remapping East Asia: The Construction of a Region.* Ithaca, US: Cornell University Press.

Plummer, M.G. (2007). Best practices' in regional trading agreements: An application to Asia. *The World Economy*, 30(12), 1771–1796.

Pomfret, R. (2011). Regionalism. In *East Asia: Why Has It Flourished since 2000 and How Far Will It Go?* Singapore: World Scientific.

Rajan, R. (2002). International trade in services in selected ASEAN countries: Telecommunications and finance. *ISEAS Working Paper.*

Rajapatirana, S. (1994). The evolution of trade treaties and trade creation: Lessons for Latin America. *World Bank Policy Research Working Paper Series* No. 1371. Washington, D.C.: World Bank.

Ravenhill, J. (2001). *APEC and the Construction of Pacific Rim Regionalism.* Cambridge, UK: Cambridge University Press.

Ravenhill, J. (2010). The new East Asian regionalism: A political domino effect. *Review of International Political Economy*, 17(2), 178–208.

Roffe, P., D.Vivas, and G. Vea (2007). *Maintaining Policy Space for Development: A Case Study on IP Technical Assistance in FTAs.* ICTSD Programme on IPRs and Sustainable Development Series Issue Paper No. 19. Geneva: International Centre for Trade and Sustainable Development and the UK Department of International Development.

Roy, M. (2012). Services commitments in preferential trade agreements: Surveying the empirical landscape. *NCCR Trade Working Paper* No. 2012/02.

Roy, M., J. Marchetti, and H. Lim (2007). Services liberalization in the new generation of preferential trade agreements (PTAs): How much further than the GATS? *World Trade Review*, 6(2), 155–192.

Roy, J. and S. Bagai (2005). Key issues in trade facilitation: Summary of world bank/ EU workshops in Dhaka and Shanghai in 2004. *Policy Research Working Paper* No. 3703. World Bank, Development Research Group, Trade, Washington, D.C.

Rudolf, A. (2006). Services negotiations in the Doha round: Lost in flexibility? *Journal of International Economic Law*, 9(4), 865–889.

Ruggie, J. G. (1992). Multilateralism: The anatomy of an institution. *International Organization*, 46(3), 561–598.

Ruggiero, R. (1996). Implications for trade in a borderless world. Speech of the Director-General of the WTO at the World Trade Congress in Singapore. Available at http://www.wto.org/english/news_e/pres96_e/pr046_e.htm.

Russett, B. (1985). The mysterious case of vanishing hegemony: Is Mark Twain really dead? *International Organization*, 39(2), 207–31.

Sampson, G.P. (1996). Compatibility of regional and multilateral trading agreements: Reforming the WTO process. *American Economic Review*, 86(2), 88–92.

Sally, R. (2007). Thai trade policy: From non-discriminatory liberalisation to FTAs. *World Economy*, 30(10), 1594–1620.

Sauvé, P., G. Pasadilla, and M. Mikic (2011). *Services Sector Reforms: Asia–Pacific Perspectives*. ADBI Institute and ARTNeT Secretariat.

Schaefer, M. (2007). Ensuring that regional trade agreements complement the WTO system: US unilateralism a supplement to WTO initiatives? *Journal of International Economic Law*, 10(3), 585–603.

Schiff, M. and L.A. Winters (2003). *Regional Integration and Development*. Washington D.C.: World Bank.

Schreuer, C.H. (1990). In Rüdiger Wolfrum (eds.), *Strengthening the World Order: Universalism v. Regionalism: Risks and Opportunities of Regionalization.* Duncker & Humblot GmbH.

Schroder, H.Z. (2011). Harmonization, equivalence and mutual recognition of standards in WTO law. Kluwer Global Trade Law Series No. 36.

Scollay, R. (2004). Preliminary assessment of the proposal for a free trade area of the Asia-Pacific (FTAAP). *APEC Business Advisory Council (ABAC) Issue Paper*. Available at www.apec.org.au/docs/koreapapers2/SX-RS-Paper.pdf.

Sell, S. (2009). Cat and mouse: Forum-shifting in the battle over intellectual property enforcement. Paper presented at American Political Science Association Meeting. Toronto. 3–6 September.

Shadlen, K.C. (2008). Policy space for intellectual property management: Contrasting multilateral and regional-bilateral arrangements. *Econômica.* 10(2), 55–81.

Shaffer, G. (2006). Can WTO technical assistance and capacity building serve developing countries? *Wisconsin International Law Journal,* 23(4), 643–686.

Shingal, A. and P. Sauvé (2011). Reflections on the preferential liberalization of services trade. *Journal of World Trade,* 5(45).

Smith, M. (1988). The free trade agreement in context: A Canadian perspective. In Schott, J.J. and M.G. Smith (eds.), *The Canada-United States Free Trade Agreement: The Global Impact.* Washington, DC: Institute for International Economics.

Snidal, D. (1985). The limits of hegemonic stability theory. *International Organization,* 39(4), 579–614.

Soesastro, H. (2003). Challenges to APEC trade policy: The Doha development agenda and RTAs/FTAs, *CSIS Economics Working Paper Series.* Jakarta: Centre for Strategic and International Studies.

Solingen, E. (2005). East Asian regional institutions: Characteristics, sources, and distinctiveness. In Pempel, T.J. (eds.) *Remapping East Asia: The Construction of a Region.* Ithaca, US: Cornell University Press.

Srinivasan, T.-N. (1995). Regionalism and the world trade organization: Is non-discrimination passe? *Yale University Economic Growth Center Working Paper Series* No. 767. New Haven, US: Yale University.

Stephenson, S. and D. Nikomborirak (2001). Liberalization of trade in services: East Asia and the Western hemisphere. Presented at PECC Trade Forum in Bangkok, Thailand. June 12–13.

Stoler, A.L. (2009). TBT and SPS provisions in regional trading agreements. Conference on Regional Integration in Asia and Europe. Sussex, UK. September 14–15, 2009.

Tangermann, S. (2002). The future of preferential trade arrangements for developing countries and the current round of WTO negotiations on agriculture. Rome: Food and Agriculture Organization.

Thanh, V.T. and P. Bartlett (2006). Ten years of ASEAN framework agreement on services (AFAS): An assessment REPSF Project No. 05/004 Final Report. Available at www.aseansec.org/aadcp/repsf/docs/05-004-FinalReport.pdf.

Trachtman, J.P. (2003). Toward open recognition? Standardization and regional integration under article XXIV of GATT. *Journal of International Economic Law,* 6(2), 459–492.

Trewin, R. M. Bosworth, D. A. Narjoko, A Mukherjee, A. Stoler, J. Redden, V. Donaldson, and G. Thomson (2008). *East Asian Free Trade Agreements in Services: Facilitating Free Flow of Services in ASEAN.* Paper submitted to the ASEAN Secretariat. REPSF II Project No. 07/004. Available at http://pc-web01.squiz.net/ __data/assets/pdf_file/0011/95942/sub032-attachment2.pdf

UNCTAD [United Nations Conference on Trade and Development] (2011). Trade facilitation measures in regional trade arrangements. Ad Hoc Expert Meeting on "Trade Facilitation in Regional Arrangements, March 30–31, Geneva.

UNCTAD (2008). *Aid for Trade and Development: Global and Regional Perspectives.* Geneva: UNCTAD.

UNCTAD-JETRO [Japan External Trade Organization] (2008). South–South Trade in Asia: The Role of Regional Trade Agreements.

Viner, J. (1950). *The Customs Union Issue.* New York, NY: Carnegie Endowment for International Peace.

Wesley, M. (1997). The politics of exclusion: Australia, Turkey, and definitions of regionalism. *The Pacific Review,* 10(4), 523–55.

Wille, P. and J. Redden (2007). A comparative analysis of trade facilitation in selected regional and bilateral agreements and initiatives in United Nations economic and social commission for Asia and the Pacific's. *Trade Facilitation Beyond the Multilateral Trade Negotiations: Regional Practices, Customs Valuation and Other Emerging Issues.*

Wilson. J.S., C.L. Mann, and T. Otsuki. (2005). Assessing the benefits of trade facilitation: A global perspective. *The World Economy,* 28(6), 841–871.

Wilson, J.S., C.L. Mann, Y.P. Woo, N. Assanie, and I. Choi (2002). *Trade Facilitation: A Development Perspective in the Asia Pacific Region.* APEC.

World Bank (2005). Beyond trade policy barriers: Lowering trade costs together. *Global Economic Prospects 2005: Trade, Regionalism and Development.* Washington D.C.: World Bank.

WTO [World Trade Organization] (2011). World Trade Report 2011. Geneva: WTO.

WTO (2010). *Measuring Trade in Services.* Training module produced by WTO/OMC. Geneva.

WTO (2007). World Trade Report 2007. Geneva: WTO.

WTO (2002). Compendium of issues related to regional trade agreements. TN/RL/W/8/Rev.1.

WTO (2000). *Synopsis of "Systemic" Issues Related to Regional Trade Agreements.* WT/REG/W/37.

Wyatt-Walter, A. (1995). Regionalism, globalization, and the world economic order. In Fawcett, L. and A. Hurrell (eds.), *Regionalism in World Politics: Regional Organization and International Order.* Oxford, UK: Oxford University Press.

Yamazawa, I. (1992). On Pacific economic integration. *The Economic Journal,* 102, 1519–1529.

Yamazawa, I. (2006). *APEC's Trade and Investment Liberalization and Facilitation (TILF): Its Achievements and Tasks Ahead.* From paper presented to the APEC International Symposium on the Catalytic Role of the APEC Process: Behind the Border, Beyond the Bogor Goals. Chiba, Japan. 14–15 March. Available at: http://www.apec.org.au/docs/06_apec_perspect.pdf

Yi, S.-S. (1996). Endogenous formation of customs unions under imperfect competition: Open regionalism is good. *Journal of International Economics,* 42(1/2), 153–177.

Zhang, Y. (2009). *China and Asian Regionalism.* Singapore: World Scientific.

Zhang, Y. and M. Shen (2011). The status of East Asian free trade agreements. *ADBI Working Paper Series* No. 282. Tokyo, Japan: ADBI.

Index

Printed in the United States
By Bookmasters